Bulldozed

Niki Savva is one of the most senior correspondents in the Canberra Press Gallery. She was twice political correspondent for *The Australian*, and headed up the Canberra bureaus of both *The Herald Sun* and *The Age*. When family tragedy forced a career change, she became Peter Costello's press secretary for six years and was then on John Howard's staff for three. Her work has brought her into intimate contact with Australia's major political players for more than 40 years. She is a regular columnist for *The Age* and *The Sydney Morning Herald*, and often appears on ABC TV's *Insiders*.

Her first book, *So Greek*, a memoir, provided rare insights into the relationship between Howard and Costello, and the workings of their government. *The Road to Ruin*, the first volume in what became her trilogy about Australia's Coalition governments that ruled from 2013 to 2022, was a bestseller, and won the 2016 General Nonfiction Book of the Year Award at the Australian Book Industry Awards. The second volume, *Plots and Prayers*, which dealt with the government led by Malcolm Turnbull and the ascension of Scott Morrison, was also a bestseller. In March 2017, the Melbourne Press Club presented Niki with a lifetime achievement award for 'outstanding coverage of Australian politics as a reporter, columnist, and author'.

Bulldozed

Scott Morrison's fall and
Anthony Albanese's rise

Niki Savva

SCRIBE
Melbourne • London

Scribe Publications
18-20 Edward St, Brunswick, Victoria 3056, Australia
2 John St, Clerkenwell, London, WC1N 2ES, United Kingdom
3754 Pleasant Ave, Suite 100, Minneapolis, Minnesota 55409, USA

Published by Scribe 2022
Reprinted 2022, 2023

Typeset in Adobe Garamond Pro by the publishers

Printed and bound in Australia by Griffin Press

Scribe is committed to the sustainable use of natural resources and the
use of paper products made responsibly from those resources.

Scribe acknowledges Australia's First Nations peoples as the traditional
owners and custodians of this country. We recognise that sovereignty
was never ceded, and we pay our respects to their elders, past and
present.

978 1 922585 98 1 (paperback edition)
978 1 922586 84 1 (ebook)

A catalogue record for this book is available from the National Library
of Australia.

scribepublications.com.au

To the next generations:
Dana
Andrew, Peter, Laura, Maria
Thomas, Christian
Nicki, Steven

Contents

CHAPTER ONE

Victory and Damnation

Peter Dutton and Josh Frydenberg knew, months out from the election, that they were headed for disaster under Scott Morrison. They knew, as long as a year before, that if the election became a referendum on Morrison, they would lose. By the end of 2021, they knew, along with almost every other member of the Coalition, including the most prominent members of Morrison's Praetorian Guard, that he was badly damaged, probably beyond repair.

But Dutton had already torn down one Liberal prime minister, so he wasn't about to tear down another. And Frydenberg was never going to challenge a sitting prime minister. Dutton and Frydenberg were immobilised, prisoners of their history and their personalities, hostage to Morrison's misplaced conviction that he could destroy Anthony Albanese as systematically as he had demolished Bill Shorten in 2019 in what he declared a miracle win. They remained locked in a deathly embrace.

Months after the election, they discovered the depths of his deception. There was a flurry of retrospective braggadocio, firing speculation that if his colleagues had known back then that he had secretly sworn himself into five additional cabinet portfolios — four of them without the knowledge or consent of those who already held them — the rebellion would have been ignited, he would have been deposed, and Frydenberg installed.

Maybe. If Morrison had refused to revoke his secret commissions, it is possible. More likely not. Much would have depended on how colleagues found out about them and when.

The consensus from post-trauma discussions is that cabinet ministers would have forced him to retreat and a broken party would have limped to the election, in much the same way as it eventually did.

The what-ifs are as tantalising as they are largely irrelevant. All the people who mattered, including those closest to him, already knew everything they needed to know about him, even without knowing about his clandestine acquisition of ministries. They knew he was secretive and that he lied; that he was stubborn; that he bullied people; that even if he sought advice, he seldom took it; and that he had little interest in policy.

They knew that Morrison was a deeply flawed personality, a duplicitous, damaged leader with limited horizons and appalling judgement even they were not certain they could trust, who rarely understood what Australians expected of a prime minister.

He ignored advice from almost every quarter to go to an early election, then grew paranoid that the Dutton and Frydenberg camps were plotting a coup. Even though they could see the ship heading straight for the iceberg, they did not mutiny. Instead, they waited on deck without lifejackets, without lifeboats, for their captain to ram it.

Morrison used, played, and deceived them, as he had so many others, in ways that were both obvious and beyond even their imaginings. He left them with a pile of rubble, feeling wounded and betrayed.

Those who stood up to him ran the risk of being frozen out.

He was petty and vindictive. Few dared challenge him, worried that if they did they would bring the show down. That reluctance ruined them, and left the Liberal Party in its sorriest state since it was founded by Robert Menzies in 1944.

Morrison's secret takeover of ministries showed a contempt of parliament, of conventions, and of his ministers, including those he called his best friends, like Josh Frydenberg and Stuart Robert. They took it very personally.

After the revelations, his former colleagues spat out all the M words: messianic, megalomaniacal, and plain mad. Dutton's shadow cabinet decided that Australians would care more about the cost of living, so muted its criticisms.

They didn't want to rake over the past. They didn't want to provoke him into forcing a by-election for his seat, which they feared they would lose, so they continued the protection racket, compounding the damage to their reputations and the party's standing.

Perversely, they accused the government of playing politics instead of focussing on more important things such as the economy. As if fundamentally undermining the proper functioning of responsible government, as the solicitor-general, Stephen Donoghue, put it, was of little consequence.

Morrison's actions were profoundly wrong on every level. They should have cut him loose immediately; instead, they showed they had learned nothing from their defeat.

There was only one senior serving Liberal who had the guts to say publicly, immediately, that he should quit parliament: Karen Andrews. She was right. He was a constant reminder of everything that had gone wrong with the Liberal Party.

After he found out that the prime minister had secretly acquired Treasury, Frydenberg, who had been loyal beyond measure to Morrison, was furious. When they eventually spoke, he said to Morrison: 'You wouldn't do it again if you had your time over!'

Incredibly, Morrison replied: 'Yes, I would.'

The longer Morrison stayed in parliament, the lower down he would drag them, and the harder and longer would be the rebuilding process.

He stayed, crumpled in his seat on the backbench next to Alex Hawke, glowering at the man who had replaced him. His near neighbours could hear him muttering, bitter and resentful that he had been beaten by someone he regarded as so inadequate.

Morrison had always underestimated Albanese, who was both resilient and street smart.

When Morrison tried to taunt him or intimidate him during terse off-mike exchanges in parliament, Albanese, a product of New South Wales Labor when it really was a political killing machine, would brush him off, saying: 'I have fought people a lot tougher than you, mate.'

Albanese constructed Labor's winning strategy, stuck by it in the face of external criticism and internal doubts, faltered at a critical time, then recovered to secure majority government—something that only three other Labor leaders had done before him since the Second World War.

Albanese knew, as surely as Dutton and Frydenberg did, that keeping the focus on Morrison would deliver victory. There were many factors that contributed to the Coalition's defeat: the desertion of women, the desertion of Chinese Australians, a yearning for tougher action on climate change, the desire to restore integrity and trust in institutions, and lingering frustrations over Covid.

Hanging over all of it like a dark mist was Morrison. There was no escape from him, not for one moment. There was not a single cut-through policy he offered to leaven the images or lift the vote.

When Albanese contracted Covid during the campaign, after an awful first week rescued by his win in the first debate, it gave members of his shadow ministry—including Penny Wong, Jason Clare, Katy Gallagher, and Jim Chalmers—the opportunity to shine. They provided a stark contrast to Morrison's one-man show, which was causing internal friction—even before colleagues knew the extent of his deceit.

Albanese's absence ensured that Morrison stayed in full focus, front and centre, not even able to air-punch his chief opponent, literally fighting shadows, desperately trying to explain the disastrous news that the Solomon Islands had signed a security pact with China, which dissolved his credentials on national security—one of the three pillars he had constructed to secure his re-election.

The second being the economy, and the third a culture war grounded in an appeal to the religious right.

Skyrocketing inflation, steep increases in the cost of living, a rise in interest rates, low wages, and a trillion dollars of debt—now Labor's dismal inheritance—ate away at Morrison's reputation as an economic manager.

Religion was central to Morrison's life. Colleagues believed it drove him, made him immoveable, more resistant to logical explanations. He surrounded himself with people who thought like him—ministers, friends, staff—who took part in regular prayer sessions in his office and at The Lodge.

He used religion in ways that no Australian leader had before in an effort to harvest votes. He flaunted it. It was there more subtly in 2019. In 2022, it was blatant and divisive as he sought to push through the religious discrimination bill that failed to protect vulnerable children.

Morrison's response to the defeat of his bill at the hands of his own MPs was typically self-pitying and revealing. His words then, along with a post-election sermon in Perth, help explain his view of life and politics, and why nothing that went wrong was ever his fault.

'I have been mocked every day because of my faith, because I am a Pentecostal,' Morrison was heard to say to colleagues after the vote on the bill. 'I have surrendered this battle to God, now. I have said, over to you.'

Weeks later, hoping to mobilise the religious right, he deliberately chose a candidate fated to exploit the sensitive issue of transgender women during the heat of an election campaign.

Occasionally, during meetings with cabinet ministers, he would recite passages from the Bible he had read that morning that had inspired him. He laid hands on colleagues in prayer. A few found it comforting; a few thought it was weird.

He would lecture them on hubris, then neglect to heed his own advice. In early June 2020, after his standing had been restored as a result of his early handling of Covid, he reminded his leadership group of the fate of Winston Churchill, who had led Britain to victory in the Second World War, then lost the election.

'We can't take anything for granted,' he told them. Then he gave people no reason at all to vote for him again.

In 2022, Morrison thought he could win by frightening people out of voting for Albanese, just as he had frightened them into choosing him over Shorten in 2019. The second time around, there was no Shorten, nor Shorten's promise of $400 billion in new taxes.

He had nothing to offer other than himself, and he had become a massive drag on the vote in Liberal strongholds. Nor was it obvious this time that he had God on his side.

One former cabinet minister who had known Morrison for many years told me that Morrison had 'this thing about *God wants this*, or *God has chosen me to be prime minister*. The overflow from 2019 was that he and others around him believed their own bullshit'.

His friends despaired that he kept repeating his mistakes and that he had misread the reasons for the 2019 victory. They complained that he refused to take advice and that he treated them badly.

'He got addicted to executive authority,' Alex Hawke said.

Another close colleague questioned Morrison's loyalty. 'He always took his friends for granted, and he wanted his enemies to love him,' he said. 'Often, he would screw his friends.'

Morrison had begun his parliamentary career in 2007 after a dirty preselection. His tenure as prime minister was conceived in deception, marked by disasters, and ended in disgrace.

A few of Morrison's colleagues, male and female, said they never had a problem with him. Others, male and female, said he was a bully or plain belligerent.

Describing himself as a 'bit of a bulldozer', he offered, a week out from polling day, to change, to be a better person and a better prime minister, if only people would give him another chance. It sounded like a come-to-Jesus moment, a plea from a condemned man for a reprieve at five minutes to midnight.

After he lost, he quoted Barnaby Joyce, of all people, to say that sometimes people just wanted to change the curtains. As if voting him out had an air of whimsy about it. No. Voters bulldozed the house with him inside it, sending tremors across the political landscape.

In wondrous, clever ways, voters did whatever they had to do to be rid of him, electing greater numbers than ever before of Greens and independents, seeing that the Liberal Party couldn't bring itself to remove him for them.

They warned the Liberals to change, or die. They put Labor on notice to perform, or else.

Only weeks after the election, the Greens and the Teals, confident that this was just the beginning, were planning which seats to target next.

Morrison did not instigate the drift away from major parties, but he indisputably accelerated it, then carried on as if it didn't matter, ignoring the damage he was inflicting on his vulnerable colleagues.

In the end, voters worked him out. They grew sick and tired of his weaving, wedging, dodging, fibbing, and fudging. They despaired at his absence at critical times, his refusal to accept responsibility for his mistakes, his stubbornness, and his slowness to respond.

Morrison would lie, get caught out, and then he would deny that he had lied, pretending it never happened, rarely if ever apologising for it, seemingly incapable of admitting it even to himself. It was stunning that the rebuttal of his lies with audiovisual proof did nothing to stem their number or frequency. Boris Johnson without the hair or the humour.

His obsession with secrecy, his insistence on absolute control, his aversion to transparency, his readiness to corrupt proper processes, and the complacency of sections of the media about his behaviour, were fully exposed after publication of a book designed to cast him as the country's saviour during a pandemic, but which unintentionally revealed him as a power-hungry control freak who lacked confidence in his own colleagues.

He amassed unprecedented powers while simultaneously avoiding responsibility and accountability.

The rich, delicious irony of the events triggered by that book,

Plagued, most of which came directly from Morrison, where his early usurpation of two portfolios was presented as an 'elegant solution', would have been hilarious if it were not so serious. We should be grateful that he believed it was such an act of genius that he needed to share it with the two authors at the time, so that after publication it would embellish a legacy he claimed he never wanted.

He swore himself in first as health minister on 14 March 2020, with the knowledge and consent of the minister, Greg Hunt, as a safeguard because the powers vested in Hunt under the Biosecurity Act were so immense. Then he took over Finance on 30 March 2020; the portfolios of Industry, Science, Energy and Resources on 15 April 2021; and Home Affairs and Treasury on 6 May 2021 — all without telling the responsible ministers.

He acquired Resources specifically to override the minister, who was preparing to make a decision that Morrison judged would cut across his political interests. Under pressure from MPs, including his friend Lucy Wicks in Robertson and inner-urban Liberals, Morrison was determined to block the PEP 11 project to drill for gas off the New South Wales coast.

The other resources minister, Keith Pitt, was planning to approve the project, using the authority vested in him alone to do it. Or so he thought. Pitt made it clear to Morrison all the way through of his intention to endorse the April 2020 recommendation of the National Offshore Petroleum Titles administrator to extend the exploration licence.

Morrison's office asked Pitt in February 2021 to delay his decision, to give the prime minister more time to resolve it with his colleagues. Pitt agreed. Soon after, he had a heated argument with Yaron Finkelstein, Morrison's chief political adviser, after Morrison was asked in Tomago on 4 March if he supported the extension of the licence, and twice said: 'No.'

Pitt was furious that Morrison had publicly stated his position, which contradicted his own as the responsible minister.

Morrison and Pitt discussed it again on the phone on 27 March, when Pitt again made it clear that he planned to approve the project. Pitt and Morrison then met in Canberra in early June. The Nationals' leader, Michael McCormack, attended that meeting. Pitt was immoveable, making it clear he would grant the extension.

Pitt, Morrison, and their staff met again a few days later, without McCormack. Pitt thinks this was around mid-June — he was not sure of the exact date, but it was before McCormack's ousting by Joyce on 21 June.

It was at this meeting that Morrison told Pitt he had sworn himself in as resources minister, and that he would decide against the extension if Pitt wasn't prepared to do so.

Pitt's first thought was *WTF*, a thought shared later by millions when it became public. Pitt asked that all staff — his and Morrison's, including Finkelstein — clear out so he could be alone with the prime minister.

'I have never had a screaming match with the guy,' Pitt said later. Pitt asked Morrison how he could swear himself into another minister's portfolio, and if that was even constitutional. Morrison told him he had advice that it was. Pitt said he would check it out for himself.

Pitt went back to his office. He read the section in the *House of Representatives Practice*, the day-to-day bible for MPs, on the operations of parliament and the executive. He could not find any precedent for what Morrison had done.

He was left with few choices. He could offer his resignation, Morrison could ask for his resignation, or Morrison could tell McCormack to sack him. Or Morrison could take it to cabinet, roll Pitt there, and Pitt could either resign or live with having to announce the rejection of the permit. Later, Morrison could offer no satisfactory explanation to Pitt why he did not do that. To this day, Pitt does not understand why he didn't.

Pitt told me he seriously considered resigning. He also discussed with his staff the option of unilaterally releasing a statement approving PEP 11 without telling anybody in advance, including Morrison—which he would have been entitled to do.

Two senior Morrison staff suggested to me later that Pitt was grateful he had been relieved of the responsibility for the decision. Pitt was momentarily lost for words when this was put to him.

The prime minister's office had asked Pitt's office if he wanted to put his name on Morrison's 16 December press release announcing the rejection. 'Hell, no,' Pitt told his staff. He never endorsed the decision; he never once said he supported it.

Pitt remembered seeking advice from Arthur Sinodinos when he was an assistant minister to Greg Hunt. Pitt says Hunt was pressing him to agree to something he opposed.

Top of mind for Pitt during his dealings with Morrison were Sinodinos's words: 'You never sign a brief you haven't read. You never sign a brief you don't understand. You never sign a brief you don't agree with.'

Within 24 hours of his meeting with Morrison, Pitt went to McCormack's office to tell him what Morrison had done and to seek his support. Pitt did not get it.

He suspected that McCormack already knew what had happened by the time he told him about Morrison being sworn in to his portfolio, because McCormack didn't act surprised.

'This is ridiculous. You are the leader of the Nationals,' Pitt says he told him. 'Either it's our portfolio or it isn't. This is a breach of the Coalition agreement.'

McCormack replied: 'He is the prime minister.'

Again, Pitt told McCormack: 'You are the leader of the Nationals.'

McCormack told me later that he did not already know. He has a different recollection of his conversation with Pitt. He said he did not 'believe' Pitt told him explicitly that Morrison had 'sworn himself in to the portfolio'—only that Pitt told him Morrison had made himself, as prime minister, 'a signatory for that decision'.

McCormack says that is when he said: 'He is the prime minister.' McCormack also disputes that Pitt told him he was the leader of the Nationals and that it was a breach of the Coalition agreement. He says he would have remembered that.

McCormack says there was a lot going on at the time, not just PEP 11. However, he said he recalled Morrison telling the National Security Committee and the leadership group that he had sworn himself in as health minister, and might have to take on other portfolios if necessary.

Pitt stands by his version of events and his conversation with McCormack. Immediately after his meeting with McCormack, he went back to his office and briefed his then chief of staff, Gerard McManus. What he told McManus that day is the same as what he told me for this book.

Barnaby Joyce coyly says he found out 'obliquely' what Morrison had done, and also succumbed. After resuming the Nationals' leadership on 21 June, not long after Pitt's discussion with Morrison and McCormack, Joyce also neglected to disclose it publicly, because he said he wanted to keep the Nationals' extra ministry and staff entitlements.

There are those who believe that Joyce was aware of what happened, and that he used it 'obliquely' against McCormack to roll him. Whatever, Joyce's pitch to the Nationals to remove McCormack was that he didn't stand up to Morrison.

Pitt describes it as a 'wild time'. With the pandemic still raging, he did not believe he would achieve anything by resigning or acting unilaterally, except to plunge the government into crisis. He wondered if anything else was going on inside the Liberal Party that made Morrison reluctant to take it to cabinet.

In fact, there was. Morrison announced his decision to block PEP 11 after parliament had risen, on the same day that Frydenberg released the midyear fiscal outlook, and after a period of high anxiety for Morrison over his leadership, when he was convinced that both left and right were out to get him.

Morrison's catalogue of known disasters prompted muttering, despair, fantasising, and regular appeals for someone or for either of the two aspirants to do something. Nothing ever came of it.

Partly, that was because Dutton and Frydenberg figured there was only one safe way to be rid of Morrison that would minimise the bloodshed and likely acts of vengeance from the most ruthless, duplicitous political player either of them had seen—and they had seen a few.

They believed Morrison might have entertained stepping down if two of his best friends in the parliament, Ben Morton and Stuart Robert, counselled him to stand aside for the good of the Liberal Party. Dutton and Frydenberg knew that Morrison would never go of his own volition. They also knew that neither Morton nor Robert would ever suggest it to him, and they never did.

Although Morton and Robert remained part of Morrison's Praetorian Guard, and would have mobilised to thwart any move against him, there had been a striking deterioration in the relationship between Robert and Morrison, which began before the election and worsened after.

Morton continued to defend Morrison, even after news of his secret ministries broke. Tellingly, Robert did not. He was one of the first to say that Morrison had acted unwisely, that he should have put it to cabinet, and that cabinet would have insisted he undo it. He said so in a television interview, then called Morrison to tell him what he had said.

'You should have told us,' Robert said to him.

Robert told people after the election that he felt dudded by Morrison. He lobbied for the home affairs portfolio, and didn't get it; he lobbied for policies late in the term, and Morrison refused to endorse them.

Robert told me that he and Morrison had continued to pray together regularly while he was prime minister. They prayed both at The Lodge and in the prime ministerial suite, particularly before big events or press conferences. They took part in regular prayer-group meetings in Canberra, every Tuesday night.

Morrison never once told him he had sworn himself into those ministries. He then rubbed salt in the wound by implying he couldn't trust those in the jobs to do them, and that others were too 'junior' to fill the portfolios he had acquired if something were to happen to the ministers who already held them. Robert was already a cabinet minister, confident he could step into any of those roles.

He says that even if 'Armageddon' had struck, it would only have taken a few minutes to swear others in. Robert was deeply wounded by Morrison's actions, and insulted by his subsequent attempts to justify them.

'Scotty's a friend, as much as one can have a friend in politics,' Robert told me. 'We are still reasonably close in that regard.' Twice during an hour-long conversation, after I had asked him if they were still friends, he laughed and quoted the old maxim: 'If you want a friend in politics, get a dog.'

As employment and skills minister, Robert had forged what he regarded as a breakthrough skills package with the New South Wales treasurer, Matt Kean. The package, which involved additional spending of $600 million for the state, as part of a planned total outlay of more than $3 billion, ensured that New South Wales would also put in extra money.

Robert told me the deal was so attractive that it would have induced other states to follow suit and provide a national approach. With streamlined conditions on spending and efficiency reviews, the package was supported by the New South Wales and federal treasuries, as well as Morrison's department of prime minister and cabinet.

Both Robert and Kean were enthusiastic about the plan.

But, as hard as he tried, just a few weeks before Morrison was scheduled to call the election, during which the government would have little to talk about except, er, him, Robert could not get Morrison to approve the agreement. It languished.

Robert subsequently told people from both sides of politics that the reason Morrison refused to sign off on it was because he hated Kean. He said the same to people in the New South Wales government and to other friends of Morrison's.

After the election, he urged his Labor successor, Brendan O'Connor, to take it up. Robert and O'Connor spoke in the chamber soon after the new parliament first met. Robert extolled the virtues of the package, and told him bluntly the reason Morrison had not endorsed it was his hatred of Kean.

While Robert confirmed he had forged the agreement, he told me he could not 'remember' telling people that Morrison had refused to back it because of his dislike of Kean. Some of the people he told, who knew how close he had been to Morrison, were stunned by his candid disclosures.

While there had clearly been tension between himself and Morrison, Robert also told me that he would never have told Morrison to step aside, and that, as his numbers man, he knew that the support was never there for either Frydenberg or Dutton to mount a successful challenge.

'The prime minister had no need to be concerned,' he said. 'They either have the numbers or they haven't. And they hadn't.'

Morton also later said that no one had ever suggested to him that he should tell Morrison to step aside—not even Frydenberg. He affirmed he would never have suggested it to Morrison, and was absolutely confident that changing the leader would not have changed the result.

Nevertheless, according to others, an increasingly paranoid Morrison felt threatened by both Dutton and Frydenberg.

Morrison was especially wary of Dutton. His approach to Frydenberg had been to bind him so close that he could not break free, including by inviting him to bunk down at The Lodge with him during Covid, which colleagues later said was one of the worst decisions Frydenberg made.

They wanted creative tension between the prime minister and his treasurer, which had been the case in previous administrations, and it (almost) always got better results on economic policy. Frydenberg's determination to stay close, to not allow a sliver of daylight between himself and Morrison, cost him dearly.

'The PM thought he owned him. And he did own him,' one Liberal MP said.

Alex Hawke, closer to Morrison than Frydenberg, never stayed at The Lodge, and he thought it was bizarre that Frydenberg had.

Morrison's approach to Dutton was to keep him at a respectful distance, to never cross him and to lock him into all government decisions by appointing him to both the Expenditure Review

Committee of cabinet and the National Security Committee.

Even if there had been divine intervention to remove Morrison, there would have been a contest between Dutton and Frydenberg. Frydenberg had no doubts at all he would have won that.

Dutton's supporters now say they also thought Frydenberg probably would have won, although they calculated it would have only been narrowly, which would have left a fractured party. The Liberal Party was effectively broken before the election, and the election split the cracks wide open.

While Robert did not believe the leadership chatter amounted to much, Hawke took it seriously. Hawke says Morrison himself was convinced that plotting was underway. He was panic-stricken. 'He flipped,' Hawke said.

Morrison knew that MPs had been trooping into Frydenberg's office. As deputy, Frydenberg had duly reported to his leader that his backbenchers were very worried they were going to lose their seats and lose the election.

Frydenberg did not tell him they were appealing to him to challenge. Morrison knew this without Frydenberg telling him, because he had heard it from others. He did not fear he would be toppled by Frydenberg; he feared it would be Dutton.

As the political year drew to a close, the atmosphere was febrile.

Hawke believed that both moderate and right-wing MPs were involved, and that it was all coming to a head in the final two sitting weeks of the year, the so-called killing season, when there would be one last party meeting, on 30 November.

Morrison was expecting Dutton to do to him what he—Morrison—had done to Turnbull. Wait for the other guy to make a move, and then come through with less bloody hands and crush him with the numbers.

Hawke insists it was real. 'It wasn't a drill,' he said. 'The prime minister took it very seriously.'

Morrison and his supporters believed that Michael Sukkar, who was known to be close to Frydenberg—to the point where he would brag to people he had him wrapped around his little finger—was pressing him to challenge.

Morrison believed that Sukkar was actually in Dutton's camp, along with others in the so-called monkey-pod group that had hatched the last plot in 2018, and had reactivated itself. He was convinced that Sukkar was secretly setting it up for the Queenslander to come through the middle to win. It was the kind of devilishly cunning plan worthy of Morrison himself.

Frydenberg says it was not true. Sukkar was not urging him to challenge, but he was discussing the leadership with him.

New South Wales moderate Andrew Bragg, one of around a dozen who talked to Frydenberg about the leadership as 2021 was drawing to a close, believed the government would have fared better under Frydenberg. But, after discussing it with him, he knew Frydenberg would never challenge.

MPs were telling Frydenberg that they no longer believed Morrison would win the election, that he had been grievously damaged by the attacks on his character, and that Frydenberg would appeal more to the sensible centre.

Dutton's supporters reckoned they were not plotting and that neither of them would have challenged. They claimed that Frydenberg was unwilling to move against Morrison and was in fact trying to shore up his numbers post-election.

Frydenberg was convinced that Morrison would retire midway through the next term if he won. If true, that would have made him the first prime minister to leave office voluntarily since Robert Menzies in 1966.

Even if no one else believed it would happen, especially given Morrison's personality and the propensity of all prime ministers to dissemble on these matters, Frydenberg genuinely thought he would.

MPs said he was telling backbenchers that, one way or another, there would be a change after the election. He was asking them if he could count on their support then.

He never expected he would not be there himself to fulfil his destiny.

Flattered as he was by the interest, Frydenberg had no intention of challenging. Not only was he loyal, but he feared what Morrison would do. He knew that Morrison would have resisted, and that the show 'would have blown up to the point where it was unsalvageable'.

The other constraining factor was the 2019 result. Perhaps Morrison would be able to do it again. Perhaps Morrison would come good, run a stellar campaign, Albanese would collapse under the pressure, and the heavens would bestow another miracle.

'He was convinced of the righteousness of his path,' Frydenberg told people later.

As one prominent Liberal MP observed, Morrison would only step down if God told him to, and given he was there because God had ordained that he should be there, he wasn't going anywhere until God decreed it. Which, as it transpired, was what Morrison actually believed.

Looking back, West Australian Liberal Andrew Hastie says there was never going to be a change in the leadership. He also believes it would not have made much difference if there had been a bloodless coup. 'It wouldn't have mattered, the Liberal brand was so damaged,' Hastie said. The damage in the west occurred early, in 2020, with the federal challenge to the state's border closure, and it was too late to reverse it.

Hastie, a conservative, held onto his seat of Canning, but the Liberals lost Hasluck, Pearce, Swan, and Tangney to Labor, and Curtin to independent Kate Chaney.

Until very late, on the religious discrimination bill — the clarion call to the religious right — Morrison's authority was seldom publicly challenged, except by one woman, Tasmanian backbencher Bridget Archer, who was rewarded with a higher vote by her electors and then punished by her colleagues afterwards.

'The whole idea that Morrison had less than 1,000 per cent support is false,' Bragg told me later. 'The idea there was an insurrection is BS. He had the full support of his party room.

'The only people that were creating division were in his office.

'Morrison had the complete support of the Liberal Party. Of course, there's always discussion about our prospects, but he had complete and united support to run the campaign the way he wanted to. Even when he provoked complex issues like the transgender matter, even then he was afforded near-universal acquiescence.

'People put the party and his leadership first. He got his go.

'He was able to run it exactly as he wanted to, it was his show.

'The [election] result was a repudiation of this style of politics and policy.

'The adoption of US-style culture wars was very damaging. When people were worried about childcare and emissions reductions, we were talking about transgender issues. And not in a positive way.

'We were talking about how we could weaponise a vulnerable minority.'

Bragg said even though Morrison had been a state director, he did not understand the character of the Liberal Party.

'We have to get back to the live-and-let-live ethos of the Liberal Party,' he said.

Dutton would express despair at Morrison's reluctance to take on reform, relying instead on his tactical, marketing, and campaigning skills to survive.

Frydenberg would say Morrison's problem was that he viewed everything through the prism of politics, not principle, citing the selection of Katherine Deves, the treatment of Christine Holgate, and the deportation of Novak Djokovic as examples. Dutton would tell people that if there was a low road, Morrison would take it.

'The reason he got to be PM is because he is very tactical in his thinking. Consistently,' Frydenberg told people.

The two never were contenders, and did what they could to mitigate disaster. Dutton had been urging the moderates early on to push for a resolution to climate change to get it off the table, which Morrison should have settled soon after his 2019 victory, but which he delayed confronting till close to the end.

Dutton was also among a group of Queensland MPs, including Trevor Evans and Julian Simmonds (both of whom lost their seats to the Greens), pressing Morrison and his office to adopt the December 2020 recommendation of the Joint Standing Committee on Electoral Matters, chaired by fellow Queenslander senator James McGrath, advocating the introduction of optional preferential voting for federal elections.

Stuart Robert was also urging Morrison to switch to optional preferential.

Morrison did not want to drop compulsory preferential voting, even though the Queenslanders believed the change would save Coalition seats. In any case, those pushing it also feared that it would have been stymied by far-right senators Alex Antic and Gerard Rennick, who went on 'strike' against their own government in protest over vaccination mandates.

In his day job as defence minister, Dutton ramped up the

threat of China, which led to accusations later from Liberals that the strident language from him and Morrison had cost them the votes of Chinese Australians in seats such as Chisholm, Reid, and Bennelong, which were lost to Labor, and Kooyong, lost to the Teals.

The then New South Wales party president, Philip Ruddock, rang a number of MPs, including Frydenberg, before the election to warn them about the impact it was having on the vote. John Howard voiced his concerns privately about the tone of some of the rhetoric.

Dutton was later determinedly unapologetic, but there were Liberals saying the party had been wiped out in metropolitan areas of Sydney, Melbourne, Brisbane, and Perth partly as a result of the desertion of Chinese Australians.

Frydenberg concentrated on the budget, which loomed as the government's last, best hope for a comeback. That was blown up by internal politics.

When defeat finally came, it flattened them both — not because it had happened, but because of the emphatic nature of the rejection. Disaster did not begin to describe it. Unchallenged, Dutton landed the one job he never really wanted: opposition leader. Long regarded as the worst job in politics.

If he had kept his seat, Frydenberg would have jumped at that, if that was all that was going, and he would have fought Dutton tooth and nail to get it.

It might have been very different if Morrison had listened to the colleagues urging him to call an election any time from around September 2021. Alex Hawke told Morrison directly that he should go as soon as he possibly could. Stuart Robert told him to go in November.

Backbench Liberal MPs appealed to Dutton and Frydenberg

to try to convince Morrison to go before Christmas. They were certain their prospects were never going to get any better, that there would either be more bushfires or another Covid outbreak. They argued that another budget would not help much anyway, and they were encouraged by reports that Bill Shorten was arcing up against Albanese.

Importantly, they argued it would give the Teals less time to prepare their campaigns. 'It was ridiculous to think we would have a good summer,' Hawke said.

Dutton agreed. He thought it was 'crazy' to wait. He was keen for the election to be held more than six months ahead of the due date, before anything else could go wrong. Frydenberg was noncommittal, but undertook to pass it on.

Morrison showed a level of arrogance and timidity. He told colleagues he was worried he would face criticism for going early. They argued that would disappear after a few days, and that he could justify it by seeking a mandate to continue his stewardship of the pandemic.

He told them that Albanese was 'not threatening', the gap was not that great between the parties, the government was solid, and the longer he left it, the more time he would have to tear down Albanese. Again, it all sounded like he thought he could do 2019 all over again.

Hawke, who was later blamed for deliberately delaying New South Wales preselections — which he denies — and which were seen as another major factor in the defeat, says the party miscalculated the threat from the Teals, then faced an assault from the left, right, and centre. In his view, '2019 proved to be Morrison's greatest success and greatest weakness.'

Hawke believes that if Morrison had gone early, he 'probably' would have won, because it would have been before the debacle of the lack of rapid antigen tests and before the Teals had consolidated their appeal.

'The rule is, go when you think you can win,' he said. Hawke despaired that Morrison 'didn't really take advice from people'.

'He wasn't the greatest listener,' he said.

He also believed that Morrison should have quit parliament almost immediately after the election, rather than stay, and risk becoming bitter and twisted.

To be fair, the advice to Morrison to go early was not unanimous. Morton was opposed to an early election because the situation in the west was so dire. The state's premier, Mark McGowan, still reigned supreme, and the closed borders presented major logistical problems.

Labor had a contingency plan for an early election if the west was still closed. Albanese was prepared to go into isolation, if necessary, so he could campaign in the west, so vital was the state to his election strategy.

Morrison's preference was to call the election around Australia Day for a Saturday in March, before the budget, scheduled for 29 March. He was hoping that a relaxed holiday period would put Australians in a better frame of mind. The arrival of Omicron ended that.

Every year of his tenure began with a disaster of one kind or another. Usually, leaders were able to use summers to reset. For Morrison, they became segues to another disaster.

Omicron ensured that the summer break was miserable. Warnings from the Australian Medical Association and others, months before, of the need for a national strategy to secure enough rapid antigen tests so Australians could speedily check themselves, went unheeded.

With record numbers of infections, supply lines and businesses were disrupted by staff who were either ill or isolating. There were empty shelves in supermarkets again, and prices were beginning to soar.

It revived memories of Morrison's failure the previous year to secure enough vaccines.

Assessing, rightly, that the end could be nigh, that he now had no choice except to delay the election until May, after the budget — although he had sought advice to see if he could extend beyond that by citing Covid — Morrison told colleagues in early 2022: 'What's happening here is existential.'

For many voters, it was the last straw. Polls were showing Labor ahead by 10 points or more on a two-party-preferred basis. The Liberals' polling showed that almost the only thing about Albanese that was cutting through was his makeover. This was no bad thing for Labor. He looked sharper, he sounded sharper, and, more importantly, he was unthreatening, although not in the way Morrison thought. Albanese did not frighten people.

The Liberals' polling showed that their position was near irretrievable. The government appeared doomed. Most of them knew it. Morrison was said to feel it, too, which probably explains some of his crankiness during the campaign.

Those dealing with him reported that he was more difficult to handle this time around, less willing to take advice, and even more insistent on getting his way. Morton decided to stay with him on the campaign trail. He ignored advice to head back home to the west after internal polling showed he was in dire straits in his seat of Tangney.

Morton knew he was in trouble even before the election was called. Two weeks from polling day, campaign headquarters told him that if he did not stay home, he would lose the seat.

He chose to stick by Morrison.

Morton told people it was more important to spend time with the prime minister rather than stay to try to save his seat. He reckoned that if he could help make a difference in the national campaign effort, it might help locally, too.

Morton hates it when people refer to him as Morrison's security blanket, and there was a lot more to his work than that. On both the Expenditure Review Committee and the National Security Committee, Morton cast his political eye over every decision. Often, when he was in Canberra, he stayed at The Lodge.

When he was in trouble, Morrison felt much better having Morton with him. Others around Morrison felt better if he was there, too. As well as calming him down, according to those in the know, Morton acted as a buffer, or a shock absorber, a shield to protect others from Morrison's poor behaviour.

One Liberal MP described Morton's decision to effectively relinquish his seat as the 'leaky taps theory'. Plumbers neglect to fix their own taps. Former campaign directors don't always do what they should to safeguard their own electorates.

In his more forgiving moments, Frydenberg would argue that, overall, it had been a competent government and that Morrison deserved credit for three great achievements. The first was winning the 2019 election; the second was the negotiation of the AUKUS agreement, which Morrison personally drove, and which saw Australia cancel its submarine deal with France to acquire nuclear-powered submarines from the United States or the United Kingdom; and the third was securing Coalition agreement on a net-zero emissions target for 2050.

Unfortunately, there were negatives associated with all those things. If Morrison had lost the election in 2019, Frydenberg would have held onto Kooyong, the Liberal heartland would not have been obliterated, and Frydenberg would most likely have become leader. There would have been something left from which to rebuild in a term. Then, again, he would never have been treasurer during a pandemic.

Before and after the election, there were Liberals who privately argued it would have been better if they had lost in 2019. Some rued the day that Morrison won, because he was destroying the party they loved.

Gladys Berejiklian was so exasperated by Morrison's behaviour, particularly during and after the Black Summer fires, when she complained bitterly of his constant bullying, that she told colleagues it would have been better if Dutton had won the leadership in 2018.

The AUKUS deal to equip Australia with nuclear-powered submarines was indeed seen as a significant achievement, but marked by concerns the vessels will only surface around the time the trillion-dollar debt is paid off, and marred by Morrison's failure to inform the French in advance of the new deal, which led President Macron to utter the immortal line 'I don't think — I know', after journalist Bevan Shields asked him if he thought Morrison had lied to him in the lead-up to the cancellation of the contract. The US had wanted Morrison to inform both the French and the ALP well in advance. That didn't happen.

Macron's '*J'accuse*' crystallised peoples' thinking. It is no small thing when a world leader calls your prime minister a liar.

A collection of crisp sentences like that of Macron's, plus the lethal trilogy that Morrison employed — 'I don't hold a hose, mate', 'It's not my job', and 'It's not a race' — provided the ammunition that helped destroy his prime ministership.

As Simon Birmingham would say when it was all over,

Morrison's ability during the 2019 campaign to synthesise sentiments into short, sharp, punchy lines damaged Shorten and helped win the election.

In 2022, they became political suicide notes.

And the net-zero deal was undermined by the Nationals, including Joyce's best political mate, Matt Canavan, who argued it was effectively dead or a flexible option, providing the independents with their killer lines against the moderates that a vote for Frydenberg, or Trent Zimmerman, or Dave Sharma, or any of the rest of them, was a vote for Joyce. When polling showed that Morrison stunk, the Teals replaced Joyce with Morrison in Liberal heartland seats.

It helped cast them into opposition.

Former cabinet minister and Nationals MP Darren Chester said later that Morrison and Joyce should have considered stepping down.

'Both Morrison and Joyce knew months in advance that they were a drag on their parties in many parts of Australia, and neither of them contemplated standing aside,' Chester said in an interview for this book.

'They should have contemplated what was in the best interests of the Coalition. Neither of them had the capacity to think beyond their own status in political life and look at the broader opportunities for the Coalition government.'

He reckons people who believed they could turn it around were 'deluding themselves'.

Former Liberal cabinet minister Karen Andrews was withering in her assessment of what went wrong, which was basically everything—from Morrison's leadership style, to the campaign, to the delay in the New South Wales preselections, on top of the issues he neglected to address or addressed too late.

Andrews believes it is 'possible' that if Frydenberg had taken over, the damage to the party electorally might not have been as great, although she reckons the government was already gone by Christmas 2021.

'People had made up their minds,' she told me.

Andrews says she was not part of any push at the time, nor aware of one, but if the switch to Frydenberg had occurred, he might have saved some seats, including his own, and possibly helped stave off independents in Wentworth and Mackellar, and the Greens in Ryan. She believes it likely they would have still lost the election, but it would not have been the calamity for the Liberal Party it turned out to be.

Andrews, who was industry, science and technology minister before taking over from Dutton in Home Affairs, was regarded as one of the government's more solid performers during Covid. Back then, when assessing their opponents, senior Labor figures would nominate her as one of the most effective ministers. Liberal backbenchers would message Morrison during Question Time, saying: 'She's on fire.' He agreed.

Andrews did two interviews for this book several weeks before it was revealed that Morrison had sworn himself into her home affairs portfolio. She only found out about it when Albanese revealed it.

Her assessment of what went wrong in the campaign and of Morrison's leadership style, along with her comments on the asylum-seeker boat on election day, were made in our interviews before she knew about his secret acquisitions. What she said about him then was frank, but it was not infected by that knowledge.

Of course, when she did find out, she was horrified, and then did what Dutton should have done — called on Morrison to quit parliament. She told me in a subsequent interview that Morrison had diminished himself as prime minister, and diminished the cabinet. When he eventually rang her to apologise, she did not ask him why he had done it, because, she said, nothing he said would have been 'plausible'.

'There was so much loyalty given to Morrison, and he has, in hindsight, squandered all the goodwill that was there,' she said.

In our first interview, Andrews listed five reasons for the defeat: voters' intense dislike of Morrison; their belief that the government had not done enough on climate change and the environment; their concern that politics lacked integrity; their desire for politicians to behave better; and their conviction that the government had not been supportive of women.

On top of that, Morrison had made the mistake of releasing an important policy — allowing home-buyers to use a portion of their superannuation as a deposit — too late, after more than 50 per cent of Australians had voted and he had surrounded himself with supporters.

She didn't say it outright, but the tenor of her remarks showed that she meant men. That also was a common complaint. Women called his office 'the boys' club'. There were frequent complaints, from both men and women MPs, that his office was 'too blokey'.

Andrews believed it was a big mistake to build the campaign around Morrison, given that he had created or failed to address every major problem confronting the government that eventually dragged them all down.

She said that the presidential-style campaign worked in 2019, but in 2022 it was 'a very bad idea', considering Morrison's unpopularity.

'We knew there were people who had issues with Scott Morrison personally,' she said, admitting she once asked her daughters why people hated him so much.

She believed that other members of the team, particularly

women, needed to be showcased during the election and in the months preceding. She had raised this gently, she says, in meetings with Morrison and other ministers.

Andrews discussed it more directly with Morrison's senior political adviser, Yaron Finkelstein, towards the end of 2021, arguing that a woman—not necessarily her, although she would have been happy to play a bigger role—should always be at Morrison's side during the election campaign, and that he should be surrounded by members of the team.

She says that Finkelstein agreed with her, but it never happened. She also raised the idea a number of times with campaign officials, who would say, 'You're right', and then, again, nothing would happen.

She says that in discussions with other ministers and campaign officials, she argued that: 'We shouldn't be doing anything that is so presidential, because no one person could have universal appeal.'

Even though she had been led to believe beforehand that campaign 2022 would be different from campaign 2019, Morrison remained 'front and centre'.

'There were multiple discussions at party level, and a lot of expectation from me and colleagues, that things would be very different. That's what we understood to be happening,' she said.

She said that neither of the two official campaign spokespersons, Simon Birmingham and Anne Ruston, featured prominently during the campaign.

She said she would have 'gladly' done more, but was not asked, and in fact was told she was doing well in Queensland.

She said that although Morrison had campaigned well, Labor had done a very good job in attacking him and constantly reminding people about his character flaws. She said that while the quality of candidates mattered, the presidential nature of campaigns meant that was what would register.

Like so many other Liberals, she said long-time party supporters either spoke politely without engaging, or would say outright to her: 'I am not going to vote for you this time because I can't stand Scott Morrison.'

Lucy Wicks, whose main ambition as a teenager had been to one day represent her community, lost the seat of Robertson that she had held since 2013. Wicks was devastated. A seasoned campaigner who joined the party as a Young Liberal, Wicks was regarded as a solid local member.

Months later, she was still trying to work out where the local campaign had gone wrong and what else she might have done to prevent defeat. The sad truth is that there was nothing else she could have done.

Like the others, she knew she was in trouble at the pre-polls. She heard the same things from voters that her colleagues had.

Labor had plastered her electorate with 'Vote Wicks, Get Morrison' posters. Yet, unlike others, she would not lay the blame solely at Morrison's feet. A member of his prayer group, and part of the team that helped him secure the leadership in 2018, Wicks said it was 'never the fault of just one person'.

She blamed Labor's character assassination of Morrison, describing it as 'devious and ruthless'.

After the election, Chester was not impressed by arguments that the Nationals had managed to hang on to all their seats. He said that soon after Joyce had deposed McCormack, MPs had been briefed on party research that showed all Nationals MPs would hang on to their seats, so he reckons the Nationals did not do any better with Joyce than they were expected to under McCormack.

That wasn't the problem, Chester said. The problem was losing government. In his opinion, they locked themselves on a pathway to defeat on the day that Joyce regained the leadership on 21 June 2021. Women deserted the Coalition in greater numbers after that, Chester said, contributing to the defeat in May 2022.

'We lost all capacity to influence regional policies dealing with issues critical to our communities, like energy security and live-sheep exports,' Chester said, lamenting that they were all now in the hands of a left-wing Labor government.

'We aided and abetted the loss of government.'

Chester, first elected to Gippsland in 2008, said he had never fought in a campaign in which the National Party was used as a weapon against Liberals.

'They were calling Dave Sharma "Sharmaby",' he said.

Another senior National told me that every time Joyce visited the seat of Nicholls, which was under threat from an independent, the party's vote dropped. The Nationals' primary vote there crashed by one quarter, down to 26 per cent, after the independent, Rob Priestly, secured a 25 per cent primary vote.

Nicholls went from one of the safest Coalition seats — territory that was once the domain of the legendary Country Party leader John 'Black Jack' McEwan — to a marginal seat.

Chester told Joyce's office that Joyce would not be welcome in his electorate during the campaign. He believed Joyce would cost the Nationals votes in every seat south of the Murray. He also told the Nationals' state director in Victoria, Matt Harris, that Joyce should not visit the state at all during the campaign, and he certainly should not visit his seat of Gippsland.

Labor's research from focus groups had distilled Morrison's great flaws to a failure to accept blame or take responsibility. It was mirrored in the Liberals' focus-group research in his home state, and in the research for the independents, which found that his inability to connect was a big turn-off, particularly for women.

Fran Bailey, who had sacked him as head of Tourism Australia in 2006, had a simple explanation. 'He is missing that part of the brain that controls empathy,' she said.

A staggering 70 per cent of voters in Liberal heartland seats, including Frydenberg's seat of Kooyong, who were defecting to the independents, were driven by their dislike of Morrison.

A pivotal moment in Morrison's downfall came when he forced the removal of Christine Holgate as the head of Australia Post in October 2020 after she had spent $20,000 to buy Cartier watches as a reward for four employees who had secured contracts worth $220 million from the banks to enable Australia Post to keep its regional offices going.

After his brutal attack on Holgate in parliament, Morrison thought he had won the meat tray in the pub lottery, that what Holgate had done wouldn't pass the sniff test down at the local. He was as wrong about that as he was about so many other things.

Professional women, seething, mobilised to bring the party to its knees. In the regions where post offices had been saved, they were furious. Thousands of them sent $5 notes to Morrison to pay for the watches.

Morrison not only harmed a woman who had done nothing wrong, but he once again inflicted considerable harm on himself. Men were equally horrified that a prime minister would use his office in such an intemperate way. He ignored appeals from prominent businessmen, and from serving and former politicians—Nationals and Liberals—to retract his remarks, apologise, and restore Holgate to the job.

Women, already deserting the Coalition, stampeded over the handling of the Brittany Higgins' rape allegations. Higgins, a young staffer, alleged she had been raped in 2019 in the defence industry minister's office only a few steps from the prime minister's suite by a fellow staffer, Bruce Lehrmann. (Lehrmann later denied sexually assaulting her.) In the wake of Higgins' allegations in 2021, the spotlight fell on Morrison and his government's political management of a highly sensitive situation. It did not help Morrison at the time that his wife, Jenny, had to explain the gravity of the allegations to him. He could not understand why people disparaged him for that.

Through their different experiences, Holgate and Higgins bonded. They became friends. Higgins says she cried on election night. That night, at least, she felt both sad and vindicated. Holgate says: 'When it was clear that he would no longer be prime minister, I went home and slept well for the first time in 22 months.'

Morrison's misjudgements continued until the very end. Katherine Deves was his captain's pick for Warringah, after he succeeded in grinding down the New South Wales division, inciting a costly civil war, yelling and thumping the table during one federal executive meeting, demanding the right to preselect the people he wanted.

In a desperate, calculated move, he thrust the complex, sensitive issue of transgender athletes and sport into the centre of the election campaign, using a woman with an extensive history of transphobic, offensive material on social media, ignoring the impact it would have on his moderate MPs, including Frydenberg, who were under threat from independents.

Deves dominated the campaign on days when Morrison should have been talking about other matters; she was completely unsuited to the electorate; the locals refused to support her; she drove the party's vote even further down than Abbott had when he lost the seat; and she cost moderates from North Sydney to Kooyong a lot of heartache and a lot of votes.

Deves did something else. She confirmed and exposed the great divide in the Liberal Party between its moderate base and the religious right that Morrison courted and fostered, who contacted MPs and campaign headquarters to insist she be supported. Moderates were also not speaking with one voice—Jason Falinski endorsed her before and during the campaign.

Marise Payne, then Morrison's minister for women, was very upset that Deves had been chosen. Payne thought she was appalling as a candidate, and conveyed her views to Morrison. According to one colleague, she had advised Morrison not to preselect her.

Others said she had appealed to him to disendorse Deves during the campaign. Payne did not deny this when I put it to her. Alex Hawke also told him not to choose her. Simon Birmingham, intervening on behalf of other moderates, urged him to dump her. Morrison ignored him, too.

He rejected demands by other moderate Liberals such as Dave Sharma and Trent Zimmerman, and advice from senior members of his campaign team, for her to be disendorsed. It now sounds perverse, but he told them if he did that, his judgement would be questioned.

If he had agreed early enough to dump her, it might have been a two-day wonder. Instead, it boomed and crashed all the way through the campaign and beyond.

He bragged he had chosen her, and he stuck by her, regardless of the damage he was inflicting on his campaign and his MPs. Campaign officials suspected that Morrison talked Deves into staying in the race when she was on the verge of pulling out.

Former Liberal senator and prominent New South Wales moderate Chris Puplick, who lives in Warringah and has stayed active in the party, was outraged by her preselection.

'Thinking about what happened, you have to assume either

that Morrison was just being an evangelical idiot in picking Deves, or else this was a deliberate tactic—a disastrously failed one—to sacrifice genuine Liberals in the hope of winning God-knows-what somewhere else, in which case it was an act of treason and he should be expelled from the party,' Puplick told the Warringah federal electorate conference three weeks after the election.

There were mutterings of support for Puplick's general proposition, although not for his call to expel Morrison. If small-l Liberals planning to vote for the Teals had any doubts, they were dispelled by the Deves debacle.

Labor managed to win majority government with a primary vote slightly under 33 per cent, its lowest since the war—something that pundits had said could never happen from such a low base.

Many political observers, their powerful outlets, and a few misguided Liberals, including Morrison, firmly believed that Albanese could never win because he was too left-wing, too timid, or too dumb.

Albanese was neither weak nor stupid. A warrior of the socialist left, he had been blooded in the factional wars of the New South Wales Labor Party, where he fought the right to the bitter end, always surviving to fight another day. Asked what that says about him, Albanese replies: 'I am tough.'

He never gave up. As the only child of a single mother raised in social housing, he was hardy and resourceful. He dragged himself and his party towards the centre. He devised the small-target strategy, which after the election didn't seem small at all. He minimised the potential points of conflict to limit the scope for Morrison to do what he loved most—to tear down an opponent.

Albanese chose a few key areas: climate change, childcare,

aged care, affordable housing, an integrity commission, and the Indigenous voice to parliament. He was determined not to repeat Bill Shorten's mistake of trying to 'govern from opposition'.

He held his nerve, withstanding relentless criticism from the media and some internal sceptics, who kept insisting that Labor needed a bold agenda to win. He bounced back after a terrible first campaign week, full of mostly self-inflicted harm that might have flattened a lesser person, and which probably denied Labor a bigger majority, then still went on to accomplish a very rare feat. He won majority government for Labor.

Albanese would say later that he had been underestimated all his life. Morrison never rated him. Some of the egomaniacal journalists travelling with Albanese brought shame on themselves and their profession by treating him with contempt.

There is a line between journalists being tough and probing — something that a few of them found difficult to comprehend in three years of covering Morrison — and being unprofessional or objectionable. A feral few crossed that line during Albanese's press conferences by orchestrating hysterical questioning, by sniggering, eye-rolling, and heckling, and then by making sure they starred in the often-misleading packages they put together.

They got it very badly wrong, just like they got it wrong when they said Monique Ryan would never be able to unseat Frydenberg, or that Allegra Spender could not beat Sharma in Wentworth.

Anyone who had spent more than a few minutes talking to the independents, the people who supported them, and the voters in those electorates — many of them lifelong Liberals — would have twigged that not only were these women exceptional candidates, but that a rebellion was brewing, much of it inflamed by a primeval dislike of Morrison.

It was visceral, as Ryan would say. Those who paid attention could hear it, see it, and smell it. Sharma said later that the Teals became a repository for anti-Morrison votes.

From the west coast to the east, from north to south, the most common refrain heard by Liberal candidates at polling booths from voters was that, as much as they liked them, they could not vote for them because of Morrison. Not even Stuart Robert, in his Queensland electorate of Fadden, displayed posters of Morrison at his polling booths. The only photos that Robert had on his corflutes were of himself.

Those of us who had been around many campaigns could not remember a time when a leader's own people disliked him so much that he could not set foot in once blue-ribbon seats.

Liberals clung to the hope that Albanese's last week would be as bad as his first, and that they could make up more ground. Waiting for your opponent to screw up is a poor substitute for an agenda.

Albanese performed well in the last week, opening up a critical point of difference on wages. With one word — 'Absolutely' — he unequivocally declared himself for increases for the poorest-paid, while Morrison showed he was not, ridiculing Albanese as a 'loose unit'.

The overwhelming emotion that Albanese felt on election night, after he realised he had won, was relief. And vindication. The burden of expectations had been a great weight on his shoulders.

After Morrison called him to concede, Albanese hugged and kissed his son, Nathan, his partner, Jodie Haydon, and the small group that had gathered at his Marrickville home. Some cried, but not him.

'I cry all the time. It's a miracle I didn't cry then,' he said later. 'I cry all the time, I'm hopeless. But I didn't then. It was like, wow. You know, like wow — this has happened.'

'I feared letting people down and letting the country down

because I also, genuinely, had just trepidation about what sort of government they would be in their fourth term. I think that the Morrison government in their last year were worse than they were the year before, and worse than they were the year before that,' Albanese told me.

'I just shuddered to think how arrogant and unworthy of our nation they would be if they got a fourth term.'

He had a very low opinion of Morrison, and it was reciprocated. He was also determined to bring a vastly different style and tone to the job and to government.

No one had ever heard Albanese say in his youth that he wanted to be prime minister, although someone later told him that his mother Maryanne had predicted it. A few of his closest friends never thought he would make it, believing it only when he prepared to give his victory speech.

After he was elected leader, particularly during the long periods of Covid lockdown, he thought a lot about how he would conduct himself if he won.

He began in office much better than many expected, but, as he keeps saying, people keep underestimating him. When he marked his first 100 days, it could have been Albo of the 1,000 days. It felt as if he had been there much longer, so settled was he in the job, so comfortable in his own skin.

Imperfect on the campaign trail, as prime minister he accurately read the mood of the electorate. They wanted civility, they wanted collaboration, they wanted honesty, and they wanted the integrity of institutions to be restored.

The immediate problems he confronted were monumental: China's increasing belligerence, cost-of-living increases, labour shortages, escalating interest rates, and a huge level of government debt. All of them were seemingly insoluble, all contributing to perceptions that the economy would crash, that he would only have one term in majority government and a second in minority government if he was lucky.

He was calm, carried himself with assurance with world leaders when he was repairing damaged relationships, gave speeches full of hope and inspiration, promised to keep his promises, refused to bend to the Greens, and set about fixing important matters left untouched or unfinished or in disrepair.

His jobs-and-skills summit, where unions and business groups concentrated on what they could agree on, rather than on what divided them, was as important for the spirit of the thing as for the decisions that followed.

After the summit, Brendan O'Connor picked up and expanded Robert's skills plan. O'Connor pushed for a national agreement to reform the vocational-education sector, foreshadowing $3.7 billion in extra spending over five years from 2024. He was positive about getting all states and territories to sign up to reform the sector by eliminating duplication, simplifying rules, and injecting more money.

People responded well in those early stages to Albanese's warmth, his authenticity, and his apparent decency.

By the end of the campaign, the Morrison government had next to no friends. There were no respected voices advocating for them, or making the case for the Coalition's re-election. Business stayed quiet. Farmers' groups were mute. They had all supported action on climate change, setting emission targets higher even than Labor had.

Businesspeople could see what was coming. They let their money talk. Not long before the election, on 12 May, Albanese attended a fundraising dinner at the home of a Brisbane businesswoman. She had hoped to get 10 people at $10,000 a head. On the night, there were 22 people seated at the tables. For the first time in a long time, there was no complaint from Labor about how tough it was to raise money.

Months before the election, I asked one leading business figure to nominate what would be the major issue of the campaign. Without pausing, even for a second, he replied: 'Well, it certainly won't be policy.'

One Liberal MP, infuriated by the lack of support, complained: 'We destroyed our economic narrative and economic DNA to save them with JobKeeper. Fucking no one remembers.'

Morrison had reinvented himself as the daggy dad after he toppled Turnbull—a persona never before seen by any of his colleagues or close associates.

Under 'personal interests' in his 2006 CV, he had listed an AFL team, the Western Bulldogs, but neglected to mention the Cronulla Sharks. He never stopped trying to reinvent himself. In the process, he never provided his government with defining values, or a mission, or a reason for being.

Nick Minchin, a former Howard government cabinet minister, former party state director, and serving male vice-president on the party's federal executive, is no catastrophist. He has seen worse defeats. He cites Malcolm Fraser's loss to Bob Hawke in 1983: Fraser, also aiming for a fourth term, lost 24 seats in a smaller parliament.

Minchin conceded that two years of Covid and lockdowns were 'considerable' factors in Morrison's defeat. He said that it had played to the advantage of incumbents in state elections, but not federally, due to problems with the vaccination rollout and Omicron.

Echoing the view of others, including Karen Andrews, Minchin believed that the government erred in not outlining an agenda for a fourth term. That failure ensured that the focus stayed on Morrison's unpopularity.

'In the absence of significant issues, leadership became more significant in voters' minds than it might have been,' Minchin said in an interview for this book.

'Albanese wasn't Hawke, but he wasn't hated or despised. People didn't think about him much, didn't really have a view of him.

'Morrison's significant unpopularity was a major factor in the defeat.

'A more sober, objective analysis would have said we needed some defining issues, policies, setting out a fourth-term agenda, to make sure the campaign was not about leadership.

'They were seduced into believing they could replicate 2019, that Albanese was not popular, and they could go into the election without any real agenda. Frankly, that was a mistake.'

He says John Howard probably saved himself in 1998 by going into the election promising to introduce a GST. Howard was out there fighting for something he believed was right for the country.

Minchin says the lesson from 2022 is: 'If you are seeking re-election after nine years, you have to give people a reason to vote for you.' And that doesn't mean promising to fix every basketball court in every marginal electorate.

Minchin believes integrity was as much an issue in the success of the Teals as climate change, which he reckons has an influence depending on weather conditions at the time.

With his old finance minister's hat on, Minchin says: 'One of the upsides of the campaign was it demonstrated rampant pork-barrelling is not going to save a dying government.

'You can't win by throwing money around like Santa Claus.'

Howard was another who said, after the election, that a major factor in the defeat was a lack of policy. He criticised the absence of a manifesto, delivering a lukewarm assessment of the former government by saying its record was 'very mixed'. In an interview with *The Australian*, Howard also attacked Morrison over his treatment of Christine Holgate.

Howard rang Morrison to forewarn him of the publication of his unflattering comments. Morrison was upset and bitterly disappointed by Howard's damning assessment, especially as Howard had been so supportive during his time in office.

'We had no agenda for a fourth term,' one prominent backbencher said. 'We didn't tell people what we would do with it, other than we were not Labor. Labor was scary in 2019; they were not scary in 2022. It wasn't going to work twice in a row.'

In fact, there were three policies agreed to by Morrison's Expenditure Review Committee ahead of the budget that might have helped dispel some of that and to set up points of difference with Labor. The first was to expand the cashless debit card; the second, to allow pensioners to work and earn more while retaining their pension; and the third, to allow people to access their superannuation for housing. There was a fourth if you included Robert's skills package.

Only one saw the light of day during the campaign. That was super for housing, which wasn't released until five days before the election. The other, to encourage older people to stay in the workforce, was adopted by Labor and trialled after its jobs-and-skills summit.

Minchin's post-election analysis reflected the most common complaint of Morrison's colleagues, which was that he stood for nothing and believed in nothing, except what would get him through the news cycle.

Often, it would be with one stunt after another, each more

ridiculous than the one that preceded it, not stopping until close
to the end when he crash-tackled eight-year-old Luca Fauvette on
a football field. It was right up there with the Mark Latham–John
Howard handshake moment. Worse, if that's possible.

Labor's national secretary and campaign director, Paul Erickson,
wound up Labor's research for the campaign on 19 May, the night
after Morrison bulldozed Luca.

The focus group was asked: 'Have you heard or seen anything
in the past few days that's altered the way you feel about Scott
Morrison and/or the Coalition?'

A voter from the Victorian seat of Casey volunteered: 'Yes. The
soccer incident. If Scott Morrison wants to lead the country again,
why is he playing silly games like football with children?'

Tim Gartrell, who worked on Albanese's 1996 campaign to
enter federal parliament, was federal campaign director for Kevin
07, and joined Albanese as chief of staff in 2019, was gobsmacked
when he saw the footage.

He reckons the crash-tackle sealed the deal in voters' minds.
Gartrell would know. He was also national secretary and campaign
director in 2004 when he saw a menacing Latham grip Howard's
hand as if he wanted to squeeze the life out of him. The image
remains seared on his brain.

Morrison had never had many friends inside the parliamentary
Liberal Party. His Machiavellian, manipulative ways enabled him
to outwit both Peter Dutton and Malcolm Turnbull. Dutton knew
what he was like all along. When Turnbull discovered the full extent
of it, he became an implacable, relentless critic.

Among his detractors, and there were plenty, Morrison was
regarded as the worst prime minister since Billy McMahon. After

news of his secret ministries emerged, they revised that to say he was worse than McMahon. Worse even than Tony Abbott, who lasted a scant two years in the job, whose chief accomplishments were that he destroyed Julia Gillard and then himself, and then, aided and abetted by Dutton and Morrison, destroyed Turnbull.

Morrison squandered the goodwill of his miracle win. Instead of using it to push for much-needed reforms, he stood still. He snuck off to Hawaii for a holiday during the Black Summer bushfires. In the end, he was seen to have failed to rise to the challenge of the pandemic. Under him, Australia's debt topped a trillion dollars. He thought reform was a vanity project. He said he never wanted to leave a legacy.

He got his wish.

Unless you count taking the Liberal Party to the brink of destruction. Or, as constitutional lawyer Professor Anne Twomey said of his secret ministries: 'It is the damage to public trust that will long outlast Morrison's tenure. It is a poisonous legacy.'

While the hard right did not mourn the passing of the moderates, they had been an integral part of the character and spirit of the Liberal Party that Menzies had created. And, as one senior New South Wales Liberal reminded the party later, after people like Abbott were arguing they should discard their heartland, it was where most of its membership resided and where most of its money was raised.

One senior member of the government, who was close to Morrison, said the Liberals had not only lost professional women, but it wasn't connecting with professional men, either. Those connections had to be restored. He said the party had hollowed out, and that the influence of those that had contributed to its success, including the Murdoch media, had diminished.

'Australian society has changed a lot. The party needs to work out how to relate to it as much in Townsville as in North Sydney,' he said. 'There is a very interesting process the party needs to go through—a long and tortuous one—and there is no guarantee of coming out the other side.'

The more thoughtful Liberals were pondering the party's future, if indeed there was one.

Morrison sought refuge in scripture and victimhood. Speaking to the Asian Leadership Conference on 14 July in Seoul, Morrison said he had 'taken the hit' for the inevitable squabbles between the federal and state governments during Covid.

Good try. It might have worked for the international audience, but it is unlikely to get traction here.

He should have been the great winner, not the biggest loser, from the pandemic. If he had done all that he was supposed to do, if he had fulfilled his promises on acquiring vaccines and organising the rollout, then maybe that would have transcended the other quarrels that Australians had with his leadership. But he didn't. He picked unnecessary fights with state premiers.

His early closure of Australia's borders was vital in limiting the number of deaths and protecting businesses, as was the spending of hundreds of billions of dollars to keep the economy afloat. He should have been able to capitalise on that. He couldn't, because it was the premiers who were seen to have done all the heavy lifting on lockdowns, rollouts, and quarantine.

One of the most acute observations about the election result came from Labor's new climate and energy minister, Chris Bowen. He likened the emergence of the Teal independents to the great Labor split of the 1950s, which led to the creation of the Democratic Labour Party.

'That didn't destroy us, but it kept us in opposition for a long time. It has that potential [for the Liberals],' Bowen told me, predicting that the Liberals would never regain government unless they re-won that constituency.

The great Liberal split may yet come if the irreconcilable differences between the religious right, the conservatives, and the moderates can't be resolved.

Which is not to say that Labor doesn't have life-threatening challenges of its own from the Greens or the Teals in inner-urban areas, or from One Nation or the United Australia Party in safe suburban areas stealing its working-class vote. It most certainly does, as a primary vote of 32.6 per cent showed.

By the time of the 2025 election, Albanese hopes those threats will be mitigated by his performance personally and by the government's generally.

The early signals were good. He promoted 10 women into his cabinet from a caucus that was at last beginning to resemble Australia. The opposition provided a sorry contrast. It had lost 18 seats to Labor, the Teals, and the Greens. Only nine Liberal women were left in the House of Representatives—the lowest number for three decades. The party's moderate wing was gutted.

Just as Labor decided in 2019 to recycle its 2016 strategy with such disastrous consequences, Morrison's strategic decision to try to repeat history, rather than to learn the lessons from it, was catastrophic for the Liberal Party.

In 2018, the moderates spurned Julie Bishop and made Morrison prime minister to block Dutton. He owed them.

Yet they stayed mute—not all of them, but enough of them, even when it became obvious they had been manipulated, even when it became obvious he wasn't up to the job. They held back at critical points until it was too late to extract concessions that might have saved them, saved him from himself, and saved the Liberal Party from near oblivion.

A few of them wished they had spoken out more. Or they sought to blame others—including this author—for being critical rather than joining the squad to cheer on the emperor they had elected, who was not only stark naked, but as they later discovered, stark-raving mad.

CHAPTER TWO

Straight to Hawaii

Scott Morrison effectively destroyed his prime ministership on 15 December 2019, when he boarded a flight in Sydney with his wife, Jenny, and their daughters, Abbey and Lily, bound for a Hawaiian holiday.

His departure during the Black Summer fires, and everything that flowed from that fateful decision—the secrecy, the lies surrounding his whereabouts, his protest that it wasn't his job to hold a hose, his attempt to force firefighters and victims in Cobargo to shake his hand—provided piercing insights into his character and his judgement that reverberated all the way through his term as prime minister, right up until election day, 21 May 2022, when posters of him wearing a Hawaiian shirt and a frangipani headdress were plastered around polling booths in targeted electorates by his opponents.

Diamond Head on Waikiki has been dormant for at least 150,000 years. The eruptions for Morrison will continue forever. It was the seminal moment of his prime ministership.

Everybody can see it now; almost everybody concedes the extent of the damage done, including Andrew Carswell, one of his closest advisers, who regrets he did not try to talk his boss out of going to

Hawaii, and wishes he had not lied to journalists about where he had gone. With the benefit of hindsight, Morrison's chief of staff, John Kunkel, says of course it was a bad decision for Morrison to go to Hawaii, but failing to advise him not to go is not at the top of his list of regrets.

Alex Hawke, one of Morrison's closest allies and numbers men, acknowledging the extent of the damage he had inflicted on his leadership by that one decision, told me that if it had not been for Covid, Morrison would not have survived as prime minister until the end of 2020.

Australia was already on fire, hundreds of homes had been lost, six people had died, and there were warnings that large swathes of the country were threatened by catastrophic fires when he and his family set off.

But Morrison had promised Jenny and the girls a family holiday, and despite the fact they had already been to Fiji in June soon after the 2019 election, and despite at least one tentative suggestion — from the Nationals' leader, Michael McCormack — that he should think carefully before going, he was determined they would have their break, where they could relax without being pestered for selfies.

In 2019, almost 300,000 Australians holidayed in Hawaii. As luck would have it, a few of them took selfies with Morrison. Ooops.

By the end of his tenure, apart from a brief revival in the first year of Covid, the deeply embedded impression among many voters was that he was the prime minister who went missing when his country needed him most, who seemed incapable of accepting responsibility when things went wrong, who always seemed to blame others for his mistakes or his failures, and who too often failed to tell them the truth.

There was no official announcement, as per convention — see

the pattern here — that he was overseas and that the deputy prime minister, Michael McCormack, was acting prime minister. Word seeped out he was in Honolulu while the bushfires were engulfing the country, thanks to the detective work of Greens MP David Shoebridge, who had followed a tip-off.

After he was flushed out, Morrison uttered the unforgettable line 'I don't hold a hose, mate' to explain his absence. Those six words now warrant being engraved on his political tombstone.

Josh Frydenberg says it's a bit of a blur, but he thinks he didn't know where Morrison was going for his holiday until he was packed and ready to go. Frydenberg says if he had known, he would have tried to persuade him not to go.

Frydenberg surmised that Morrison felt safe going then because it was not that long after the election, and he had felt secure politically. He would also have been exhausted by the election, and probably felt he would not have been able to have a proper escape in Australia.

Alex Hawke did not know that Morrison was going. If he had, he says he would have counselled him against it. He cannot believe that none of his staff advised him not to go. Apart from the fact that Morrison lacked a senior female political adviser, he thought the office was weak and should have offered more resistance.

Hawke believed Morrison had booked to go to the family's usual holiday spot on the New South Wales south coast, then switched to Hawaii and went, despite the fires. 'That's triple bad,' Hawke said.

'When you become prime minister, the sacrifices are, you have to give up your life.'

Morrison told Simon Birmingham about his plans at Christmas drinks to mark the end of the parliamentary year, which concluded on 6 December. He told Birmingham he would have been happy to go to their usual vacation spot on the New South Wales south coast, but Jenny and the girls had put up with a lot. The constant requests for selfies had started to grate. They found it impossible to relax.

Birmingham understood. He was also planning to holiday in England with his family, where he mixed in a bit of work by announcing a new tourism campaign, which later had to be abandoned. He saw no reason to counsel Morrison against it. Everyone needed a good break.

Morrison tried to take out some insurance by texting Albanese on 15 December to say he was taking leave with his family. He did not say where he was going, nor did Albanese ask, and nor did he disclose Morrison's text.

McCormack, a cautious politician, refuses to detail his discussion with Morrison when the prime minister first told him he was going to Hawaii, which McCormack thinks was around 10 days before he went, because they were 'private conversations'.

However, he admitted he had expressed his reservations, suggesting that Morrison think carefully about it, asking him: 'Are you sure that's a good idea?'

Morrison told him what he had told everybody else: he had promised Jenny and the girls a holiday, it had been booked, and they were going.

Even now, McCormack is not critical of Morrison for going. He believes he deserved a holiday with his family, says the Black Summer fires were not raging when he left, and that it is wrong for people to continue to hold it against him.

Despite that, he and Morrison's staff knew it would become an issue once people realised he was gone and that McCormack had become acting prime minister. He assumed those duties from 9.20 pm on 15 December to 8.00 pm on 21 December, when Morrison returned.

McCormack told the prime minister's office on the usual early-morning phone hook-up—he thinks on the day after Morrison left—that he would be doing media and was bound to be asked by journalists where the prime minister was.

They were not keen for him to advertise the fact that he was acting in the job. McCormack says they did not ask him to lie, but it is clear from the conversation they had, which was the political equivalent of tooth extraction, that the office did not want him to draw attention to the prime minister's absence.

McCormack told Morrison's staff—he says he can't remember who was on the call—that he would not avoid answering by telling journalists they should direct their questions to the prime minister's office. He told them if he was asked, he would say the prime minister was overseas. If pressed further, he would say Morrison was in America, and if pressed further still, he would say Morrison was in Hawaii.

He told them he would not lie, because he would be held to account for it later. He was not prepared to say the prime minister was somewhere he wasn't.

'I don't lie, I have never lied,' he told me later. Even though he thinks much of the criticism was unfair, McCormack concedes the damage was done. 'If only he had gone to the south coast,' he says now.

Andrew Carswell was one of Morrison's most trusted advisers. He had worked as a journalist for Sydney's *Daily Telegraph* before beginning as a speechwriter with then treasurer Morrison two weeks before the budget in April 2017. He became press secretary soon after. A mutual acquaintance, Ben Fordham, had put Carswell in touch with Morrison.

Carswell was not a political writer, but obviously knew of Morrison through his public and private persona. Carswell admired him, and they shared something important: their faith. Carswell was also Pentecostal.

He now concedes that while Morrison was able to rebuild during Covid, the Hawaiian holiday damaged him. He agreed it was a seminal moment in Morrison's prime ministership that resonated till the end.

'That was a mistake,' Carswell told me. 'He admits that openly, and we should have stepped in, yes. It was one of my mistakes as well, not having the courage to stop him and prevent him from going.'

Carswell said all the senior staff knew, and as far as he was aware no one counselled Morrison against it. He knows now he should have said something. 'You are paid to give advice,' he said.

'I didn't realise the consequences.

'All the senior staff would say that was something that should have happened.'

He also admits he was wrong to lie to journalists about the prime minister's whereabouts.

'I made the wrong decision. I tried to be too clever by half,' he said.

'I made many mistakes in that time. You don't get every call right. Sadly, this was a major miscalculation.'

Carswell wasn't aware if Morrison had told his colleagues, but assumed he had.

Ben Morton knew Morrison was going to Hawaii. Morton also did not try to talk him out of it, nor did he begrudge him a holiday with his family. Morton was holidaying in Singapore with his family when things really went belly-up.

He cut short his holiday and flew back to Australia. He missed the Cobargo fiasco; however, he was with Morrison when he went to devastated Kangaroo Island. Morrison committed double faux pas there when he commiserated with locals by saying at least no one had died. In fact, two people—a father and son—had died trying to get to their property.

Then, after he was corrected, Morrison said: 'Yes, two, that's quite right. I was thinking about firefighters firstly.'

Morton, who had an office inside the prime minister's suite before he became a minister, was seen as a political fixer; however, there was no fixing this. The damage was well and truly done. It meant that Morton had to be beside Morrison, literally, at every critical moment of his prime ministership.

Before he left, Morrison had resisted calls from Albanese for exhausted firefighters to be paid for their efforts, because he reckoned they wanted to be there. And he, obviously, did not.

It was in no way a normal fire season. Nor had the situation eased by the time of his departure. A catastrophic fire danger had already been declared in the Greater Sydney region on 12 November, for the first time since the measure had been introduced in 2009. Total fire bans had been declared in seven regions of New South Wales, including Greater Sydney.

On 14 November, there were reports that 23 former fire and emergency leaders had tried for months to warn Morrison that Australia needed more water-bombers to tackle bigger, faster, and hotter bushfires.

Former New South Wales fire and rescue chief Greg Mullins, one of the founders of the Emergency Leaders for Climate Action group, said on ABC radio that the group had sought a meeting with the federal government to discuss the issue in April and again in May, immediately after the 2019 federal election.

On the day Morrison left, 15 December, a massive fire, estimated to be 400,000 hectares, was burning at Gospers Mountain, threatening residents in several Blue Mountains towns. By then, an estimated 724 homes, 49 facilities, and 1,582 outbuildings had been destroyed since the start of the fire season in September. Six people had died, and 2.7 million hectares scorched.

Dozens of buildings were feared damaged or destroyed, with reports that some firefighters might have lost their homes. By that night, 108 fires were burning in New South Wales, 57 of them uncontained, with more than 2,000 firefighters battling them. Temperatures in the mid-40s were being predicted for later in the week.

The first intimation that Morrison had vanished came in a tweet from the New South Wales Greens MP, now senator, David Shoebridge at 11.17 am on 16 December 2019.

> Where's the prime minister? We just confirmed with the Deputy PM's office that he's acting PM until at least Thursday. Have they noticed the country is on fire? We have heard rumours @ScottMorrisonMP is in Hawaii #ClimateEmergency.

It was retweeted 592 times. Shoebridge recalls the events of that day with clarity.

An hour before he tweeted, Shoebridge's office had been contacted by a trusted source, one he says was well connected to the Liberal Party. Shoebridge will not say who it was, except that it was someone credible. The source advised that Morrison had left for a Hawaiian holiday. No proof was provided, but Shoebridge surmises the source was dumbfounded, so wanted the story to get out.

After discussing it with his staff, Shoebridge rang McCormack's office. He asked the woman who answered if McCormack was acting prime minister, because he had heard the prime minister was overseas.

He got a cagey, noncommittal response, so he said he wanted

to send correspondence to the prime minister. Could he send it to McCormack as acting? Yes, he could, she replied. He then asked if McCormack would be acting on Tuesday (yes) then Wednesday (yes), and Thursday (yes). After that, she clammed up.

It was enough. That night, after Shoebridge's tweet appeared, Samantha Maiden posted her first story for *The New Daily*, quoting Morrison's office as saying it was 'wrong' to say he was in Hawaii. His office also denied it to other journalists, then cited 'national security' as a reason for not divulging his whereabouts.

Two days later, Maiden reported confirmation that he had boarded a Jetstar flight with the family bound for Honolulu, travelling business class. Soon after, photos appeared of Morrison in Waikiki smiling happily with other tourists, giving a thumbs-up.

On Thursday night, 19 December, a tree fell on the truck of two volunteer firefighters, Geoffrey Keaton, 32, and Andrew O'Dwyer, 36, both fathers to young children, killing them both. The national disaster and emergency management minister, David Littleproud, who did not know that Morrison was in Hawaii until the story broke, texted him to tell him about the accident.

Littleproud and Morrison did not get along, but Littleproud was giving him a big hint: *Come home.*

Morrison's office had already been in touch with the prime minister.

The next morning, Morrison called in to 2GB from Honolulu. He told interviewer John Stanley he would be coming back 'as soon as I can'. His enemies scoffed at that, saying he should have jumped on a plane immediately.

They couldn't believe what he said next. 'The girls and Jen will stay on and stay out the rest of the time we had booked here. But I know Australians understand this, and they'll be pleased I'm coming back, I'm sure,' he said.

'They know that, you know, I don't hold a hose, mate, and I don't sit in a control room.'

Those six words—'I don't hold a hose, mate'—were jarring to almost everyone who heard them; however, he liked them so much he repeated them when he returned at a doorstop on Sunday 22 December, after he visited the New South Wales Rural Fire Service.

'I get it that people would have been upset to know that I was holidaying with my family while their families were under great stress,' he said. 'They know that I'm not going to stand there and hold a hose. I am not a trained firefighter, nor am I an expert like those in the next room doing such an amazing job.'

When he visited Cobargo, one of the worst-affected areas in New South Wales, he tried to force people to shake hands with him. They did it grudgingly, or refused. Locals swore at him to 'fuck off'. Littleproud, who was with him that day, says Morrison was deeply shaken by the reaction.

The footage from that day remains a perpetual reminder of a man seemingly incapable of offering empathy or comfort.

The day the story broke that Morrison was in Hawaii, Victorian backbencher Russell Broadbent was picking up the former member for Kooyong, Petro Georgiou, to take him to the Bamboo House, the popular Chinese restaurant favoured by Victorian Liberals, for their regular lunch with the former Victorian premier Ted Baillieu.

Georgiou told Broadbent in the car he had just heard on the radio that Morrison was in Hawaii on a holiday. 'Bullshit!' Broadbent said. He couldn't believe it was true, so they didn't talk about it and moved on to other things.

They didn't get back to it until they were seated at the table with Baillieu, who checked his phone and, yes indeedy, the story was off and running. Morrison was in Honolulu.

They were incredulous. As experienced political operators, they were horrified. As Australians, they were aghast. They were shocked that a prime minister would leave the country for a holiday while it was on fire. They were in furious agreement: here was a man with no judgement.

They believed that Morrison had done incalculable damage to his prime ministership that could probably not be undone, and that the only option was for him to come home immediately.

They reached a unanimous conclusion: Morrison 'was stuffed'. Broadbent agrees that Covid helped Morrison resurrect his prime ministership, and then says: 'Covid buried him as well.'

'It was probably his undoing. He thought he could do anything and get away with it,' he said. That was even before Broadbent knew about the secret ministries.

Broadbent had never been a fan of Morrison's, mainly because of his approach to refugees. When Ben Morton approached him to vote for Morrison during the leadership turmoil, Broadbent says he flatly refused, telling Morton, 'Listen, your bloke is an arrogant arsehole.' Morton replied: 'Yeah, there is that, but there is another side to him, too.'

After the election, Broadbent, who suffered an 8 per cent swing against him on primaries in his seat of Monash, but held on, said it was no accident that Labor had installed photos of Morrison in Hawaiian gear at countless polling booths. Often, there were no words or slogans on those posters. They were not needed.

One cabinet minister, aghast at hearing that Morrison was in Hawaii, told people at the time that Morrison was 'terminal'.

Bridget Archer says all leaders deserve to holiday with their family; however, she thought the timing of the Hawaiian trip was all wrong. She described it as the beginning of the end for Morrison.

When Karen Andrews asked her three daughters—aged 18, 22, and 26—why people 'hated Morrison so much', they told her it was because he went to Hawaii during the fires.

'He should have been back here,' Andrews said. 'The optics were awful.'

She agreed that everyone deserved a holiday but added: 'If you are in the top job, you are giving up your personal life.'

She also thought her daughters' opinion might have been influenced by the number of times she had to forgo family events because of the demands of her job.

As it happened, the New South Wales Liberal Forum's Christmas Party, the traditional gathering of moderates, was held that year on 21 December as Morrison was winging his way home. It was at the Mosman home of Kevin McCann, a prominent party fundraiser and former chair of Macquarie Bank.

The gathering of around 100 was addressed by Julie Bishop, who had resigned her once-safe seat of Curtin before the election, after it became clear to her that she was not welcome in the Morrison cabinet.

Speaking from a balcony in a knockout white dress, Bishop 'happily' remarked about Morrison: 'The further from the fires, the easier the solution.' Those present said she was in top form.

Unsurprisingly, there was a lot of love for Bishop in that room, but not so much for Morrison. Both Marise Payne and Trent Zimmerman copped criticism for failing to support her. Morrison's coal stunt—when he had taken a lump of coal into Question Time, brandishing it like kryptonite while urging Labor MPs not to be frightened of it—had gone down very badly with those moderates. They were wondering how some sense was going to be injected into the climate debate.

'There was huge support for what Julie was saying about the response to the bushfires,' one moderate said.

Morrison seemed temperamentally unsuited to leadership, at

whatever level or in whatever organisation.

Fran Bailey wishes people had paid more attention to what had happened in 2006 when she sacked him from Tourism Australia.

'It was all out there for everyone to see,' she said. 'I think he is missing that part of his brain that controls empathy. Everything had to be his way, he would not accept advice, he would not collaborate unless it was with the cheer squad that he surrounded himself with.'

She is another who does not believe Morrison 'won' in 2019, but that Bill Shorten lost. She says she was not surprised by what happened in 2022, although she is in despair about what has happened to the Liberal Party.

'It was a disastrous experiment from start to finish for the country and for the Liberal Party,' she said. 'He has decimated the Liberal Party.'

After Morrison returned from Hawaii and before he declared a pandemic, his popularity nosedived. Albanese passed him as preferred prime minister.

Labor frontbenchers recalled a meeting in February 2020 with the party's national secretary, Paul Erickson, where he cited three examples of prime ministers who had suffered similar crashes: Howard after the 2004 election, when he introduced WorkChoices, which he had not taken to an election; Paul Keating after the 1993 budget, when he rescinded the l-a-w law tax cuts; and Julia Gillard in 2011, after she introduced a carbon tax after she had promised in the 2010 campaign that she wouldn't.

They got the message. The reputations of those prime ministers were so damaged that none of them had won the subsequent election.

Albanese was conspicuously bipartisan during Covid, when

Morrison's standing was restored. Then, when he really began to falter, politics re-emerged. It was a better climate for Labor to highlight Morrison's character flaws and to remind people how costly his mistakes were.

Just in case they had forgotten.

By the second-last week of the parliamentary sitting, on 22 November 2021, Labor decided it was time to play hardball. Albanese was in a strong position; people did not see him as negative or carping. It was the right time to flick the switch.

In any case, Morrison had laid the groundwork himself.

Morrison's problem with the truth blew up on 9 November, when he announced measures to encourage Australians to take up electric vehicles. In 2019, he had ridiculed Bill Shorten over electric vehicles, warning tradies that it would 'end the weekend'.

'How can you honestly spruik electric vehicles when you campaigned against them in the last election?' one journalist asked.

'But I didn't. That is just a Labor lie,' Morrison said. That night, his quotes from 2019 contrasting with those in 2021 ran on every news bulletin.

When parliament resumed, Labor's Tony Burke, the manager of opposition business in the House, drafted a question for Fiona Phillips, whose electorate of Gilmore had been ravaged by the fires and where people were still homeless.

Burke wanted to revive memories of Hawaii. He wanted Morrison to wear a big L (Liar) on his forehead all the way to the election, and another big L (Loser) afterwards. He knew that just because the opposition had run an issue for a week, it didn't mean that voters would remember it. He believed it was time to hark back to the bushfires; otherwise they would fade from memory.

Burke says he framed it carefully because Morrison had a habit of turning questions like that into an attack on his family. It had to come from someone other than Albanese, someone Morrison could not attack.

Not even Burke anticipated Morrison's response, which fell neatly into the category of lying about lying. Morrison shredded his own credibility on the floor of the parliament—not once, but twice.

'When my electorate was burning, the prime minister's office told journalists he was not on holiday in Hawaii,' Phillips said. 'Why did the prime minister's office say that, when it wasn't true?'

It was Tony Smith's last day in the chair as Speaker. Smith, one of the few prepared to stand up to Morrison, who became the best Speaker of the parliament in modern times, and who would often sit Morrison down in the chamber when he was straying, allowed the question.

'I can only speak to what I have said, as the leader of the opposition will know, because I texted him from the plane when I was going on that leave, and told him where I was going, and he was fully aware of where I was travelling with my family,' the prime minister responded.

Albanese told him across the despatch box that what he had just said wasn't true. Morrison insisted it was. Albanese was both incredulous and deeply grateful to Morrison for stuffing up.

'Mate, I've got the message here,' Albanese kept saying to him.

Albanese then made a personal explanation. 'I kept that text message confidential, as you do with private text messages between private phones,' he said.

No one missed the ping of that torpedo-laden submarine. It was a hit at Morrison for leaking a private text message from French President Emmanuel Macron to Morrison after Macron had accused Morrison of lying to him.

Albanese said Morrison had never told him where he was taking his holiday.

When Morrison later rose to 'clarify' what he had texted Albanese, he directly contradicted, in among the gobbledegook, what he had said minutes before.

'I simply communicated to him that I was taking leave. When I was referring to, "He knew where I was going and was fully aware I was travelling with my family," what I meant was that we were going on leave together,' Morrison said.

'I know I didn't tell him where we were going because, Mr Speaker, that is a private matter where members take leave, and I know I didn't tell him the destination — nor would I and nor would he expect me to have told him where he [*sic*] was going. I simply confirmed to him that I was taking leave with my family, and he was aware of that at that time. Thank you, Mr Speaker.'

It was dreadful. He had used a private text message to try to dispute something so easily proved because Albanese still had the original on his phone, and he did it on the floor of the parliament — all without actually answering the question, including why his staff had lied.

At every opportunity, Burke made sure there was a reference to 'going missing' in questions or commentary. Even so, Burke is not sure what would have happened if Morrison had decided to call an election at that time for December.

There was another eruption a few months later without any help at all from Labor. It was Morrison's own doing, maybe with a nudge along from the Nine Network's Karl Stefanovic.

Morrison had made a number of half-hearted apologies over time, then, in a memorable *60 Minutes* interview with Stefanovic, broadcast on 13 February 2022, his wife, Jenny, with carefully rehearsed and delivered lines, took full responsibility, saying it was her fault they went to Hawaii because she had insisted on a family holiday. Morrison sat very close beside her on the couch as she apologised. He could have interjected to say it wasn't her fault, it was a family decision, and he was deeply sorry for it. He didn't.

After Stefanovic and the crew had arrived at Kirribilli, during their pre-film chat, Morrison told him his daughters were having guitar lessons. He volunteered that he was learning the ukelele.

'You have to get that ukelele out,' Stefanovic told him. No, no, Morrison said. He cooked lunch for them. It was a good curry, Stefanovic remembers. With the meal over, as Stefanovic and the crew began making noises to leave, Morrison rushed off to get his ukulele, and, with cameras rolling, played 'April Sun in Cuba' for an awkward family singalong around the table.

Stefanovic says he can't remember if he had mentioned the ukulele again and that this was what had prompted Morrison to get his instrument. In any case, Morrison should have stuck with his original no. Stefanovic, who had been trying for around a year to set up the interview, was flabbergasted and delighted with the result, realising immediately what would happen. His interview was made, and Morrison was cactus. Again.

Morrison was oblivious to the way it would go down, which was very badly indeed. Another new political year, and another opportunity for a reset went up in smoke.

First, he had allowed his wife to take the rap for one of the worst decisions of his prime ministership, adding weight to Labor's claims he never owned up to any mistakes; and, second, he chose to strum an instrument that the whole world associates with Hawaii.

That year, like every other year of his tenure, began with a disaster.

In 2020, as if he had not behaved badly enough, there were briefings from inside his office against the New South Wales premier, Gladys Berejiklian, who had not taken a single day off during the fires. They blamed her for not calling on him to deploy defence forces sooner to help.

Then, after the troops had been deployed, Scotty from marketing swung into action with an advertisement featuring uniformed personnel appealing for donations to the Liberal Party.

A year later, on 7 January 2021, after a desultory summer, thanks to Covid, Morrison was asked at a press conference about the insurrection on Capitol Hill on 6 January, which Donald Trump had incited in an effort to overturn the US presidential election result. Unlike other world leaders, including Germany's Angela Merkel and Britain's Boris Johnson, who had publicly and robustly condemned Trump, Morrison declined to criticise Trump.

There was more than enough known even then about Trump's actions to condemn him, yet Morrison opted to go softly, softly.

'It's not for me to offer commentary on other leaders,' Morrison said. 'I don't do that out of respect for those nations. And that's where I'm going to leave that matter. I've expressed my great concern and distress about what has been happening in the United States, just as other leaders of the world's democracies have, and I concur with their view.'

Then, following his usual pattern, he later tried to pretend he had said what other world leaders had said.

On 2GB on 18 January, Jim Wilson asked Morrison if he was disappointed in Trump's behaviour, Morrison said: 'I've echoed the comments of other leaders about those things.

'I think it was disappointing, very disappointing, that things were allowed to get to that to that stage and, you know, the things that were said that encouraged others to come to the Capitol and engage in that way were incredibly disappointing, very disappointing.

'And the outcomes were terrible. But I think what's more important now is not for me to be providing lectures to anybody.

'That's not my job.'

Of course not. Not his job as a democratically elected leader to defend democracy from a democratically defeated leader refusing to accept the will of the people, inciting a mob to seek to overturn the election result, who storm Congress to find the vice-president so they can lynch him and kill the Speaker.

In that same interview, Wilson asked him about Australians still stranded overseas because of border closures while tennis players appeared to be getting priority. Morrison said that tennis players were not taking their places, adding: 'But there is the issue that you highlight of people trying to get back into Victoria now, and that's why I say to the premiers, and again, it's just not my job, I think, to be critical of other premiers or other jurisdictions.'

After all, he was only the prime minister.

'Not my job' would also feature prominently in Labor's negative advertising during the campaign. Liberals complained that the advertisement was misleading.

The deadly trilogy of punchy lines would be completed a few months later to explain yet another disaster.

Before Morrison's ill-fated Hawaiian holiday, Labor was in pieces — broken and broken-hearted by a defeat they had never seen coming. After the 2019 election, so shattered were they that Labor frontbenchers believed he might go on to rival John Howard's record as prime minister — that he was a leader so rat-cunning he could outfox his opponents and govern well enough to win as many terms as he wanted.

They, briefly, elevated Morrison to the class of political invincibles. In the early stages of grief, they misread the result, as badly as Morrison and those around him. He had campaigned well, he was disciplined, the Liberal Party campaign team under Andrew Hirst performed superbly, but the critical factors were Bill Shorten and his $400 billion in new taxes.

Morrison's great miscalculation, born of hubris or deep faith, or both, was to believe that he could make mistakes and still pull off another miracle victory.

Morrison might have survived, he might have gone on to be one of the longest-serving Australian prime ministers, if he had been a little bit smarter, a lot less convinced of his own political genius, and less confident of another miracle. But he wasn't. He doomed himself and his party.

One man who didn't fall for the myth was Albanese. He worked out his strategy early, and stuck to it. One by one, he ditched all the taxes that Shorten had proposed, including negative gearing and the hated retirees' tax.

He wanted the focus kept firmly on Morrison and Morrison's character, and he—correctly, as it turned out—resisted all the pressure to succumb to demands for a bolder agenda.

After Hawaii and before Covid, Tony Burke had been telling colleagues that he did not believe they would be fighting Morrison at the next election. He thought the situation for Morrison was so dire that Liberal MPs would be compelled to move against him. He believed Peter Dutton would have the numbers to take over.

In Burke's view, when Covid hit, it not only restored Morrison's standing, but it also deprived his colleagues of any opportunity they might have had to remove him.

Liberal MPs, including those closest to Morrison, agreed with that. They complained that he kept making the same mistake. After being rescued by Covid, he thought he could replay the 2019 election.

'Covid saved him, then damned him,' one of his closest allies said.

Liberal MPs were so angry with him over his behaviour that not even Hawke—who was firmly of the view that Morrison would not have survived but for the pandemic—Morton, and Robert would have been able to save him.

Not even the new rule he introduced in December 2018, which required a two-thirds majority to trigger a spill, would have saved him.

The rule change had troubled a few MPs at the time, including Trevor Evans and Tim Wilson, both of whom lost their seats in 2022.

'We elect a leader, not an emperor,' Wilson told the meeting where it was debated.

This undemocratic rule was meant to act as a deterrent. It meant MPs would have to think long and hard before launching a challenge, although if they could muster a majority, they could theoretically still succeed in dislodging the leader without getting 66 per cent, because few leaders would hang on knowing they had lost the confidence of a majority of their party room.

The change also gave the leader a licence on two fronts, one positive and one negative. It meant the leader felt free to act with impunity to ignore or ride roughshod over his MPs. Another inhibiting factor on poor behaviour and against poor leadership was thereby removed.

Liberal MPs said it was rare for anyone to stand up to Morrison. They said Mathias Cormann had, which was one reason why Morrison disliked him so much and why he did everything he could to ensure Cormann won the chairmanship of the OECD.

The rule also gave the leader cover to act against a troublesome minister. Yet Morrison was reluctant to employ it. Think Alan Tudge or Christian Porter.

One cabinet colleague, who said he had not seen Morrison bullying anyone—he thought the word was overused anyway—says he had seen him get frustrated and 'vent that frustration' because people were not getting things done or not getting them done quickly enough.

'He was belligerent a lot of the time,' another said. 'He would pretend he was listening, but he wasn't. He was dismissive.'

A senior staffer who observed his interactions with ministers, said Morrison would give 'short shrift' to those he thought had turned up with nothing more than talking points from their departments.

All the way through his tenure, there was intense frustration with Morrison's refusal to embark on any kind of reform. He did not hide his aversion. He bragged about it.

In a speech at the National Press Club on 1 February 2021, Morrison promised to oversee the vaccine rollout and manage the economic recovery. The *Australian Financial Review*'s Phil Coorey thought he should have shown more ambition.

'To purists probably listening in, there is a lack of bold reform ideas or proposals. You're not talking about large-scale economic reform or anything like that,' Coorey suggested in his question to Morrison.

In among his typical word-salad reply, Morrison said: 'So I'm now, see, I'm not one that likes to pursue things for the sake of vanity.'

Suddenly, reform and bold policy had become vanity projects. A year later, he told Deborah Snow in an interview published in *The Sydney Morning Herald* and *The Age* that he was not interested in leaving a legacy.

Albanese agrees that without Covid, Morrison might not have lasted as leader. 'I think that is right. Because his inner circle was so small, as you know, and he's so disliked,' he said later in an interview for this book.

He said Morrison went out of his way to avoid even the most

common courtesies. 'He never showed me any respect. And, you know, that's fine,' Albanese said.

And it was fine, because when he said that it was a chilly Canberra evening in winter 2022, and Prime Minister Albanese was seated on a couch in a small lounge room at The Lodge with a log fire blazing, sipping a glass of white wine.

CHAPTER THREE

Bless You

Ken Wyatt was sitting in a chair in the prime minister's office one night, along with six or seven other colleagues, both ministers and backbenchers, chatting over a glass of red wine, when Scott Morrison and Stuart Robert quietly approached him.

What happened next was highly unusual, to say the least. Morrison and Robert stood either side of Wyatt, then each placed a hand on his shoulders and began praying for him. They prayed for God to give Wyatt the strength to succeed in what would be an extremely challenging portfolio.

Wyatt, born on a mission station six weeks prematurely, whose mother was advised to find a priest to give him the last rites because it was doubtful he would survive, who became the first Indigenous person to be elected to the House of Representatives, then the first Indigenous person to hold a federal ministry, was unperturbed.

He said he had no issue with what Morrison and Robert had done. He found it both comforting and reassuring.

'I knew the strength of the prime minister's faith,' Wyatt said in an interview for this book. 'They were both genuine in wanting me to succeed, to have the fortitude and strength to take on the reforms.'

He appreciated they understood the pressures that would be placed on him as the first Indigenous person to hold the Indigenous affairs portfolio, both from the Indigenous community demanding change and from the right wing of the Liberal Party resisting it.

The expectations, particularly those he placed on himself, could be crushing.

Wyatt had set up the cross-party Indigenous caucus, telling his fellow Indigenous MPs that there would be people in their own ranks who would not like it, and certainly people on his side who wouldn't like it, but they had a common purpose.

After losing his seat in the 2022 election, he graciously and effusively congratulated his friend Linda Burney, offering to do whatever he could to help her succeed.

Burney told him she would honour the work he had done, and might seek his counsel occasionally. She later appointed him to a 21-member Indigenous working group to advise the government on its referendum strategy to enshrine an Indigenous voice to parliament.

Wyatt knew he was done for when he visited polling booths in his Western Australian seat of Hasluck, then on a margin of 6 per cent. People kept their heads down; they wouldn't look him in the eye. Or they would say what so many other of his colleagues had reported: 'We want to vote for you, but we can't vote for Scott Morrison.'

Voters complained about being called cave dwellers by Morrison during the pandemic, citing what Wyatt called 'the attack' on Western Australia's closed borders. Or young women and older women responded in disbelief when Morrison's wife, Jenny, had to counsel him on Brittany Higgins' rape allegations, or they hadn't liked the way Grace Tame had been treated.

'We did not send our senior ministers out to talk to the women,'

Wyatt said of the mass protests outside Parliament House in the wake of the Higgins allegations.

'One of our problems is we are too blokey. We have to look for quality people, not our mates.'

On the night he lost, when his staff were in tears, he told them not to be sad but to be proud of what they had accomplished. He was already thinking of writing a memoir, and had chosen the title: *From Mission to Minister.*

Although he would later express regret for having been unable to legislate the previous government's policy for an Indigenous voice to advise parliament—and he did subsequently come out in support of the referendum to give constitutional recognition to a voice—Wyatt was full of praise for Morrison.

He said that Morrison supported him at every point, and he takes pride in what he achieved, including the purchase of the copyright of the Indigenous flag from its creator, artist Harold Thomas.

'I have seen the good side of Scott,' Wyatt said. 'His faith is his strength.'

Karen Andrews had a different view. Andrews, who finished in government as home affairs minister in Morrison's cabinet, did not witness overt displays of faith from Morrison, but she could not believe all the religious references she had heard in maiden speeches or during debates from the time of her election in 2010.

'I was horrified, because my view is, keep politics, religion, and sex separate,' she told me.

'It was a hot bed of all those issues at Parliament House. I was surprised at the extent of it.'

It was telling that in a 2006 CV, when he was job hunting after Fran Bailey sacked him from Tourism Australia, Morrison listed under his personal interests: 'Church (Hillsong Church, Waterloo), Family,

Politics, Reading (biography, travel, history, Australian fiction), Kayaking, Rugby (Randwick, Waratahs), AFL (Western Bulldogs)'.

Not only was there no mention of the Cronulla Sharks, but he placed his church ahead of his family. He also named Pastor Brian Houston from Hillsong as a referee.

Despite the cloud hanging over Houston, Morrison sought an invitation for him to attend the White House for the state dinner that Donald Trump was hosting in Morrison's honour in September 2019. After *The Wall Street Journal* broke the story that his request had been denied—not even Trump would have Houston there—Morrison spent months denying or dismissing the story as gossip. He finally had to admit it was true.

At that time, police were investigating historical sexual-abuse charges against Houston's father, Frank. Brian was later charged with concealment for allegedly having failed to report the abuse. Subsequently, in March 2022, Brian was forced to resign from Hillsong after two women levelled allegations of inappropriate behaviour against him.

When asked about Houston's exit, Morrison said he was shocked by the allegations, but welcomed his resignation, saying it was appropriate.

'My first thoughts were with the victims, as they've rightly been described, and so very concerned,' he said.

'I mean, I haven't been at Hillsong now for about 15 years. I go to a local church in my own community, a Pentecostal church.'

Morrison was allowed to walk away from his long, close relationship with Houston, despite having attended a conference at Hillsong in 2019, and despite asking that he be invited to the White House in September that same year.

It's also instructive to note how Morrison saw himself back in 2006.

Under the heading of personal attributes, he listed: 'Positive, direct, determined, decisive, pragmatic, articulate, passionate, outcome focussed, innovative, discrete [*sic*], personable, motivated, committed, reasoned, analytic, responds to challenges, loyal, works well under pressure'.

This was very far removed from the way many of his colleagues and associates saw him. Politicians who dealt with him over the years found him a complex character, difficult if not impossible to shift once he had determined on a course. And not always as pleasant to deal with as Wyatt found him to be.

Morrison's religion and his use of it was problematic and sensitive. Labor trod warily after getting burned in 2019. MPs had thought Australians wouldn't vote for a Bible-bashing bastard. Instead, Morrison succeeded in gathering up the religious right, including conservative Christians.

It was an issue inside the government, seldom discussed openly.

One cabinet minister bemoaned the fact that Morrison had surrounded himself with his 'church mates' and left more talented people, such as Julian Leeser or Dave Sharma, to waste away on the backbench. Another complained he was tired of frequent out-loud (*Praise be to God*) oaths from Robert.

A few past and present Liberals, Christians themselves, believed that Morrison's religion affected his approach to politics and not always in a good way. They worried that praying became a substitute for good political practice, and that his circle of advice—which came from people as religious as himself—was too restricted.

'He thought starting a religious war would provide an alibi for a failure to have an economic narrative,' one Liberal MP said.

After it emerged that Morrison's preferred candidate for the New South Wales seat of Dobell was a Pentecostal preacher, Jemima Gleeson, Queensland senator James McGrath, frustrated beyond measure by the delays in the New South Wales preselections, and rightly fearing that continuing civil war could cost government, told colleagues that Morrison wanted to turn the division 'into a branch of Hillsong'.

No matter where he was or what job he was doing, Morrison always wanted to be in control. And he always seemed to have ulterior motives, as the former New South Wales Liberal leader John Brogden discovered.

As leader, Morrison insisted that the party apparatus had to deliver exactly what he wanted; it was there to do his bidding. As a party official, he insisted on directing the politicians; they were there to do his bidding.

After Brogden announced on 25 March 2002 that he was going to challenge Kerry Chikarovski for the New South Wales Liberal leadership, he received an unexpected phone call from Morrison, the party's state director.

Morrison launched into an expletive-studded tirade, asking him what the fuck he thought he was doing. Brogden was taken aback, firstly by the frequent use of the f-bomb, which he says he did not expect to hear from someone so religious, and secondly by the intervention itself.

Brogden told Morrison it was not his job as state director to get involved in parliamentary leadership matters. He warned Morrison to stay out of it and not to come to Parliament House. The next thing he knew, Morrison turned up at Parliament House. Brogden told him to leave the building; he had no right to be there. He reckoned that Morrison was there to help Chikarovski with her numbers. Brogden won by a single vote, on his 33rd birthday, on 28 March.

About a week later, Morrison called Brogden to suggest a reconciliation dinner. They went to a restaurant at Woolloomooloo.

During the meal, Morrison tried to explain to Brogden that what he had been planning to do was to get Malcolm Turnbull into parliament to make him premier. He had it all worked out. Turnbull refers briefly to this cunning plan in his autobiography, *A Bigger Picture*.

According to Brogden, Morrison was angling to get the prime minister, John Howard, to appoint an upper house MP, Jim Samios, to an overseas post, move Turnbull into the vacancy, then knock off Chikarovski and make Turnbull leader, even though he would have been in the upper house.

While Morrison was laying this out, Brogden was thinking *Stranger things have happened*, but also how strange it was for Morrison to be telling him about it over a dinner meant to settle their differences and to find a way to work together.

For months thereafter, Morrison kept insisting that Brogden visit his church, Hillsong. Brogden, who describes himself as a 'smorgasbord Catholic', did go eventually, after considerable pushing from Morrison.

He found it puzzling that Morrison was so keen to get him to go there, surmising that either he wanted people to understand the importance of his religion to him, or to show other devotees that he was able to get high-profile people to attend, or maybe he hoped it would help secure a few converts.

Morrison was also angry with Brogden for supporting drug-injecting rooms, pressing him to reverse his position. He refused. They were a similar age—Morrison was 34—but they had very different worldviews.

'We were on the same road with different paths,' Brogden would say.

The New South Wales party president, Chris McDiven, described them as 'two young bulls in the paddock'.

'Too much testosterone,' McDiven told people. 'They were always competing.'

During the 2003 state election, Brogden and Morrison were barely on speaking terms.

Brogden's chief of staff, David Gazard, whom Brogden says Morrison suggested for the job, got along much better with Morrison than he did with Brogden. Brogden thought then that Gazard, who ended up acting as a go-between, was better suited to the job of press secretary than chief of staff.

Gazard, also deeply religious, remains one of Morrison's best friends. According to friends, he became a Pentecostal and prayed regularly with Morrison.

Brogden was not surprised when Morrison became leader, not surprised that he had manipulated his way there, and definitely not surprised he was ill-suited to the prime ministership. He always thought of him as a puppet master.

But Brogden, the chair of Lifeline Australia, pays tribute to Morrison for funding mental health packages during Covid. It was a valuable contribution to help people struggling to cope. 'He was excellent,' Brogden says now. 'I couldn't fault him.'

Aileen Weissner, a Liberal Party stalwart, found that it didn't pay to refuse Morrison's requests to go to Hillsong. There were few staffers around who knew as much about marginal-seat campaigning and how to deal with MPs and their problems as Weissner did. She was indispensable in the prime minister's office during the Howard years and throughout the hard slog of opposition.

During the 2019 election, she had worked at campaign headquarters in Brisbane. Afterwards, when everyone had to reapply for their jobs, she submitted her extensive, impressive CV to Morrison's office. She never heard back.

Weissner puts it down to a run-in she had with Morrison back in 2004. At the victory party on election night, when John Howard thumped Mark Latham, Morrison, still the New South Wales state director, walked up to her and told her to 'get Howard' to the Hillsong Church at 9.30 the next morning to celebrate his victory with the congregation.

It was not framed as a request, more like a command. Weissner told Morrison he was dreaming; it wasn't going to happen. Howard always went to the Anglican Church in Kirribilli the morning after election night, and he would be going there again. Morrison, furious, stalked off. Howard went to his church as per usual on the Sunday, and somehow Weissner ended up without a job after the 2019 election.

At the very least, if she had been there, the prime minister's office might have avoided the grief of the sports rorts saga.

As prime minister, Morrison would host gatherings of his prayer group in his Parliament House office. Robert, who kept a musical keyboard in his office, would call his staff in, and together they would sing hymns.

Lucy Wicks found the meetings helpful. 'It was simply a time to meet with friends who share a love of faith and politics, and I really appreciated being part of a group of people who would both encourage and challenge me, especially during some of the tough moments in my personal and political life,' she said later.

Others found them unsettling. 'There were prayers in the prime minister's office, and crap like that,' one MP said. 'People were going in there and praying. It was just fucked.

'He believed, whether because of God or whatever, that people voted for him to be prime minister, not against Bill Shorten,' one non-religious MP said. 'He thought he had a mandate when he had an anti-mandate.' Another MP, a devout Christian, pointed to Morrison's waxing and waning on religious discrimination. 'He began as Scotty from marketing from the left, then ended as Scotty from marketing for the right,' he said.

This conservative MP said there were unrealistic expectations from the right of Morrison's ability to deliver on issues such as religious freedom, and that he was unfairly maligned by people on the left for trying.

Another reason why using it as a political tool is unwise.

One former cabinet minister, who had worked with him and observed him closely over many years, said: 'I have never been able to get my head around evangelism.

'He did seem to have this thing about *God wants this*, or *God has chosen me to be prime minister*. He didn't brook much opposition to his course, once he set his mind on it. It was a my-way-or-the-highway approach, which I suspect was inspired by his evangelism, and this feeling he had been anointed.

'He was overly self-confident, in a way. There was a lack of humility, which is a necessary part of being a wise leader. I do think he lacked that. The overflow from 2019 was that he and others around him believed their own bullshit.

'The meme was he just wanted to select a whole lot of God-botherers in those seats. That's what was being suggested.'

Another former MP, also a practising Christian who had been subjected to Morrison's controlling ways, was decidedly unimpressed by Morrison's faith.

'The happy-clappy orthodoxy is largely unacceptable to me. The Morrison happy-clappies are part of that,' he said.

'He can be there clapping his hands and holding them up, and singing loudly. All that is largely irrelevant to me. It's how you live your life and how you conduct yourself that's more relevant.'

Another cabinet minister said it was impossible to say whether his determination or his confidence were driven by his faith or sourced from it.

'I doubt anybody outside his wife or his pastor could possibly have heard him express that it was his religion,' he said. 'You can't do those jobs without a fair degree of confidence.'

Soon after the defeat of his religious discrimination bill at the hands of his own backbenchers, Morrison preached from the pulpit of St Maroun's Maronite church in South Australia. In a confused retelling of the Old Testament story of Solomon, he cast himself as the real mother of the baby that the wise leader had threatened to cut in two, to explain why he had withdrawn the bill.

At the time, one cabinet minister wholeheartedly endorsed Morrison delivering that sermon, saying it had enabled him to show his 'passion and commitment to the issue', and that the way was now open for him to use the issue against Labor in its western Sydney seats with high percentages of people of faith.

It was obvious that religion would become the third pillar of Morrison's re-election bid, alongside economic management and national security.

Labor frontbenchers, who trod warily on his religion, were quietly confident that Morrison's use of it would not be as successful in 2022 as in 2019, when his signals were more artful. They reported little or no negative feedback from their communities, but did have a few words of caution for Morrison.

One Labor frontbencher pointed out that he had actually killed his own bill, so his recounting of the story of Solomon was inaccurate.

Another, Michelle Rowland, a practising Catholic from the western Sydney seat of Greenway, who had also been predicting well before the election that 'the only person who can kill Morrison is

Morrison', was uncomfortable with politicians flaunting their faith. Rowland, re-elected with an increased margin, quoted scripture essentially advising that when you pray, pray quietly. (Matthew 6:5).

Her views were echoed by Liberal senator Andrew Bragg.

'Australians respect religion,' he said.

'Many Australians are cultural Christians and appreciate the special role religious institutions play in our society. But my sense is Australians don't want to see religion feature heavily in public life.

'They want it to be a private matter and not in the public domain.'

In April 2020, from his prime ministerial office, Morrison participated in a national Zoom prayer marathon organised by the Australian Prayer Network and the Canberra Declaration, a fundamentalist Pentecostal group claiming a national membership of more than 80,000 that counts Margaret Court, former tennis champion, as a leader. Court oversaw Morrison's prayer session in the final hour of the 24-hour prayer session.

According to various reports from inside the meeting, Morrison shared two scripture verses. One of them was Psalm 34:17–19:

> The righteous cry out, and the Lord hears them; he delivers them from all their troubles.
> The Lord is close to the broken-hearted and saves those who are crushed in spirit.
> The righteous person may have many troubles, but the Lord delivers him from them all.

The Canberra Declaration claims that an earlier national prayer effort, for 21 days, was responsible for Morrison's 2019 electoral victory. 'The team at the Canberra Declaration have never seen such a level of unified pushback against overtly evil political policy in an election,' the group enthused on its website. 'Furthermore, the team at Canberra Declaration have never seen such united fervent prayer and fasting for an election in the recorded history of our nation.

'The prayer effort for our nation in the 18 May 2019 Federal Election was unprecedented and so was the miracle!'

It was a belief obviously shared by Morrison when he declared on election night: 'I have always believed in miracles.'

A similar effort in 2022 with 21 days of prayer and fasting did not achieve the same result.

In July, Morrison gave a soul-searching 50-minute sermon in Perth to mark the 27th birthday of Margaret Court's Pentecostal Victory Life Centre church and to open its Perth Prayer Tower. It was also the former tennis player's 80th birthday.

At a time when trust in government was at its lowest ebb, partly thanks to the behaviour of politicians like him, when conspiracy theories were abounding, pushed by his footy buddy, QAnon adherent Tim Stewart, whose wife was housekeeper at The Lodge and Jenny's best friend, the man who had been prime minister for almost four years—who had spent decades in politics running for office or running campaigns for others to get into office, often playing dirty to achieve his ambitions, including clandestinely acquiring the ministries of his colleagues—urged people to put their faith in God and not in governments.

'God's kingdom will come. It's in his hands. We trust in Him. We don't trust in governments. We don't trust in the United Nations, thank goodness,' he said.

'We don't trust in all of these things, fine as they may be and as important as the role that they play. Believe me, I've worked in it and they are important.

'But as someone who's been in it, if you are putting your faith in those things as I put my faith in the Lord, you're making a mistake. They are earthly, they are fallible.'

He would know. He was the government.

'Do you believe if you lose an election that God still loves you and has a plan for you?' he asked.

'I do, because I still believe in miracles.'

The sermon was largely about anxiety. After watching, it was impossible not to think he was suffering from it. Most of what he said was about himself.

His friend David Gazard, who appeared regularly on television panels to make the case for Morrison, tried to clean up afterwards.

'You would never trust government with your salvation. That's what he was saying,' Gazard said. According to Gazard, Morrison had been trying to say that governments were fallible, but God was not.

Morrison didn't care what people made of it. Privately, later, when people expressed concern about his remarks and the interpretation placed on them, Morrison shrugged. He was unrepentant. He did not resile from what he said, nor try to excuse it by saying people had misunderstood what he said.

There was the pungent aroma of absolution about it. For him from Him. Everything that happened was part of God's plan. The Lord giveth and the Lord taketh away.

This also meant, of course, that in his mind no blame could attach to him for the lost decade of opportunity, or for the decimation of the Liberal Party.

CHAPTER FOUR

Hello Comrade!

The early surefooted handling of Covid enabled Scott Morrison to resurrect his leadership. Australians set aside their misgivings and gave him a second chance.

The initial management of the pandemic was difficult and incredibly effective. On the advice of the chief medical officer, Brendan Murphy, Morrison imposed restrictions on travel from China in February 2020, began the stockpiling of masks, and limited travel from countries where Covid was spreading rapidly, such as Iran and Italy.

Recognising that the country could slip into recession following the Black Summer fires, and the increasing anxiety about the impact of Covid, the government announced a $17.6 billion economic-support package on 12 March.

In what looked like a masterstroke—and in those early days it was—Morrison moved quickly to abolish the creaking Council of Australian Governments, a cumbersome forum for the prime minister and state and territory leaders to discuss matters of national importance, and to replace it with the national cabinet, which came into being on 13 March 2020.

It worked well initially, but then it began to fray. Morrison veered between supporting and opposing lockdowns, closures, and mandates. He was caught in a pincer between the majority of Australians who supported the tougher measures proposed by the state and territory leaders, and a noisy, influential minority—which included state and federal Liberals—aggressively attacking governments, and fighting for 'freedom' from vaccines, conventional protection measures, and democratically elected leaders they called dictators, whom some of them threatened to kill.

Inside his own government, some ministers and backbenchers chafed at the usurpation of his authority by the premiers. They wanted him to be in charge, not to be seen to be following their directions. One Liberal MP thought he should have flown to Perth to challenge Mark McGowan's border closures.

The national cabinet also sidelined the federal cabinet. Cabinet ministers complained at the time of their irrelevance. 'The NSC [National Security Committee of cabinet] became the supreme decision-making body of the government,' according to one minister.

It turned the premiers into national figures, more popular than rock stars, and more powerful than the prime minister, whose personal and constitutional limitations were soon exposed.

Morrison was pushed or pulled by them to do what they wanted. He would get there eventually, whether it was on border closures or wage subsidies, but in areas other than spending that were considered to be his responsibility—such as acquiring vaccines, or providing quarantine, or caring for the aged—he was seen to have failed.

While Morrison moved quickly on some measures, on others he dawdled or baulked. Although he saw it very differently, state and territory leaders ultimately did all the heavy lifting, then carried the can when things went wrong, and shared the kudos with him when they went well.

Nevertheless, despite all the inevitable tensions and errors, Australia still fared better than any other country. More lives were saved, the economy was stronger, and social cohesion largely remained as it was.

The premiers were full of praise for Morrison's early handling. He chaired the meetings well, he allowed everyone to speak, and they were impressed with his command of his brief.

They were also impressed by the quality of the briefings lined up from Treasury and health officials on the likely impacts of Covid on the community and the economy.

Morrison was the national cabinet's chair, and became its chief spokesman. His press conferences summing up next steps were compulsory viewing, as were the daily briefings from the other leaders with their chief medical officers.

In those early stages, they were all flying blind. No one really knew what the future held, or had a complete handle on what exactly was needed to prevent the spread of the virus and to protect the community without destroying businesses.

'Everyone was operating under radical uncertainty,' one senior member of the Morrison government said. 'There was no such thing as an expert. Often, the politicians had better instincts.' Mistakes were made at every level of government. 'The blizzard of decision-making is a blizzard,' he said.

Actually, there were experts, operating under intense pressure, often facing impossible demands.

Brendan Murphy was asked in late February by Greg Hunt to produce a primary-care plan to deal with the pandemic. Hunt told Murphy he wanted it done by the next day. Murphy had the Australian Health Sector Emergency Response Plan for Covid-19 published on 18 February 2020, but no specific detailed plans for primary care.

Fortunately for Murphy, Professor Michael Kidd, who had been living in Toronto and was a leading world expert in primary care, was back in Australia visiting his family. He had been scheduled to return to Australia to begin work with the health department as deputy chief medical officer in May, but ended up starting a lot sooner than expected.

Kidd had been watching news of the outbreak since early January, and was extremely concerned by the rapid spread of the virus, which was sneakier than the SARS virus that appeared in 2002. He worked with colleagues across the Department of Health to put together the plan in 24 hours. It was presented to Hunt, shared with the nation's peak primary-care organisations, costed, and announced on 11 March.

It comprised a $2.4 billion outlay to cover everything, including telehealth; research on vaccines; protections for Indigenous and other vulnerable Australians; funding for infection-control training; programs for health and aged-care workers; a national advertising campaign to provide practical advice on how to stay healthy; and more than $1 billion for personal-protection equipment for patients and staff.

That last was important. Kidd had learned from the SARS outbreak in 2002 in Toronto, when three healthcare workers had died — a general practitioner and two nurses — how important it was to keep healthcare staff well protected, including those working outside hospitals.

Annastacia Palaszczuk was vastly impressed with those early days. In an interview for this book, she said there was a lot of goodwill and a collegiate atmosphere.

She remembers they had dinner at Kirribilli on Thursday 12 March 2020, the night before what would turn out to be the last COAG meeting and the inception of the national cabinet. She remembers, because it was when Tom Hanks and his wife, Rita Wilson, then in Queensland for the filming of Baz Luhrmann's *Elvis*, made news around the globe by announcing they had tested positive for Covid.

Dinner was a pleasant affair. Jenny was spotted walking down the stairs by one of the other premiers, who invited her to join them for a drink. She did briefly, holding the family dog, and then left.

One feature of the gathering was the coolness of the interactions between Morrison and the New South Wales premier, Gladys Berejiklian, who arrived late, missing drinks outside and the selfies. The relationship between Morrison, Western Australia's Mark McGowan, and Victoria's Daniel Andrews was described by the other premiers as love/hate. Relations between the premiers could also be tense, particularly when one sought to lecture the others on what they should be doing or where they had gone wrong.

Berejiklian rubbed them up the wrong way, and they rubbed her the wrong way, too, although it was her frosty relationship with Morrison that stood out.

McGowan remembers the Thursday-night dinner. It was the first time he had been to Kirribilli. When Morrison appeared, he was still wearing make-up from his first-ever televised address to the nation, where he reassured people that everything was under control and that 'we'll get through this together, Australia'.

McGowan and Morrison, in the early bromance stage of their relationship, were standing outside on the rolling lawns, looking out at the harbour, having drinks, when two massive cruise liners, one of them the *Spectrum of the Seas*, which can carry more than 4,000 passengers, sailed past.

'There go some floating petri dishes,' Morrison joked.

A week later, the *Ruby Princess* docked in Sydney, 2,700 passengers were allowed to disembark without being tested, and

28 passengers subsequently died, triggering a blame game between the New South Wales and federal governments over who was responsible.

In the early stages, Morrison's messaging was meant to be reassuring, but occasionally it was careless, bordering on reckless. In March–April, by far the highest number of infections among Australians — 26 per cent — came from cruise ships, or, as he called them, the floating petri dishes.

The Covid outbreak on the *Diamond Princess* ended in Japan on 20 February, weeks before the *Ruby Princess*, when Australians had to be evacuated and flown to Darwin for quarantining.

Even after that, just a week before the *Ruby Princess* set sail from Sydney on its ill-fated round trip, Morrison was still telling Australians to keep doing what they were doing.

On 28 February, he agreed with the country's then highest-rating radio host, Alan Jones, that Australians could still travel internationally, except to China.

Despite having declared a national emergency the day before, Morrison said on Jones' show: 'There is no need for us to be moving towards not having mass gatherings of people. You can still go to the football, you can still go to the cricket, you can still go and play with your friends down the street, you can go off to the concert, and you can go out for a Chinese meal. You can do all of these things, because Australia has acted quickly, Australia has got ahead of this at this point in time.'

Two weeks later at Kirribilli, on 12 March, there was still an air of innocence or naivety about what lay ahead. The leaders relished the beauty of their surroundings.

They cut across to the gardens of neighbouring Admiralty House, the governor-general's residence. Kirribilli was an amazing piece of real estate. Admiralty House was completely jaw-dropping.

They took selfies with the prime minister as dusk was falling.

The next morning at breakfast, Dan Andrews told McGowan he was about to cancel the Grand Prix, which was already revving up in Melbourne. *My God*, thought McGowan. *That's an incredible decision to take.*

Andrews told the race organisers that they could have a Grand Prix without spectators, or none at all. Competitors were already pulling out because of Covid, so they abandoned the race.

The COAG meeting itself was boring. Moribund, McGowan remembers. The agenda had already been ticked off in advance, and they were all going through the motions. Then, during a break, a small group of people, including Brendan Murphy, walked in. They crowded around Morrison, whispering to him.

Morrison told the premiers there had been an upgrade to the threat level and that they should resume their meeting. Saying it was a very serious situation, a very worrying one for the country, he asked the public servants and advisers to stay outside, leaving him with the health officials, the premiers, and the chief ministers.

He told them the situation was much more serious than first thought. He proposed the setting up of a national cabinet chaired by him to manage the pandemic. They all nodded in agreement. 'That's a great idea,' McGowan said.

At that meeting, they decided that from the following Monday there should be an end to 'non-essential' public gatherings of more than 500 people. Australians were also advised to reconsider their need for travel.

There was some unexpected theatre during the subsequent press conference, when Morrison declared he would still go to watch the Sharks play the Rabbitohs on Saturday in the first round of the NRL. Urging people to stay calm, he said: 'There is every reason for people to go about their usual business.'

That sparked outrage. He had set up a national cabinet to handle a national emergency, yet he was allowing his desire to go to the footy to undermine the message to people to restrict their contact with others and even to avoid touching the surfaces of packaged goods in supermarkets. He had to be talked out of it by his staff and medical experts, who convinced him he would be setting a bad example. It was yet one more sign from him that the gravity of a situation had completely eluded him.

Two days later, cruise ships were banned from entering Australia.

Six days later, Morrison announced that Australia's borders would be closed to all foreigners from the next day.

There was a hunger to know what was happening, what might happen, and what he and the other leaders were going to do to protect people.

That was why, after meetings of national cabinet, very long press conferences were held, sometimes late at night. Sometimes, the messages coming from him and them were contradictory. They felt he failed to convey the decisions in a nuanced way, or that he did it in ways that misled people about what had actually been decided. Clearly, leaders had different ideas about what needed to be done or what was best for their state.

Initially, they were prepared to let such irritants go. They were all trying to do their best under incredibly difficult circumstances.

It slowly fell apart. There were many reasons for this, as expressed subsequently to me by a number of them. The premiers—though, thankfully, largely normal people—were not an homogenous group. They noticed that a key focus for Morrison was the next day's headlines or that night's news bulletins.

They also noticed that if one of them came up with a good idea during the meeting, he would later parlay it as his own. Even though the tensions between Morrison and Berejiklian were obvious to all of them in the meetings, they resented the fact that Morrison held up New South Wales and Berejiklian as the gold standard for managing Covid.

The red states noticed that when things went wrong in the blue states, particularly in New South Wales, he and his ministers bit their tongues, but when they went wrong in the Labor states, particularly in Victoria, he and Frydenberg didn't hold back.

Of course, Berejiklian had a different perspective here. She did not believe that Morrison was being supportive enough. When she was preparing mass-vaccination centres, Morrison was dismissive of the idea. They proved vital to ensuring that the rollout caught up to its deadlines from a disastrous beginning.

The first signs of tension emerged early on. Morrison announced on 13 March that he wanted a national approach on school closures. His stated preference was for them to stay open.

Berejiklian had become increasingly concerned by the spread of the virus through the school system and into the community. She contacted Andrews, and together they agreed they would shut them down.

They then contacted the ACT's chief minister, Andrew Barr, who also agreed, so the trio released a joint statement on Sunday 22 March, announcing that their schools would close from Tuesday 24 March to transition to online education, that there would be stricter social-distancing laws, and that there would be shutdowns of non-essential businesses.

The growing impatience of the leaders of the two largest states, and their decision to pre-empt national cabinet, forced Morrison to organise a hook-up of the national cabinet that night rather than wait until the meeting that had been scheduled for the following Tuesday night.

Morrison was angry that they had canvassed their plans

publicly in advance, and let everyone in the room know it. He was furious that he was being challenged by the New South Wales and Victorian premiers. After all, he had a long-running bromance with Andrews. It hadn't occurred to Morrison that Andrews might forge an alliance with Berejiklian.

Berejiklian and Andrews delivered compelling arguments for their actions during the meeting, according to others present.

The time to act was now, they argued. Any further delay, or half-measures, risked the virus running out of control. The international experience was making their case for them. They had to act now, and it had to be decisive.

Barr, who supported Andrews and Berejiklian, thought Morrison was taken by surprise by the strength of their intervention. He reckoned that Morrison saw it as an undermining of his authority to make the big calls on behalf of the national cabinet. He realised he could not stop them, so the next-best thing was to pivot to try to limit the extent of the control measures.

They set about the laborious task of deciding which businesses could remain open and which had to close, which had to limit contact, and which could continue operating.

'The premiers were acting on the strong advice of their chief health officers, and, as would be demonstrated repeatedly over the next two years, had the power to act independently of the prime minister,' Barr said later.

'It wasn't the last time Morrison faced this situation.'

Andrews and Berejiklian had been concerned that Morrison was putting the economy first. They had to pull back a bit from their original plans, and while they forced Morrison that day to accept the reality of lockdowns, there would be continuing tensions about states shutting down or opening.

Berejiklian remained determinedly unapologetic. She had a

'no regrets' approach to doing whatever she believed was right by her state, even if the other states didn't like it and Morrison didn't approve.

Reluctantly, despite detecting increasing public and political sentiment in favour of stricter measures, a tetchy Morrison warned people at a late-night press conference to 'be careful what you wish for' as he announced stage-one restrictions.

Pubs, gyms, cinemas, restaurants, and churches were to close, possibly for six months, from midday the following day. Next morning, the queues outside Centrelink offices stretched for kilometres. The Centrelink computer system crashed. It showed how unprepared the government was for what was to come.

Morrison had been reluctant to follow the UK's lead on wage subsidies to protect workers affected by closures. He even warned that it could be very 'dangerous' to introduce a scheme similar to the UK's. Very quickly, the spectacle of jobless people lining up for benefits in their hundreds of thousands forced him to raise the white flag. He claimed he was working on an 'Australian' solution, but Frydenberg was already onto it with the head of Treasury, Steven Kennedy.

Kennedy offered three options for payments that would keep employees tied to their jobs and their employers—$1,000, $1,300, and $1,500 a fortnight. It was, as Frydenberg would say later, a break-glass moment.

Frydenberg immediately chose $1,500, got the Tax Office to agree to administer it through its existing payments system, and then convinced Morrison, the Expenditure Review Committee, and cabinet to go with it.

Frydenberg was fond of quoting John Howard's advice to him at the time that during such a crisis there was no place for ideology.

He worked in his office until midnight the night before

the announcement, getting only four hours' sleep before he and Morrison revealed the biggest single program ever announced by a federal government.

Morrison paid tribute to Frydenberg for sticking with it. 'You did it, Josh. You ran it, you had control of it, you took it over the line,' he told him.

More than two years later, after Frydenberg lost his seat, he received a heartwarming message from economist Chris Richardson, congratulating him on his stewardship during the crisis. Richardson said that Australia had fewer deaths and the lowest unemployment rate since Abba won Eurovision (in 1974).

'Governments are designed to go slow, but you managed to make one go fast, and the results were spectacular. It wasn't perfect, but that's an impossible yardstick,' Richardson told him.

'That's a record that will absolutely stand the test of time.'

Morrison and Frydenberg announced a $130 billion package called JobKeeper, which ended up costing $90 billion. It saved 800,000 jobs and countless businesses, and averted untold misery.

It might have been the most expensive measure ever; it was also one of the most important. Unfortunately, it was also one of the most wasteful, thanks to a design flaw. The independent Parliamentary Budget Office estimated that $20 billion went to businesses that were not entitled to receive it, and yet there was no mechanism to force them to pay it back. Despite Labor condemning this failure, they could do little to retrieve the money when in government, other than ask businesses to voluntarily repay the funds.

'That horse has bolted,' Labor frontbencher Andrew Leigh said after.

As they walked out together to the press conference on 30 March to announce JobKeeper, Morrison turned to Frydenberg.

'Josh, I thought we would be building the nation, not saving it,' he said.

He wasn't far wrong.

At that day's national cabinet meeting, McGowan greeted Morrison with: 'Hello comrade!'

'You have taken over a factory, nationalised hospitals, and put in place the biggest social wage in Australian history,' McGowan told Morrison. He congratulated him for emulating the great Labor leader Ben Chifley, who had sought to nationalise the banks.

Everyone had a good laugh, including Morrison.

Morrison's popularity was restored and then some. The standing of the premiers soared. But it was destined not to last. The national consensus initially forged by the national cabinet slowly began to disintegrate.

States went their own way on border closures, lockdowns, and the implementation of rules on who could do what, where, and when. Morrison's control of the agenda and his authority began to weaken.

He picked fights with the premiers, and they retaliated. It got nasty and counterproductive. Palaszczuk went from supporter to implacable opponent, without an ounce of pity for him when he lost the election. She did not call or text him to commiserate.

Their relationship had slowly deteriorated, then collapsed completely in early September 2020 when he rang her to press her to intercede on behalf of a Canberra woman wanting to visit her dying father in Queensland. The story, like so many others, was heartbreaking. Families were being separated by border closures. They could not see their gravely ill relatives or go to their funerals if they were interstate.

Cases like these garnered lots of headlines. They incited pressure on the premiers to intervene. Queensland had an exemptions review board that handled hundreds, if not thousands, of similar requests to waive the rules.

Palaszczuk has a clear recollection of the call that Morrison made to her, insisting that she intercede personally. She told him she did not approve exemptions; the board did that. She told him she would not intervene.

He responded by saying: 'You will do this, or it will break you.'

She appealed to him not to weaponise the issue. She and her chief medical officer, Dr Jeannette Young, were already receiving death threats. As a politician, Palaszczuk had received threats before; however, the pandemic had taken them to a whole new level of virulence. It was the first time that Dr Young had experienced anything like it. They and their families were stressed. Palaszczuk herself had not been able to go to her grandmother's funeral.

The two women had to make difficult decisions every day with potentially devastating impacts on peoples' lives. It weighed heavily on them, but Morrison seemed completely unsympathetic.

'If you go down this path, I will get increased death threats,' she told him.

'Well,' he replied, 'I get them.'

Publicly, later, he accused her of being inhumane. She responded by accusing him in the Queensland parliament on 10 September of bullying her. She said the level of abuse and number of death threats directed at her and Dr Young was 'horrific', and blamed Morrison and his ministers for it.

Two years later, she still hadn't forgiven him. 'He knew what he was doing. It was deliberate. He was launching a grenade,' she told me in an interview for this book.

'In the early days, everybody was in the same position. We didn't know what was going on. In the early days, national cabinet also worked collectively in the national interest,' she says. 'It could have gone on like that for two years, and he chose not to.'

She said that Morrison could have gone into the election campaign, if not with the premiers all supporting him, at least not campaigning against him.

'He squandered the greatest opportunity a prime minister could ever have. He could have united the entire country. But he divided states; he abused premiers. He backgrounded, he sent his media unit out deliberately to get journalists to ask us questions, pitting premier against premier. It was exhausting.'

Morrison also helped sow the seeds of his own destruction and that of the Liberal Party in Western Australia when he joined Clive Palmer's lawsuit to force McGowan to keep his borders open.

McGowan insists that he got along well with Morrison during the management of the pandemic, and got along 'fine' with him afterwards. McGowan says he is not one of those who 'hates' him. He says Morrison was forceful, but he understood that, because a prime minister had to show authority.

McGowan watched Peter Gutwein move first, on 19 March, to effectively close off Tasmania. Gutwein decreed a two-week quarantine period and screening for all people entering the state. McGowan was intrigued by that idea, although he admits the first time it was suggested to him for Western Australia, his response was: 'My God, that's a big step.' He began reading up on Western Australia's border closure in 1919 during the so-called Spanish flu pandemic, when the state even impounded the transcontinental train.

He was dubious about school closures when Andrews and Berejiklian first pushed for them, struggling to see how essential services workers such as nurses and others would be able to keep doing their jobs.

He said it was 'ironic' that Berejiklian was the one proposing closures, when later she was arguing to stay open, then of course had to lock down again after the Delta outbreak that was triggered by a limousine driver.

McGowan's solution, announced soon after the 22 March meeting, was not to close down the internal operations of his state, but to keep everything going and to seal off his borders to all other Australians. He announced his hard border closure on 2 April, with 14 days' quarantine for any exemptions.

'These are extreme steps, but these are extreme days ... we all need to step up and play our part in one of the greatest crises facing our state in its history,' McGowan said at the time. 'Western Australia is now in a war, the type of war we have never seen before.'

'I want the message to be absolutely clear to any Western Australian over east who is thinking of coming to Western Australia. If you need to get home to Western Australia—come home now.

'If you are an eastern stater, and thinking about visiting Western Australia—forget about it.'

That triggered another kind of war, a legal one, initiated by Palmer, supported by the Western Australian Liberals, then later joined, to his great cost, by Morrison, who was pushed along by the two senior West Australian cabinet ministers, the attorney-general, Christian Porter, and the finance minister, Mathias Cormann.

It seemed like a good idea at the time, although not to Alex Hawke and Stuart Robert, who told Morrison not to do it. 'No way in hell,' was Robert's reaction when he heard what was happening. 'This will kill us. It's wrong, it's nuts,' Robert says he told Morrison at the time.

Robert reckons that the west was lost the moment Morrison joined the challenge, and that by the time he withdrew, it was too late.

McGowan insists that the border closure was the best thing

he did. It kept businesses going, it saved the state, and it kept the country afloat. Barely a day was lost in the mining sector. For two years, life within its borders went on as normal, except for a few days of lockdown.

'Morrison, Frydenberg, Porter, Berejiklian all bagged us about it. They were all totally wrong,' he told me.

If it had not been done, he says, it would have been a political, economic, social, and health disaster, and the rest of the country would have suffered also from the loss of export income.

McGowan says that he and Morrison worked well together. But.

'He made a grievous error,' McGowan said. 'What happens to the Liberal Party is they get sucked in by the Commonwealth bureaucracy — this idea that everything has to be the same, everything has to be done the same way. It's a very Canberra attitude to Australia.'

He says that Porter — whom McGowan mockingly describes as smarter than everybody else — was the most vigorous in pursuing the legal action.

McGowan spoke to Morrison about the legal challenge a number of times. 'I told him: "Don't do it. You have got to get out."'

Morrison insisted there were technical reasons why it had to be done.

'"There is no law that says you have to. Get out of it now,"' McGowan says he told him.

Morrison was convinced that his legal arguments stacked up. He told McGowan his advice was that they would win, that McGowan was the one who would lose, that he would end up with egg on his face, and that it would be shocking for him.

McGowan says he could not see how the High Court could rule

that Western Australia would have to infect itself. 'I just couldn't see that,' he said later.

McGowan was not the only westerner urging Morrison to back off. Andrew Hastie, who was finding it difficult personally because he couldn't visit his family in Melbourne, and his wife couldn't visit hers in the United States, could still see how popular McGowan's move was on the ground, and how much it was hurting the Liberals politically. People had little sympathy for those with loved ones in other places. They just wanted to be safe.

Hastie talked to his friend Ben Morton to get him to speak to his friend Morrison to convince him to abandon the legal action.

He was not the only one who spoke to Morton. Other Liberals also spoke to him and to Michaelia Cash. Morton and Cash relayed their concerns.

Morton held great sway with Morrison. Unlike so many of Morrison's closest friends, Morton was not a member of Morrison's prayer group, nor was he particularly religious.

Nor was he frightened to give alternative advice. In 2003, aged 20, coming from a family of tradies, he ran for Liberal preselection for the state seat of Wyong in regional New South Wales. Present that day in Tumbi Umbi was Morrison, the state director. After Morton failed to win the safe Labor seat, he had the choice of two jobs: one, to join an accountancy firm; the other, to join Morrison at the Liberal Party's New South Wales division and to work on the 2004 federal election. He took the second option, later moved west, went on to become the Liberals' Western Australia state director, then won Tangney in 2016.

Liberal MPs on both sides of the country believed that Morrison mishandled the dispute with the west over its lockout. They argued that he should have challenged McGowan, but not done it with Palmer through the courts.

One frustrated backbencher even suggested it would have been better if he had got on Shark One—Morrison's name for the RAAF VIP aircraft used to ferry the prime minister—and headed for Western Australia. He could have landed in Perth, and, in front of a media posse, dared the premier to arrest the prime minister, the man charged with representing all Australians, for crossing the border. It would have made for an interesting contest.

Finally convinced by colleagues that it was a disaster, Morrison withdrew from the legal contest.

At the height of his popularity, McGowan had a 91 per cent approval rating. At the March 2021 state election, Labor won an astonishing 53 out of the 59 seats in the Legislative Assembly, the largest victory ever by any federal, state, or territory leader since Federation. The Liberals held just two seats; the Nationals, four.

It was only part of the story of how the west was lost. When Morrison and Frydenberg shacked up together in The Lodge between late August and early September 2021, they watched an animated movie called *The Croods* about cave dwellers.

Prompted by that movie and anxious to get the country reopened—which would leave him with the option of calling an election by the end of the year—Morrison thought it would be clever to use cave dwellers as an analogy to urge the reopening of borders and to exert pressure on the premiers, particularly McGowan, to weaken.

'Now, it's like that movie—in *The Croods*, people wanted to stay in the cave … and that young girl, she wanted to go out and live again and deal with the challenges of living in a different world,' Morrison said on the Nine Network's *Today*.

'Covid is a new, different world, and we need to get out there and live in it. We can't stay in the cave, and we can get out of it safely.'

Morrison was defending the plan, agreed to by national cabinet in July, to begin opening up the country once 80 per cent of Australians were vaccinated, and was suggesting that those who refused could face repercussions. It backfired badly.

McGowan wrote on Facebook:

> This morning the Prime Minister made a comment implying Western Australians were like cave people from a recent kids' movie.
>
> It was an odd thing to say. I think everyone would rather just see the Commonwealth look beyond New South Wales and actually appreciate what life is like here in WA.
>
> We currently have no restrictions within our State, a great quality of life, and a remarkably strong economy which is funding the relief efforts in other parts of the country.
>
> West Aussies just want decisions that consider the circumstances of all States and Territories, not just Sydney.

The failures over quarantine and vaccines were also costly. Morrison refused to act on recommendations from a committee headed by Jane Halton, which he had commissioned, that had recommended purpose-built quarantine centres. The only one on the mainland was at Howard Springs in Darwin. It was expanded, and there was not one single leak of infection from there, but there was no way it could cope with the number of returning Australians.

The federal government did not want to spend the money on facilities. Morrison insiders argued they would become 'white elephants' when the pandemic was over, although they might have been useful to house vulnerable people, farm workers, or people rendered homeless after floods or fires. Just saying.

It was Andrews who had suggested hotels be used for quarantine, and it was Victoria that was hardest hit and became the lockdown capital of the world, first from leakages of the virus from quarantine hotels, and then as a result of seepage from New South Wales.

In July 2020, as a result of an outbreak from hotel quarantine, Covid infiltrated Victorian aged-care facilities. The protracted closures that followed led to assaults on Andrews that Frydenberg—as the leading federal Liberal from Victoria—joined enthusiastically. He was pleased that one particularly robust attack in parliament won unsolicited endorsements from government backbenchers.

Andrews fought back, describing Frydenberg as 'not a leader, he is just a Liberal', who liked to 'play politics all day, every day'.

'Victorians are sick of it,' Andrews said.

Frydenberg still has no regrets about what he did, believing he was speaking up for Victorians who were struggling mentally and financially from the closures. He argued there was no evidence to suggest that what he did backfired. Labor contends that the attacks alienated those Victorians desperate for the harsh measures to work.

It all contributed to the unravelling of national cabinet. Morrison's own unravelling was exacerbated by the slowness of the vaccination rollout.

On 1 February 2021, Morrison kicked off the year with a speech at the National Press Club. He listed his five priorities for the year, with the very first to 'suppress the virus and deliver the vaccine'.

It turned out that the most successful suppression strategy was the one meant to catalogue and publicise the progress of the rollout. It turned into a bog, full of incomplete, conflicting, or inaccurate data that could not even be relied on as a guide to how many vulnerable Australians and their carers had been inoculated.

On Sunday 21 February, Morrison received his first vaccination—Pfizer—to officially kick off the rollout that was later dubbed a strollout by the ACTU's Sally McManus. The government had pinned its hopes on the AstraZeneca vaccine, which was being produced locally; however, it was later found to cause blood clots in a very small number of cases. Morrison announced the problem in a breathless late-night press conference, declaring that people under 50 should get the Pfizer vaccine.

Slight problem. Pfizer's offers early on to supply Australia had been ignored by the government. Australia signed a deal for just 10 million Pfizer doses in November 2020, four months behind other countries. Demand for it far exceeded the supply.

When it was obvious that the rollout was in deep trouble, Morrison said: 'It's not a race, right. It's not a competition.' This snappy line became the third to be tied around his ankle like a ball and chain — joining 'I don't hold a hose, mate' and 'It's not my job' — because people actually knew they were in a race for their very lives.

Morrison had picked up on remarks the previous day at a joint doorstop he had with Dr Brendan Murphy, who was by then head of the health department. Murphy had said: 'This is not a race. We have no burning platform in Australia. We are taking it as quickly and carefully and safely as we can. We're not like the US, or the UK, or most other countries in the world where they've got people in hospital dying. We can take our time, set up our systems, do it safely and carefully. We are expanding our rollout every day.'

When Morrison was challenged about his remarks, he sought to argue that he had said it when referring to the time that experts were testing the vaccines to make sure they were safe to use. Like so many other things he said when he was in strife, that was demonstrably not true. The rollout had already begun weeks before in February when he was given his first Pfizer shot.

The states and territories were geared up, ready to go. The only problem was that they had no vaccines — or at least not the ones that people wanted. Morrison had to beg, borrow, and scrounge around the world for Pfizer. A senior member of the government conceded later that it had been a mistake over the summer not to stress-test the health department to ensure it was up to the job, although the main problem was the unavailability of Pfizer.

In July 2021, Laura Tingle revealed that former prime minister Kevin Rudd had used his contacts in the United States the previous month to urge Pfizer to make its vaccine available earlier than had been contracted.

Everyone was worried. The former CEO of Ford, Jac Nasser, who grew up in Melbourne after migrating there with his family from Lebanon when he was four, confirmed to me he was the businessman who had interceded to secure supplies for Australia. Based in the US, using his impeccable business and political contacts, he made direct appeals to Pfizer to deliver doses sooner.

The government claimed that the success in bringing forward millions of doses was a result of its own negotiations with Pfizer Australia. Of course.

It turned out to be a costly delay. The number of Covid cases was rising in New South Wales, with the Delta outbreak forcing another lockdown in Sydney on 27 June. Victoria closed its border with New South Wales on 11 July, then went into lockdown again on 15 July. Labor blamed the length of the lockdowns on the slowness of the rollout.

Red-state leaders looked on as Morrison first praised Berejiklian for holding out and not locking down the state (a big swipe at Andrews), then watched him change his tune when she was forced into another lockdown.

Conservative columnist Katrina Grace Kelly dubbed Morrison

'The Prime Minister for New South Wales'. Andrews plagiarised it to use against Morrison.

Andrew Barr says the recurring theme became Morrison criticising the Labor states, but never criticising the Liberal states such as South Australia and Tasmania.

During our interview in June 2022, Barr said that the full spectrum of Morrison's character was on display during the meetings of national cabinet — from hectoring and bullying to quite calm and considered. Barr was prescient in his assessment of Morrison back then. He said then Morrison would have been happier running the entire operation on his own.

'If he didn't have to include us, he wouldn't have,' Barr said. 'But he had to.'

He argued it showed that those who drafted the constitution had got it right by distributing power between the federal government and the states.

After the news broke about Morrison's clandestine takeover of ministries, Barr told me: 'I wasn't really that surprised. It was entirely consistent with his operating style.'

Barr's handling of the pandemic was rewarded in October 2020, when he led Labor, then in its 20th year of governing in the ACT, to another election victory. Less than two years later, at the 2022 federal election, Canberrans showed no sympathy and no gratitude to Morrison at all. The Liberals' only representative, the conservative senator Zed Seselja, lost his seat to independent David Pocock.

McGowan was generally much more benign towards Morrison, although he did find his flip-flopping hugely annoying, particularly when he was publicly arguing for Western Australia to open up.

As if McGowan was going to give Covid a passport into his

state. Then, when Morrison realised that West Australians actually supported McGowan's handling of the pandemic, he became pro-closure.

McGowan also believes that Morrison and Frydenberg were wrong to attack Andrews over Victoria's lockdowns, saying that their language was both extreme and unedifying.

Morrison was the one who had suggested in national cabinet that there should be mandatory vaccinations for aged-care workers. After health officials baulked at this proposal, he told them to come back with a way to do it. It was later mandated for aged-care employees, then Morrison hopped on the anti-mandate bandwagon — because of pressure, McGowan thinks, from his own backbenchers, rather than from the Palmer party.

McGowan was pretty cranky about that, too. 'I thought that was a pretty low blow, considering the anti-vax community was threatening to kill me and other premiers,' he said.

He pressed on with his plans, turning Western Australia into one of the highest-vaxxed places on the globe.

He said that Morrison was never aggressive with him. In one of those strange quirks, McGowan had met Morrison years before. In 2005, McGowan was Western Australia's tourism minister when Morrison ran the Australian Tourism Commission.

'I thought he was quite impressive,' McGowan told me. 'He was very impressive in his presentations.'

McGowan reflected on what an extraordinary time it was to be a leader at the time of Covid-19, and what he learned from it.

'It all came out of nowhere,' he said. 'There was no manual, no preparation, no understanding of what the processes were or the systems that could be activated to deal with it.

'What it showed me is that when times are difficult, overwhelmingly, not entirely, people do the right thing, that there is a sense of responsibility towards each other in Australia that is very strong.

'There is a willingness to accept the advice of government that is very strong and work well together—as opposed to the US.'

A key lesson for him was: 'When you have to do difficult things, do them, don't hesitate.'

'It worked well. The national cabinet process worked well,' he reflected. 'While Scott Morrison made some poor calls, particularly in relation to Western Australia, overall it was pretty good.

'We worked pretty well together.'

Where Australia also got lucky, he said, was that, overwhelmingly, the nation's leaders were a 'relatively sane, normal, reasonable group of people'.

He wondered what would have happened if there had been 'a Joh Bjelke-Petersen, or a Henry Bolte, or even a Jeff Kennett' around the table.

'What the hell would have happened then?' he asked. 'It could have been a disaster if some person hadn't fitted into the collegiality of the thing.'

Australia was also lucky with the quality of the medical advice that the government was receiving, particularly in those early days from Murphy and those around him, including Michael Kidd, Paul Kelly, Jenny Firman, Ruth Vine, and Nick Coatsworth, and the Commonwealth chief nursing and midwifery officer, Alison McMillan.

Their urgings to close borders, their knowledge of what action was needed to contain the virus and how to treat those infected, saved thousands of lives. The medical officers, too, were impressed by the quality of the politicians around the national cabinet table, despite the inevitable mistakes at a time of great uncertainty.

Their questions were intelligent, the discussions respectful, and the meetings were chaired well by Morrison.

'Leadership under fire,' one said. 'I found them incredibly impressive. The national cabinet approach was very wise, very sensible. They were very respectful of the advice given. They each had huge confidence in their chief health officers.'

They praised Hunt as the right man at the right time. Like almost everyone else, they were not told that Morrison had been sworn in as health minister. They dealt with both as a matter of course.

Hunt, who can be prickly and hypersensitive to criticism, told his medical officers at the outset that he did not want them to be 'yes people'. He told them he wanted honest advice, and if they thought he was on the wrong track, they should tell him. He worked hard, wanted to be across everything that was happening, and paid great attention to detail.

The medical officers worked incredibly long hours in highly stressed environments. They often had to deliver the worst news as case numbers rose in the second wave and greater numbers of Australians died, particularly in nursing homes, while dealing with their own personal traumas.

One of Professor Kidd's closest friends, a bridesmaid at his wedding, was the second person in Australia to die of a stroke caused by a blood clot after being vaccinated with AstraZeneca. His mother contracted Covid in a Melbourne nursing home, but thankfully survived. She had been vaccinated.

As for the lessons learned, that will have to wait for the pandemic to end and for an inquiry to be held, but the health professionals were pleased that many of the practices implemented during the early stages of the pandemic endured, including telehealth and e-scripts. There was particular attention paid in the early stages of the pandemic to the welfare of vulnerable people — Indigenous people, the disabled, and the mentally ill—which they hoped would continue, along with the tremendous community spirit that saw people look after one another, ranging from neighbours having drinks on the driveway to taking food to people unable or unwilling to venture out.

McGowan rang Morrison a few days after the federal election to commiserate. They had spent something like 65 meetings together. McGowan was concerned, because he knew that, often, leaders couldn't cope psychologically with electoral defeat.

He says that Morrison sounded 'philosophical' and was proud of what he had achieved. McGowan told him he should be proud. He was one of only a couple of dozen people to become prime minister of Australia.

Morrison told McGowan he was 'looking forward to becoming a quiet Australian'.

McGowan spoke to Morrison again after his visit to Perth, where he had delivered his sermon urging people to trust in God rather than government. McGowan told him, in the gentlest, nicest possible way, that the best thing he could do now, for his own wellbeing, was to quit parliament.

When news broke initially that Morrison had acquired Health, the premiers believed that nothing much turned on it, unless he had taken decisions secretly. McGowan admitted he got that wrong when he found out how many ministries Morrison had acquired, and that he had done so secretly.

He was right to worry about Morrison's state of mind.

Barr said that the leaders from this period have agreed to reunite when they are all in nursing homes to reminisce over these incredible years.

With many of the physical demands on hold—such as attending meetings or functions—it was the mental exhaustion that took its greatest toll. McGowan would exercise, either by himself or with his teenage kids, if they could bear to have him around.

Barr would unwind by putting his headphones on and listening to pop music, including 'Mad World' by Tears for Fears, 'Under Pressure' by Queen/David Bowie, 'One Step Ahead' by Split Enz, 'Holiday' by Madonna, and Cher's 'If I Could Turn Back Time'. Definitely a few not-so-hidden meanings there.

The pandemic had followed the bushfires, which had also taken their toll on the ACT. He says he would never want to go through it again, but learned a lot in those two years, particularly about how to get the best out of a team, and how to work collaboratively with people with whom he might not always agree.

'For all the trauma, I think I emerged as a better leader than before,' he says. The other leaders suffered different fates. Tasmania's Peter Gutwein was burned out. So was the Northern Territory's Michael Gunner, who also suffered a heart attack and ended up leaving politics. Gladys Berejiklian resigned and left politics. Stephen Marshall, the person in the room that Morrison could always count on for support, was mowed down by Peter Malinauskas in the South Australian state election in March 2022.

Barr says that Morrison's best days were in the early part of the pandemic, and makes a sharp observation about why Morrison ended up so damaged.

'When other people grew in the role, maybe he didn't,' Barr said.

'Everyone is going to be hit by events, but if you were to go through it point by point, how much of it was self-inflicted? Quite a lot of it was.'

CHAPTER FIVE

Clusterf..k Alert

The first concrete sign that Labor had smartened up since 2019, that it could run a successful campaign, came on 4 July 2020 when Kristy McBain won the by-election for the marginal New South Wales seat of Eden-Monaro.

It was only by 735 votes, but, as everybody keeps saying, and they are right, a win is a win is a win. It was vital for Anthony Albanese to show that he was capable of winning. A loss would have fired up leadership chatter, and prompted open questioning of his decision to be bipartisan on Covid and of his determined dumping of Bill Shorten's tax agenda.

McBain, the former mayor of Bega, was Albanese's handpicked candidate. He met her with other local mayors, was impressed by her, particularly as she had handled herself well during the Black Summer fires that had devastated the electorate, and decided then and there that she would be Labor's ideal candidate for the seat about to be vacated by Mike Kelly.

It was Albanese's first major test, but he was not the only one being tested. So was Labor's new national secretary, Paul Erickson, along with his campaign team.

Erickson, a fresh-faced 38-year-old, had spent five years as assistant secretary before taking over from Noah Carroll, who, along with Bill Shorten, paid the price for the 2019 loss.

Erickson had mixed experience in by-election campaigns. He had worked on the Western Australian seat of Canning in 2015 under George Wright, which had been shaping up as a Labor victory until Malcolm Turnbull unseated Tony Abbott. They had to cut Abbott's head off all the prepared bunting before polling day.

He had also worked on Braddon in Tasmania, another disappointment, and the inner-urban Melbourne seat of Batman (now Cooper) in 2018, when Labor fought off an assault from the Greens.

Eden-Monaro was going to be tough. Although the devastating Black Summer fires were still fresh in peoples' minds, the by-election came at a time when Morrison's popularity had hit a new peak.

According to Newspoll, released days out from voting day, Morrison's personal approval rating had hit its highest level since he'd been elected leader in August 2018. It had gone up two points to 68 per cent, with his dissatisfaction rating falling by two points to 27 per cent. The Coalition's primary vote was a healthy 42 per cent, giving the government a slight 51–49 lead in the two-party-preferred vote over Labor. Morrison's preferred-prime-minister rating had risen two points to 58 per cent, with Albanese on 26 per cent. A branch-stacking scandal in Victoria appeared to have no impact on Labor's federal primary vote, as measured by Newspoll, which had risen by one point to 35 per cent.

Fear of Covid meant that every leader in the country was riding high. Labor feared there would be a flight to safety by voters.

The Liberals had also settled on a good local candidate: Fiona Kotvojs, who had stripped back longtime Labor incumbent Mike Kelly's margin to less than 1 per cent at the 2019 election, without any help from head office. Because they didn't think she had a hope in hell of winning the seat, they had allocated little money, no resources, and few high-profile visits to her campaign.

Kotvojs got another go only after a public mud-wrestle between the deputy premier of New South Wales, Nationals leader John Barilaro, and the New South Wales transport minister, Liberal Andrew Constance, whose run of bad luck continued into the federal election.

Morrison and Alex Hawke wanted Constance. Internal polling showed he was the most likely candidate to win the seat, having distinguished himself during the fires by joining in the fight with neighbours, and then by telling the world that Morrison deserved what he got when he went to Cobargo, where the locals swore at him and refused to shake his hand.

Morrison, in a remarkably familiar power play, thought he could get Constance up as the candidate without a preselection or as the sole candidate. The locals, including a chap called Jon Gaul, were furious. Morrison and Hawke did not count on the wiliness or determination of Gaul, who had been immersed in politics for a few decades more than both of them put together.

Gaul, who had worked for William McMahon as press secretary and speechwriter, and then on almost every Liberal campaign thereafter, had migrated from Canberra to the New South Wales far-south coast, stayed involved with the Liberal Party, and had run Kotvojs' campaign in 2019, when she shaved 2.1 per cent from Kelly's margin.

While Barilaro and Constance were trading public insults, Kotvojs quietly lodged her nomination. Despite his bluff and bluster, Barilaro soon realised that he was never going to win the seat, and withdrew from the contest. Constance was under heavy pressure from the locals, including Gaul, to also pull out.

Albanese was alerted to Constance's impending withdrawal via a text message screaming 'clusterf..k alert'. Impossible to argue with that. It was a farce.

Morrison never learned not to mess with the locals. Sick of the manoeuvring, they had a simple message for the powerbrokers: if the party wanted another Gilmore, then abandoning a fair preselection was the best way to achieve it. That referred to Morrison's imposition in 2019 of Warren Mundine on the electorate of Gilmore. Liberals refused to campaign for him, and the disunity ensured that he lost the seat.

Locals argued that if the party expected volunteers in Eden-Monaro to turn out in bitterly cold weather in late June or early July, when the by-election was expected, then members deserved the right to choose the candidate.

Voters in the electorate who had been to hell twice in less than a year—first with the fires, then again with Covid, and who were still living in tents or caravans—were also unimpressed by the carry-on.

Even so, Kotvojs increased the Liberals' primary vote by 1.3 per cent. Having both the Nationals and the Shooters and Fishers Party running against her did not help; however, it was also clear that Morrison's high approval ratings had not been enough to deliver victory. Labor, partly thanks to its improved postal-vote campaign, flopped over the line to win.

It was an important confidence boost for Erickson, and it helped Albanese consolidate his leadership. Erickson, one of four sons of teachers Tim and Lois, grew up in Melbourne's inner-northern suburbs of Fawkner and Pascoe Vale. The by-election over, he packed his car and drove to Victoria. His mother was gravely ill. He just made it across the border before it closed for a stage-three lockdown caused by the leakage of Covid from hotel quarantine.

Lois, who had taught at Broadmeadows TAFE for 20 years, and had then quit to get a law degree, died six weeks later. It was an awful time for his family, and the restrictions on movement were onerous, but Erickson learned things, too.

Such as the resilience of the community and the preparedness of people to make sacrifices to stop the spread of Covid, minimise deaths, and limit the load on the health system. From where he was in Pascoe Vale, he concluded that the federal government was misreading the mood of Victorians, and that subsequent attacks by Morrison and the treasurer, Josh Frydenberg, on the premier, Daniel Andrews, were ill judged.

Victorians wanted Andrews to succeed, not fail, because failure would lead to more illness, more deaths, and more pressure on the hospital system.

Erickson didn't make it back to Canberra until September, but he was convinced by then that there had been a shift in sentiment against Morrison. Labor's research confirmed it.

In 2022, in the general election, Eden-Monaro fell victim to Morrison's grinding down of the New South Wales division. There was no preselection. Constance, nicknamed Bega after his state seat, had switched to the adjoining seat of Gilmore, where it was thought he had a better chance of winning because it contained his old seat. Thanks to the insistence of locals, Constance was required to face preselectors.

Gaul does not lay all the blame for the loss with Morrison, but he has to wear some of it. Jerry Nockles was chosen as the Liberal candidate for Eden-Monaro at the death knell, shortly before Morrison called the election. Morrison had tried to recruit a number of celebrity candidates — the former deputy chief medical officer, Dr Nick Coatsworth, and Erin Molan, daughter of Jim, a former TV sports presenter, and now a Sky After Dark host. Both refused.

Nockles was a good candidate, but it was mission impossible for him so late in the piece, even though Gaul believes the campaign was too long.

Gaul made a submission to the post-election review by Brian Loughnane and Jane Hume, recommending—among other things—that joining fees be slashed to $25, that only one year's membership should qualify for voting for preselections, and that preselections be held at least a year out from the final due date of the election.

Gaul was scathing about the campaign, believing the party did not offer young people a reason to vote for the government or attract them to join the Liberals. He complained that the grunt work was being left to an ageing membership. People like him.

He firmly believes that the party cannot win without winning back its heartland. He does not believe they are lost forever, but that they could be for a long time, and he doesn't think the party should give up on trying to get them back. Gaul, 83, plans to keep fighting for as long as he can.

The task will be even more difficult next time. In 2022, McBain won Eden-Monaro with a swing to her of more than 7 per cent on a two-party-preferred basis, taking her to 58 per cent, with a strong showing of 9 per cent for the Greens.

Eden-Monaro was once a classic bellwether seat. On the surface it now looks like a safe Labor seat, but as everyone keeps saying, and they are definitely right, there is no such thing as a safe seat anymore.

CHAPTER SIX

Jenny Says

After everything she had been through, and after everything that had flowed from her allegations, all the political and social ramifications — not to mention the cost to her personally, which made her question her decision to go public — Brittany Higgins broke down and cried on election night.

She is a great believer in the maxim that Australians always get it right at the ballot box. Nevertheless, after the result became clear, she says she went through a 'grieving period'.

'I was really sad,' she told me a few weeks after the election. 'I felt I had played a part in this big change for the Liberal Party. I was a small-l Liberal. People I had worked with and knew vaguely lost their seats.

'I knew it was the best thing for the country. It was quite sad. I cried. It wasn't a joyous occasion.'

She watched it unfold all day and through the night on 21 May.

'When Anthony Albanese gave his speech, I thought it was hopeful, beautiful, that it was great,' she said.

'When Morrison made his concession speech, I didn't feel sadness towards him. I saw Yaron [Finkelstein, Morrison's political adviser], Carswell [Andrew, the press secretary], and Kunkel [John, the chief of staff] getting out of the car.

'I felt vindicated seeing them. I had no warm feelings towards them.'

Then, as she spotted others in the crowd, particularly John Howard, her relief turned to sadness.

Summing up the feelings of so many small-l Liberals, Higgins said: 'It was not a good government; it didn't deserve to be re-elected.'

The Nationals' leader, David Littleproud, always believed that women stopped listening to Morrison after his tin-eared responses to Higgins' allegations that she had been raped in the office of then defence industry minister, Linda Reynolds, by another staffer on 23 March 2019, only metres from the prime ministerial suite in Parliament House.

Thereafter, whenever Morrison appeared, or failed to, such as outside Parliament House to address the thousands who had joined the March for Justice, he just made them angrier.

Women were already angry with Morrison. The bonfire was smouldering. At almost every point, he seemed utterly incapable of understanding what was expected of him. Whether it was the handling of the allegations against Christian Porter and Alan Tudge, or the fact that after he heard of the Higgins allegations, his wife, Jenny, had to explain their seriousness to him.

Morrison lit the fire on 22 October 2020, after Labor senator Kimberley Kitching asked the CEO of Australia Post, Christine Holgate, a series of questions during Senate estimates that elicited an admission she had given four senior executives Cartier watches worth $20,000 as a reward for securing multi-million-dollar contracts.

Labor thought this would turn into a huge embarrassment for the government. So did Morrison, who sacked her on the floor of the parliament without even bothering to hear her version of events. Saying he was appalled, that it was disgraceful, he yelled into the microphone: 'The chief executive … has been instructed to stand aside. If she doesn't wish to do that, she can go.' Those last three words were delivered with particular emphasis and in a menacing tone.

At that moment, people saw for themselves his nasty streak.

Former Queensland Nationals senator Ron Boswell was watching Question Time, and saw what Morrison did. Boswell thought it was 'the craziest bloody thing I have ever seen'.

Boswell, who had met Holgate, was full of praise for her role in helping save regional post offices. Almost immediately, he says, he contacted people close to Morrison—members of his prayer group and his staff—urging them to get the prime minister to go back into the House and fix it. Boswell says that all Morrison had to do was to say that since Question Time he had received additional information that had clarified the matter, it was now resolved, and Holgate would stay. In other words, he should admit that he had made a mistake. Simple.

Morrison's political adviser, Yaron Finkelstein, even well after the event, continued to defend his boss, on this and on many other issues. Finkelstein believed at the time that handing out expensive watches would not pass the pub test, and that the punters would be infuriated. Speaking to me for this book, he refused to concede it was a problem.

Boswell, who coached Holgate ahead of her subsequent appearance at the Senate inquiry, says he warned people close to Morrison that every woman journalist and every economic journalist would rip them to pieces. 'You can't win this one,' he warned. When nothing happened, he urged Barnaby Joyce, Matt Canavan, and Bridget McKenzie to back Holgate, which they did.

McKenzie was already on to it. She was scathing about Holgate's treatment.

'I personally pursued the Christine Holgate matter through the Senate inquiry process specifically to highlight the unfairness of what had happened,' she told me.

'A whole lot of professional women outside politics had watched a highly regarded and competent corporate leader, who appeared to have acted within company policy, publicly humiliated, and effectively sacked during Question Time.

'That was unjust, and a lot of women identified with that experience. And you have to wonder whether they privately asked, *If it can happen to her, could it happen to me?*

McKenzie was also one of the women who attended the March for Justice outside Parliament House. She said she felt it was important to go, because she fundamentally believed that women should not be subject to sexual harassment or violence at work or in the community.

'This didn't mean I was signing up to the log of claims put up by the organisers, but [it was] an opportunity to show that it wasn't just left-wing activists who were concerned about the treatment of women in the workplace and in broader society,' she said.

The communications minister, Paul Fletcher, as one of the two portfolio ministers involved, heeded his master's voice on Holgate. He failed to step in to try to fix it, and instead went along with Morrison.

When Simon Birmingham took over Finance on 30 October after Mathias Cormann's departure, which made him the second shareholder minister for Australia Post, he urged Morrison to patch it up. He wouldn't.

Nick Minchin thought it was 'terrible' that the prime minister had launched a public attack in that way against Holgate over something so trivial. He thought it was wrong, and 'the beginning of a downward trend for Morrison'.

John Howard joined in the criticism of Morrison after the 2022 election, saying it was egregious and that Holgate had done nothing wrong.

Frydenberg also nominated it as one of Morrison's low points.

It was judged by many as a pivotal event in the decline of women's support for the Liberals.

Executives were free to pay themselves millions in bonuses and salaries without eliciting a prime ministerial demand for their dismissal. The government had paid undeserving businesses billions via JobKeeper and not demanded repayment, because, according to Morrison, that would have been giving in to the 'politics of envy'. But gifting a few baubles to executives for nailing down contracts that helped secure the future of Australia Post franchises in regional areas was appalling and disgraceful, and warranted dismissal.

What was appalling and disgraceful was the way that Morrison had used his bully pulpit and the privilege of parliament to force a highly successful woman executive out of a job.

Holgate was furious when she heard that Morrison had been secretly sworn into the finance ministry, welcoming Albanese's decision to proceed with a formal inquiry into Morrison's secret ministries 'including examination of his influence and actions as an undisclosed Australia Post Shareholder Minister'.

'Australia needs safeguards in place to ensure no one can assume power covertly, and that all people are afforded safety, respect, and equity—inside and outside of parliament,' she told me.

Updating an earlier interview for this book, she said: 'The saying democracy dies in darkness has never been truer.

'Being secretly appointed to the most important cabinet positions, with statutory authority, is extremely problematic for our democratic values, and for any decisions made during that period.

'Mr Morrison thought it appropriate to publicly admonish me, when I had done absolutely nothing wrong, at the same time as he was withholding critical information from his colleagues and the public.

'When a Senate inquiry exonerated me and recommended he apologise, he refused to. To this day, I have never had any contact from him.'

Holgate still cannot bear to watch the video from that day when Morrison sacked her. She responded in detail to my questions after the election and before knowing that Morrison had assumed the finance minister's role in March 2020.

She was as disturbed by that, demanding answers about what role he had played in ultimately determining her fate, as she was disgusted by his initial dismissal of her.

'I continue to believe that this was one of the most public and brutal acts of bullying,' she told me. 'I was simply used as a pawn for distraction from other political issues that were hurting the prime minister at the time.'

This referred to a revelation the previous day from the auditor-general, Grant Hehir, that he had referred to the Australian Federal Police for investigation the Commonwealth purchase of a 12-hectare plot, near the Western Sydney Airport, in mid-2018 for almost $30 million. A valuation a year later showed it was worth just $3 million, and an Australian National Audit Office report was scathing about how the Commonwealth had handled the deal.

The infrastructure minister at the time was Fletcher. There were no findings of wrongdoing by Fletcher.

Holgate says that within two hours after she had finished answering questions in the Senate, she was effectively dismissed by Morrison. Neither he nor Fletcher spoke to her.

'If the former prime minister had done what he did in a corporate workplace, or outside of parliament, he would have been immediately dismissed and faced significant legal action,' she said.

'I have been very public regarding the deep disappointment that I felt regarding the prime minister and the chair of Australia Post [Lucio Di Bartolomeo], and the significant impact their actions had on my mental health.

'However, almost 22 months later, I feel the scars of those events fuel me to be a stronger leader myself. Apart from being more determined, I have learnt a lot through this period. Particularly regarding the weaknesses in workplace law to protect individuals against corporate injustice, the breadth of bullying and abuse that happens in workplaces, and the depth of mental health issues many individuals are suffering across the country.'

She said she passionately supported implementation of the 55 recommendations of the Respect@Work review, so that what happened to her couldn't happen to anyone else.

She said the agreement she had forged not only saved community banking in regional Australia, but it also made a significant financial contribution to the viability of community post offices.

'I had the authority to reward the individuals who secured this agreement up to $150,000 each as a bonus; however, I chose to give them a watch with an average value of less than $5,000.

'The former chairman of Australia Post [John Stanhope] jointly presented these gifts with me and signed a card for each of the recipients. But for politically expedient purposes to a prime minister under pressure over multiple issues, it was perceived as I had been handing out gold watches in the middle of the pandemic, and this needed to be investigated.

'No effort was made publicly at the time to correct the facts. It was highly misleading, to not just the general public but also to the rest of government, including their own party members.

'My lowest moment was when I was depicted in a cartoon in a national newspaper as a prostitute leaving Scott Morrison's bedroom. The fact that anyone could think that was appropriate probably helps explain why we have such a gender imbalance in leadership in Australia.

'The investigation ordered by the former prime minister proved I had done no wrong, nor broken any rules, and so the government tried to bury it. It was only via a sustained campaign of pressure brought to bear by a handful of my supporters, most notably Angela Cramp, that it was released, and that is what turned the tide.

'In many ways, I have felt I was lucky. Several important people reached out immediately and offered help,' she said.

She named public relations consultant Ross Thornton as a stand-out.

'He knew I would be silenced, and that I was too unwell and unable to speak to the media due to the terms of the government's investigation. He dealt with every inquiry, and did not seek one dollar in compensation,' she said.

'The community post offices across Australia, in particular Angela Cramp and the Licensed Post Office Group, campaigned for me to be reinstated. They put posters up in their shop windows saying #westandwithChristine; they went on television and asked members of the public to send $5 to the prime minister, which thousands did; and in the days up to my hearing ran newspaper adverts, calling for public support, asking people to wear white to unite behind me.

'The Wear White to Unite campaign was an idea of the late Carla Zampatti. I wore her white jacket to parliament. She sadly died days before I gave evidence. One colleague from Australia

Post, Taeressa [*sic*] Fawthrop, risked her career, helped edit my submission, and sat by me in the inquiry. Many other colleagues wore white on the day as a sign of solidarity.

'Business leaders like Andrew Forrest, Ian Silk, Tim Reed, Drew Abercrombie, and particularly both Marcus Blackmore and Shaun Bonnet openly supported me. Shaun and Marcus sat with me throughout the Senate inquiry hearing. Politicians with broad and differing views from all main parties reached out and tried to help.'

She said that she and Boswell, as the former National Party leader in the Senate, set aside any political differences. She says he 'coached' her through the process, which had been initiated by Pauline Hanson. Bob Katter constantly raised the 'injustice' in parliament.

She says the committee's report ultimately vindicated her, and that tens of thousands of people contacted her after she appeared on ABC TV's *7.30* program with Laura Tingle.

Recounting her life, she says she left at home at 18 with no job, no money, and a one-way ticket to London.

'I have lived and worked in several countries, and often took risks with my career, because I was prepared to "have a go" to be able to progress. Everything I have achieved in my career is because I worked very hard. To have that taken away from you, in a flash of one person's political desire to distract the country, felt almost criminal.'

She says that she, Grace Tame, Georgie Dent, and around a dozen other women united to speak out and advocate change. They met on Saturday mornings to plan their campaign.

'Then Yasmin Poole and Lucy Turnbull suggested a video to get our message across. We released #SafetyRespectEquity on the eve of International Women's Day.'

Holgate says that more than one million people viewed it in

24 hours. Within weeks, it had crossed the globe. She was told it had been shown in universities across the UK and the US. She said she had heard that more than 10 million people watched it within a month.

On 13 May, Women in Leadership Australia gave her the National Award for Excellence in Leadership. She regarded it as a great honour, but also as a recognition of the great wrong done to her.

'I think that a lot of Australians started to see the former prime minister for what he really was through his treatment of me,' she said.

'It became increasingly obvious the comparison on how he treated me, to shout he was "shocked and appalled", but was not when he was informed a member of his cabinet (whether rightly or wrongly) was accused of rape, or … another cabinet member massively overpaying for land at the airport, or the debacle of Robodebt, which used taxpayers' money to settle $1.8 billion after unlawfully raising debts against innocent people.

'None of these appalling accusations warranted an investigation or criticism of the individual. These leaders all stayed in his cabinet or government.

'Undoubtedly, the disrespectful treatment of women, of which I was just one, played a role in the election result.

'The most significant cohort of voters in the result of the election were professional women, and their vote undoubtedly impacted many key Liberal seats turning Teal. Yet Scott Morrison appeared to be deaf to women.

'I know many men who have written to me and said that Scott Morrison's disrespect for women impacted them to vote differently at the last election, even when they had been lifelong Liberal voters.

'All of us want our loved ones to flourish and be safe. We all have either a mother, sister, daughter, or female friend. Personally, I found it very encouraging that so many men supported a safer, more respectful, and equitable future for women in our country.'

Asked how she felt on election night, Holgate said: 'When it was clear that he would no longer be prime minister, I went home and slept well for the first time in 22 months.'

Weeks after Holgate's traumatic experience, Louise Milligan's *Four Corners* documentary, 'Inside the Canberra Bubble', aired on Monday 9 November 2020. Focussing on two cabinet ministers, Alan Tudge and Christian Porter, it plunged the government into another crisis.

The program interviewed Rachelle Miller about her affair with Tudge while she was his press secretary. Malcolm Turnbull was also interviewed about his 'counselling' of Porter in 2017 after he had been informed that Porter had behaved inappropriately in a Canberra bar with a young woman who was not his wife.

Morrison responded by sooling Paul Fletcher onto the ABC. He also defended his ministers by saying that everyone did it—Labor, the Greens, the media—and that the ABC needed to look at them.

He refused to inquire into the behaviour of Tudge and Porter, saying that the activities had occurred in 2017, before Turnbull had added the so-called bonk ban to the ministerial code of conduct, stipulating the sacking of ministers who had sex with their staff. Ipso facto, the ban had fixed whatever problem there was.

'I think Australians understand human frailty, and I think they understand the people who work in this place are just as human as anyone else, and subject to the same vulnerabilities and frailties as anyone,' he said at the time.

Tudge admitted the affair, and apologised.

'I regret my actions immensely and the hurt it caused my family. I also regret the hurt that Ms Miller has experienced,' he said.

Porter threatened to sue. He denied kissing the woman in the bar. According to my sources at the time, Tudge had sought to protect Porter's reputation by demanding that a journalist destroy a compromising photo of him in the bar with the woman.

The photo was taken on the phone of an ABC journalist by a public servant said to have a deep interest in matters of national security. He had just been talking to the journalist about the recently departed Labor senator Sam Dastyari, who had been forced to quit over dodgy Chinese connections, when he spotted Porter with the woman. Concerned by what he believed to be inappropriate behaviour by Porter, and to show how easily people can be caught in potentially compromising situations, the public servant grabbed the journalist's smartphone and took a photo.

According to *Four Corners*, Tudge, prompted by Miller, who was with him in the same bar that night, approached the journalist to ask that she delete the photo of Porter and the young woman. The journalist refused.

According to my sources, Tudge then rang the journalist the next day to plead with her to delete the photo. She did. Tudge refused, through a spokesman at the time, to respond to my questions about the photo.

The chair of the ABC, Ita Buttrose, who was appointed by Morrison, effectively dismissed a formal 'Please explain' letter from Fletcher, which demanded to know why the private lives of politicians were newsworthy, why Labor had not been investigated, and why the ABC was hostile to the Liberal Party.

Buttrose replied that there was no bias and that all proper processes had been followed. It marked a sharp deterioration in relations between the government and the ABC. That was just the beginning.

After Brittany Higgins' allegations became public, Milligan reported on 26 February 2021 that the Australian Federal Police had been notified a letter had been sent to Morrison detailing an alleged historical rape by a cabinet minister in his government. The offence was alleged to have occurred in 1988, well before the man had entered parliament.

Days later, Porter identified himself as the cabinet minister. He tearfully and flatly denied the allegations. After Porter announced he would sue the ABC, Morrison moved him from the attorney-general's portfolio to Industry. That was one of the portfolios Morrison had acquired after Porter showed Morrison's office in 2020 how to do it.

Allegations that Porter had received anonymous donations via a so-called blind trust led to his resignation from cabinet on 19 September 2021. He did not recontest the 2022 election, and his seat of Pearce was lost to Labor.

It was in between these two scandals that Tame and Higgins emerged. Tame, a survivor of child sexual abuse, gave a powerful speech when she accepted the Australian of the Year award on 26 January 2021, an award that the prime minister's office was convinced would go to Dr Brendan Murphy, the chief medical officer, for his handling of Covid.

Not for the first or last time, Morrison showed, when Tame had finished, how much he didn't get. 'I shit you not, he leant over, and right in my ear he goes, "Well, gee, I bet it felt good to get that out,"' Tame later revealed.

It was a fateful night. Tame's speech helped Higgins decide to go public.

Higgins told me in early June 2022 that she was not sure that she would go public if she had her time over again. She believed that important changes had been made, but the personal cost to her had been enormous.

She also said it 'defies belief' that Morrison did not know of her allegations until they became public.

She was 24, smart and keen as, working in her 'dream job' as a press secretary for the defence industry minister, Linda Reynolds, when she went back to Parliament House with a fellow staffer, whom she alleged raped her in Reynolds' office while she was intoxicated.

She says she felt demoralised by the internal processes, so she had no option but to go public after struggling with it for almost two years.

'I was at my lowest point,' she told me. She described herself as a 'Liberal, through and through', a small-l one.

'Speaking out was the nuclear option, even though I knew I would be hurting myself and hurting the Liberal Party,' she said.

She told her story to Samantha Maiden at news.com.au and to Lisa Wilkinson for Ten's *The Project*. Maiden put questions to the prime minister's office on Friday 12 February 2021, notifying them that her story would appear on Monday morning 15 February.

Because of privacy considerations, Reynolds says she was unable to tell Morrison what she had been told. But his two most senior staff members, John Kunkel and Yaron Finkelstein, were certainly aware that 'an incident' had allegedly occurred in her office.

In June 2021, Reynolds alleged in Senate estimates that a fortnight before it became public, on 2 February, Kimberly Kitching had approached her in the Senate chamber and told her—wrongly, as it turned out—that the allegations of a rape had been discussed in Labor's tactics committee and that the opposition was planning to 'rain down hell' on her over it.

Almost immediately, Reynolds says she contacted Finkelstein to brief him on what Kitching had relayed on the floor of the Senate chamber about Labor planning to weaponise the issue.

She does not know what he did with that information. Finkelstein says he cannot specifically recall that conversation. He said people assumed that 'certain people knew names'.

'Some of us just didn't know who the people were who were involved. We knew about an incident,' he said.

Initially, Reynolds was angry with Morrison for publicly rebuking her for not telling him what had happened. That disappeared after she collapsed in the Senate following intense questioning about the matter when it did become public. As soon as he found out she was unwell, Morrison went around to see her.

'I was incoherent. I was in pain. I was just a mess. It was just the two of us. I will never forget his kindness,' she said. Reynolds, who has a heart condition, was hospitalised on 24 February, then went on sick leave.

She says everyone knew that Dutton wanted Defence. Morrison could have dumped her then and there. 'Nobody would have blinked an eye, nobody would have said a word,' she said later. She was moved out of Defence for Dutton at the end of March, but maintained her cabinet position.

Reynolds talked about the two sides of Morrison — the side she had seen when he was solicitous of her, who showed exceptional leadership during Covid, and the other side, spurred on by the 'bros' around him who viewed women as a tactical problem to be fixed. She said he had appointed eight women to his frontbench on 'merit', but his ability to relate to women was an issue.

'He is very blokey,' she said. And, she believes, this was not helped by the company he kept.

'He also had his band of bros — John Kunkel, Yaron Finkelstein,

Stuart Robert, Ben Morton, Scott Briggs—around him. Those people, he associated with all the time. They stayed at The Lodge with him,' she said.

'He didn't actually have anyone in his inner sanctum who saw women as anything other than a problem that needed fixing. It was all transactional,' she said. 'I became a problem to fix.'

Morrison's senior press secretary, Andrew Carswell, says the first that the press office knew about the allegations was when Maiden contacted the office.

Carswell insists that even after getting questions from Maiden on the Friday afternoon, he did not tell his boss because he wanted to try to establish what had happened before informing him.

Kunkel now wishes he had told Morrison about it before the story broke. 'In terms of things I regret, I regret not having told him earlier in some form. We let him down,' Kunkel said.

There was speculation that Morrison's staff had been trying to shield him, or that they were providing him with plausible deniability, or that they were too frightened to tell him, or that they did not think it important enough to disturb his weekend.

According to one former senior staffer, it was not true to say that Morrison did not encourage staff to speak out. He said that Morrison would often get exasperated when they did not offer alternative views.

Another claimed that staff were reluctant to be the bearers of bad news, claiming that the environment did not encourage people to speak out. '"Frank and fearless" did not apply in that office,' according to this staffer, who claimed that anyone who did speak out was sidelined. Those who were in the inner circle—all men—wanted that circle kept tight.

Those outside the inner circle complained it was cliquey, hard to break into.

One cabinet minister, who described Morrison as a bully and who, after watching them interact, concluded that Morrison's staff were intimidated by him, believes that in this instance they were protecting him, deciding not to tell him so he would be able to say later that he knew nothing about it.

Carswell disputes this.

'I found a good working environment and leadership style,' he said.

'The values connected, and there was a faith connection. He was not only a good boss, he took great interest in his staff.

'One of the things he put in place was a flat structure. Everyone could walk in and give him advice.

'You put your foot in the door and go in.'

He said the fact that his staff remained loyal proved that he treated his staff 'exceptionally well'.

Remarkably, none of them thought it necessary to tell Morrison that an important story with potentially massive political ramifications was about to break. Kunkel says that it was a stuff-up, and that they had spent the weekend trying to piece it all together.

'It is 100 per cent true he found out that Monday,' Carswell told me, insisting that most of that weekend was spent trying to deal 'with the situation'.

'I think we were just working through the process. It was a horrific process to understand ourselves,' he said.

He said they spent the weekend going through documents and notes held by Fiona Brown, who had been chief of staff to Reynolds at the time of the alleged incident, and who was by then in Morrison's office. He said he also spoke to Finkelstein and Kunkel to establish what they knew.

'There was a mountain of work that had to be done that weekend,' he said. 'We had not got to the bottom of the story yet.

They were incredibly sensitive issues we were dealing with.

'He definitely did not know.'

Finkelstein later admitted they had discussed whether or not to tell Morrison, before deciding against it. He defended not telling him in advance, saying it would not have made any difference. He said it was important to try to establish the facts, and that Carswell had handled it appropriately.

Carswell could not pinpoint the exact time he told Morrison, except that it would have been around the time of the leadership meeting that Monday morning, usually held around 8.15 or 8.30, so surmises it would have been before that—perhaps half an hour before it became public on the news.com.au website.

Morrison has always insisted he was not told by anybody until the story appeared. Few believed him. According to others present at the leadership meeting that morning, Morrison alerted them to the story, telling them that he had only just been told about it by his office, and, in a rare criticism of his staff, said he had been let down by his office.

Those present were incredulous that his staff had not told him, saying that if they had, it would have given him time to prepare mentally, to process what he had been told, as well as to make his own inquiries, then consider what action to take.

Even other men thought perhaps part of the problem was that it was a blokey office. With a boofy, blokey leader in charge. It was another huge mistake, on top of other huge mistakes, and more mistakes would follow.

Higgins accepts that he might not have known around the time that the alleged rape occurred, as it was close to the 2019 election, and it was being handled privately, including by Kunkel.

But it was different after media questions had been put to the office.

'I don't think he found out on Monday morning,' she says. 'It beggars belief.'

She surmises that Morrison may have 'misspoken'—her characterisation—when he said he didn't know until it came out.

'It goes to his personal credibility and the authenticity of his response. It defies belief.'

Almost a year later, Brittany Higgins released text messages that Barnaby Joyce had sent to a third party on 22 March 2021, which he wanted to be sent to her, clearly showing he was one of many who did not believe Morrison:

Tell BH [Brittany Higgins] I and Scott, he is Scott to me until I have to recognise his office, don't get along.

He is a hypocrite and a liar from my observations and that is over a long time.

I have never trusted him and I dislike how he earnestly rearranges the truth to a lie.

Higgins had been angered by Joyce's hypocrisy in demanding that a minister who had texted Gladys Berejiklian calling Morrison a 'psycho' out himself or herself.

'He sent the message to me through an intermediary earlier on in 2021 when he was a backbencher. The message was sent to me in response to the prime minister's public commentary about the date he was alleged to have found out about my alleged assault in Parliament House,' she said later.

'Once Barnaby Joyce became deputy prime minister, his public opinion of Scott Morrison had clearly shifted. I completely understood that this is the nature of politics, and the wheel of favourability is always turning.

'It was only when the deputy prime minister was really turning up the heat and was publicly calling for the cabinet minister to put their name to the unfavourable comments made about the prime minister.

'Only then did I decide to share his message. I felt at that point he was being quite hypocritical and it was in the public interest for his own comments about the prime minister to be known.'

Morrison sought to recover some ground on the Tuesday morning, the day after Higgins' allegations had been made public and she had appeared on Ten's *The Project*. He announced at a doorstop that he had asked backbencher Celia Hammond to look at what other processes were needed for staff to report such incidents.

'I have listened to Brittany. Jenny and I spoke last night, and she said to me, "You have to think about this as a father first. What would you want to happen if it were our girls?"' he said.

'Jenny has a way of clarifying things, always has. And so, as I've reflected on that overnight, and listened to Brittany, and what she had to say, there are a couple of things here that need to be addressed.'

He was nonplussed when Tegan George, then at Network Ten, asked pertinent questions, like why he hadn't thought of it as a human being, and what if men didn't have wives and children, would they be as compassionate?

'Well, look, in my own experience, being a husband and a father is central to me, my human being. So I just can't follow the question you're putting,' he said.

Soon after, at the National Press Club, Grace Tame was asked about Morrison quoting Jenny.

'It shouldn't take having children to have a conscience,' Tame said. 'And, actually, on top of that, having children doesn't guarantee a conscience.'

It was devastating. It drove many women mad, including some

of his MPs and female relatives of his MPs, to hear him quoting his wife in this way.

Scandals would abate and erupt throughout the course of the year, inflaming tensions inside the government.

Senior Liberals believed that Morrison's office had briefed journalists at the end of 2021 that Tudge would not be returning to the education portfolio. In a fresh outbreak, Tudge had been accused by his former lover and staffer, Rachelle Miller, of emotional, and in one instance physical, abuse.

After Miller had lodged a complaint alleging bullying, harassment, and discrimination while working for Tudge and the former attorney-general, Michaelia Cash, Tudge announced he was stepping aside.

He was found not to have breached ministerial standards; however, Morrison announced in December, after Ten reported that Tudge's name plaque had been removed from his ministerial office, that Tudge had informed him he would not return to the frontbench so he could focus on his re-election.

Articles appeared saying that Miller had been awarded $500,000 in compensation. With the election campaign underway, it all got very confusing and very murky.

After the election, it was revealed that Miller had received $650,000 for damages and loss suffered while she worked for Tudge and Cash. There was no admission of liability from the two former ministers, who denied any wrongdoing.

It appeared that Tudge was a backbencher and a cabinet minister at the same time. Under questioning on the day he called the election, Morrison said Tudge was still 'technically' a member of cabinet and still 'formally' education minister, even though he was a backbencher and even though Stuart Robert was acting as education minister.

It was an inauspicious beginning to the campaign for Morrison, soon to be eclipsed by Albanese's first-day blues, but later compounded by Katherine Deves.

Morrison refused to disclose the reasons for the payment to Miller, saying it was a private, sensitive matter. Fears that Tudge would quit and that the Liberals would lose his seat of Aston at the election were cited in private by senior Liberals as reasons why Morrison would not clearly resolve Tudge's status.

Jason Clare skewered them. 'I don't think Scooby-doo could find Alan Tudge at the moment,' he said.

Surveying the wreckage later, one senior Coalition MP recalled the advice that former Nationals leader Warren Truss used to give to MPs newly arrived in Parliament House: 'Sleep with your conscience, not your staff.'

CHAPTER SEVEN

I Am the Prime Minister (and you are a fuckwit)

Gladys Berejiklian loathed Scott Morrison. Dominic Perrottet never trusted him or his closest allies, because he believed they tried at every point to wreck his career. Politics demanded that Berejiklian and Perrottet put on a show in public that they got along well with the prime minister. Few were fooled. Morrison called them his friends. They weren't.

At least he never pretended to like Matt Kean. Because he so hated the New South Wales treasurer, Morrison took a machete and sliced off his own nose when he refused to sign off on a policy that would have helped him in the election. He resented it when Kean as environment minister tried to prod his federal colleagues to get cracking on climate change. Morrison dismissed him publicly as a nobody, which triggered guerrilla warfare before, during, and after the election, to Morrison's great cost.

Berejiklian believed that Morrison, his office, and his surrogates undermined her during the Black Summer bushfires to shift attention from his own shortcomings. She felt that he belittled, bullied, and patronised her all the way through her premiership.

In late July 2021, senior New South Wales Liberals privately accused Morrison of using the same background-briefing techniques against Berejkilian that he had used against Brittany Higgins and Julia Banks. They accused him of gaslighting their premier.

Berejiklian authorised her senior communications adviser, Sean Berry, to call Morrison's senior press secretary, Andrew Carswell, to ask him to stop briefing journalists against her. Carswell responded by saying he had simply been relaying facts.

Berejiklian regarded that as confirmation.

Around the same time, Morrison abused — in front of witnesses — her treasurer, Dominic Perrottet.

On 28 July 2021, Morrison announced to media the final iteration of the JobSaver package to help New South Wales workers facing ruin almost a month after Sydney had gone into lockdown following another Covid breakout.

Morrison was asked if Perrottet was right to claim responsibility for securing it, after Perrottet referred to himself as a pain in the arse for having pushed for the extra help for the beleaguered state. Morrison had a ready riposte designed to elevate himself to the higher ground.

Morrison loftily quoted former US president Ronald Reagan as saying: 'You get a lot more done if you don't care who takes the credit.' Then Morrison added tetchily: 'Whoever wants to take the credit for the payment, knock yourself out, OK. I'm just happy we're getting payments to people.'

Next morning, on 29 July, interviewed by Laura Jayes on Sky, Perrottet said that the two governments had worked constructively together. He agreed it was a partnership, and he agreed with Morrison's sentiment about who cares who takes the credit.

Perrottet then couldn't resist correcting the prime minister. Perrottet reckoned it wasn't Reagan who had said who cares. It was president Harry Truman. Truman had said: 'It is amazing what you can accomplish if you do not care who gets the credit.'

It was both funny and pointed, and was meant as a bit of payback for Morrison's behaviour the day before on a video hook-up to finalise the details of the package. Morrison had lost it, and had sworn at Perrottet.

A tired and cranky prime minister had allowed his temper to get the better of him. He was angered by Perrottet's public interventions, including calling for the reinstatement of Jobkeeper, which Morrison felt undermined or usurped the federal government.

Weeks before that, Perrottet had publicly lamented a lack of national leadership, which also would have infuriated Morrison.

In May, frustrated by the prime minister's increasingly ridiculous stunts, and his failure to outline under what circumstances Australia's borders could reopen, Perrottet took aim, saying on Sky: 'What's most important is the judgement in 10 years' time. It's not about the 24-hour news cycle, and rocking up and being successful at a news conference. It's about making sure we have a strategy to open up the economy.'

Warming to his theme, Perrottet followed up on ABC Radio National: 'We are not in politics to follow public opinion — we are here to lead.'

It sounded like an echo of Paul Keating's Placido Domingo speech, which set the scene for his challenge to Bob Hawke's leadership, when he complained that there was more to leadership than tripping over television wires in supermarkets.

It sounds like an unlikely coupling, but Keating and Perrottet are friends. Perrottet often seeks his counsel. They are both Catholics, and they both have similar worldviews, particularly about not wasting time in government.

All that was bubbling away in the background during the video conference call to finalise the Jobsaver package in late July. Morrison became increasingly belligerent in response to Perrottet's questioning of elements of the package. He thought Perrottet was being too picky and focussing on the flaws.

Finally, Morrison let loose, calling Perrottet a 'fuckwit'. Berejiklian and the federal treasurer, Josh Frydenberg, were also on the call, so it was far from a private exchange, unlike the florid call to the Tasmanian treasurer and later premier, Peter Gutwein, a few years before.

Perrottet bit back, reprimanding Morrison for his poor form and indulging in such an ill-disciplined outburst during a serious discussion on an important subject. Morrison backed off and apologised. Still, it left a sour taste.

In October, Berejiklian resigned after the Independent Commission against Corruption announced it was investigating her secret relationship with former MP Daryl Maguire.

Perrottet was the obvious choice for leader. Or so you would have thought. Yet, after Berejiklian quit, Perrottet's supporters complained that Morrison's staff and allies were running an anybody-but-Perrottet campaign to block him.

They accused Morrison and Alex Hawke of trying to stymie Perrottet's advancement at every point, as payback for a bitter falling-out between them that had occurred some years before. It was so serious during the negotiations over the leadership that Perrottet appealed to John Howard to intervene. Howard went on TV to tell everyone that Perrottet was the obvious and only choice to replace Berejiklian. The interference stopped.

One of Perrottet's first acts as premier was to declare that Sydney would remove quarantine requirements and lift caps on overseas arrivals from 1 November. Perrottet made a unilateral decision; a member of his staff informed a member of the prime minister's staff just before he announced it.

Morrison was not impressed. He told the media he would decide when international borders would reopen.

Around this time, Morrison was ramping up his efforts to get his way with New South Wales preselections. He was trying to poach state MPs and ministers, including the police minister, David Elliott, who was in the Morrison–Hawke faction and was toying with the idea of jumping ship, and Melanie Gibbons, who was prepared to leave her state seat of Holsworthy to run in Hughes after Craig Kelly's defection to the crossbench. Morrison also wanted a Pentecostal preacher, Jemima Gleeson, to run in the seat of Dobell.

Two days before he made his border announcement, Perrottet, worried about facing possibly four simultaneous by-elections—with Andrew Constance running for Gilmore—rang Morrison to ask if it was true he was behind the plan to get Gibbons to shift to Hughes. Morrison pretended it had nothing to do with him.

Dutton told people that if these kind of shenanigans were happening in his home state of Queensland, members would have 'burned down the division'.

Another federal MP, who believed that proper preselections protected the party, described Morrison's approach thus: 'I am a fucking genius, and you are all idiots.'

New South Wales Liberals were growing increasingly frustrated by the delays in the preselection process. They accused Morrison's designated representative, Alex Hawke, of avoiding meetings to vet prospective candidates, thereby slowing down the process.

They believed that Hawke, with Morrison's backing, was doing this because his own preselection was under threat. Morrison argued that others, including cabinet minister Sussan Ley and the member for North Sydney, Trent Zimmerman, were at risk.

Those defending Morrison said he would have been pilloried if he had allowed a woman to be turfed out. They also argued that the Liberals had little chance of holding on to North Sydney without Zimmerman.

Hawke told me that the accusations he deliberately delayed processes are 'demonstrably false'. Hawke insisted he was available to attend, but that the delays were caused by party factionalism, which meant that agreement could never be reached on which candidates should be put forward.

He agreed that it was a problem when up to four state ministers wanted to transit to the federal sphere.

He also agreed that the division is dysfunctional. Hawke rejected accusations of self-interest, saying he was always confident he would hold his preselection — as would Zimmerman — and that Morrison's manoeuvring was all designed to save Sussan Ley.

'She was dead, she was finished,' he said later.

Repeated attempts were made by the New South Wales state director, Chris Stone, directly to Morrison or to his office, to appoint someone other than Hawke to sit on the vetting body, the Nominations Review Committee. Previously, Morrison had allowed Paul Fletcher to act on his behalf.

Morrison refused to nominate someone other than Hawke. Party rules decree that all four members of the NRC or their representatives must attend — there has to be a full complement, not just a simple quorum — which include the prime minister or his delegate. It was always open to Morrison to allow someone else to attend on his behalf if Hawke was indeed too busy.

One source familiar with what happened said that Morrison's

attitude, expressed forcefully during meetings, was that he was prime minister, so the executive should accede to his wishes.

'Morrison was determined to be able to choose his own candidates, and he was going to get them, by hook or by crook,' he said. 'He had a view that "I am the prime minister. I choose, and you should deliver."'

At three state executive meetings, in October, November, and December 2021, attempts were made to force a resolution of the preselection stalemate. They went nowhere. Morrison also got nowhere.

According to the minutes of the state executive meeting on 19 November:

> The state director [Stone] has advised he has been consulting with the Prime Minister since the last meeting of state executive and it is his strong view that the state executive should not set nominations closing dates at this point in time.

A long debate ensued; then, with a vote of 15 in favour, eight against, and one abstention, it was decided that preselections for Warringah, Parramatta, Hume, Hughes, Farrer, Cook, Bradfield, and Bennelong, should be resolved by 3 December. That didn't happen, according to party sources: the vetting committee could not meet, because the prime minister's representative was not available.

At its meeting on 17 December, the state executive also resolved to implement a timetable for Bennelong, Hughes, Dobell, Parramatta, and Warringah, with rolls closing on 21 January 2022, and with the nomination-review processes to be completed by 28 February.

Unable to prevail, Morrison first sought in November 2021 to get the federal executive to intervene in the state division. There was pushback.

Nick Minchin, the serving male federal vice-president, a conservative, a former cabinet minister in the Howard government, and a former high-ranking party official who had authored the rules outlining the powers of the federal executive, offered the most resistance to Morrison's plans.

He says that the executive was later 'ambushed' into going along with Morrison, who was angry that anyone would dare try to challenge sitting members. Party officials were angry that the leader was seeking to bypass due process on such a grand scale to get his own way.

'I thought that every MP in the Liberal Party was always open to challenge,' Minchin told me later.

'It was a fundamental part of our party; we didn't protect anyone from preselection challenges. I saw no basis whatsoever for the special powers of the federal executive to avoid those three members facing a preselection.

'I expressed my considerable vehemence, as one of the authors of those powers, not to protect existing MPs.

'There's an issue of principle that we don't preserve the position of sitting MPs, everyone is open to challenge, and in New South Wales this would have been the first time that new [more democratic] rules would come into play.

'He didn't get angry with me; he just reiterated his position that if New South Wales couldn't sort this out, it would be a matter for the federal executive.

'It was like the sword of Damocles hanging over our heads.'

Three days before the scheduled February meeting, Minchin texted Josh Frydenberg to say the federal executive would be meeting on Thursday. 'Trust PM will not be seeking federal intervention in New South Wales,' Minchin wrote.

Frydenberg did not respond.

Some members were in the room with Morrison for that meeting; others, like Minchin, Zoomed in.

Morrison's increasing frustration with the New South Wales division boiled over. His detractors, with a mixture of humour and dread, feared what would happen if Morrison got his way and then went on to win the election. The division would become a wholly owned subsidiary of Morrison, Inc. Or, as McGrath had put it, a branch of Hillsong.

According to sources, in between yelling and thumping the table, Morrison felt compelled to remind members of the executive who they were dealing with.

'I am the prime minister,' he told them. As if they could possibly forget.

'He was exerting his authority to seek to have an outcome he wanted, without question,' Minchin said later. 'People were very frustrated with the whole New South Wales situation.

'The executive was placed in a difficult situation.

'A Liberal prime minister was facing a difficult election, and demanding to resolve preselection problems we all knew was the result of machinations of people close to the prime minister.'

Even the president of the New South Wales division, Philip Ruddock, the former immigration minister who was the first to stop the boats, and who had been an attorney-general in the Howard government, was powerless to sort it.

Ruddock and Morrison were neither friends nor allies. When Tony Abbott appointed Morrison as shadow immigration minister in 2009, Morrison made it clear to Ruddock that he did not want any help from him. In fact, he told Ruddock to stay out of it, that he was not to speak at all on matters relating to the portfolio. Clearly,

Morrison did not believe he needed any help from Ruddock.

Morrison had a habit of doing things like that. As minister, he treated his junior portfolio minister, Michael Keenan, appallingly, which later led to Keenan describing him at a lunch with colleagues as an 'absolute arsehole'.

Minchin told me that the three preselections could have been resolved in November or December, or even in February, but the nominations committee still had not been able to meet.

'The federal executive was ambushed into having to make the call,' Minchin said.

He abstained from voting. He understood why the others went along with the proposition, but 'it was terrible'.

Most people had assumed it was all about saving Hawke. They accused Morrison of hiding behind Ley, whom they also accused of not working her branches. Few seriously believed that Zimmerman was at risk.

Zimmerman also believed that both he and Hawke would have prevailed, that it was actually all about Ley, and that the delay robbed him of valuable campaigning time. He couldn't spend any money until he became the endorsed candidate.

Morrison didn't give up trying to get David Elliott to switch from state politics to run for Parramatta, and only landed on Maria Kovacic as a last resort. It was completely shambolic.

He wore everyone down, and won the internal battles. Then he lost the war. The delays cost the party very dearly in the state that held the key to the government's fortunes. Whereas his supporters once used both hands to count probable or possible gains, Morrison did not pick up a single seat in his home state.

It left a bitter taste for those who tried to oppose him and failed, and who wondered what else they might have done to stop him and perhaps mitigate a disaster that was all of his own making.

CHAPTER EIGHT

Listen to the Voices of the Women

The Liberals reacted late to the threat posed by the Voices movement and its carefully selected issues of climate change, gender equity, and integrity. They underestimated it; then, when they did react, they chose to abuse or belittle its accomplished women candidates, and, by implication, their supporters.

Their challengers were doctors, surgeons, journalists, and small-business operators. They were daughters or nieces of Liberal royalty, yet they were mocked as puppets of millionaire Simon Holmes à Court, the son of billionaire Robert, who founded Climate 200, which raised $13 million to help fund their campaigns.

They were called fakes and stooges. John Howard dubbed them anti-Liberal groupies.

It was insulting, offensive, and typically off-key from a government already in deep trouble with women.

They were the kind of women who, once upon a time, the Liberal Party would have killed to recruit. It hurt all the more because, once upon a time, women like them were the lifeblood of the Liberal Party.

Margaret Guilfoyle was an accountant and party official before she became the first-ever woman in cabinet, appointed by Malcolm Fraser as finance minister. She set the path for Julie Bishop and Kelly O'Dwyer, both lawyers, to follow—both of whom left parliament after Morrison ascended. That was no coincidence. Bishop and O'Dwyer had made many sacrifices for the Liberal Party during their stellar careers, and they were no longer prepared to do it under Morrison.

Bishop has made a few forays into the political arena since she left. She was a prodigious fundraiser, and one of the most popular figures in the government. Given what followed, she could have threatened his leadership or been a focal point for discontent.

Howard was swung into the campaign to help. Bishop was not invited, except by individual MPs.

O'Dwyer has remained silent. Until now. She believes that if people don't tell the truth about what happened and why, nothing will change, the party will not be reformed, and lessons will not be learned. She actually loves the Liberal Party too much to allow that to happen.

O'Dwyer worked on the staff of former treasurer Peter Costello before entering parliament at a by-election for his seat of Higgins in 2009. Malcolm Turnbull promoted her to cabinet as the minister for small business and assistant treasurer when he became prime minister in 2015. After the 2016 election, she was made minister for revenue and financial services, and minister for women.

She worked closely with Morrison, first when he was treasurer, then when he became prime minister.

O'Dwyer had a bruising time as assistant treasurer, particularly during the 2016 election campaign, largely thanks to controversial superannuation changes enacted by the government. She willingly carried the can for those changes, which were particularly unpopular in her own electorate, quickly becoming aware her senior minister, the treasurer, Scott Morrison, was seldom seen making the case for them.

That seemed to her to be so typical of the party's attitude to women. Women were there at the table — actually waiting on the table — cleaning up messes, or expected to go out and attack other women.

In January 2017, with O'Dwyer now in the more senior economic portfolio of minister for revenue and financial services, Morrison rang to inform her that, the next day, fellow Victorian Michael Sukkar would be appointed assistant treasurer. She was stunned.

She asked Morrison if he was aware that Sukkar was a well-known branch-stacker in Victoria and that his mission, along with that of former powerbroker and Sukkar ally, the state party president, Michael Kroger, was to destroy her. She reminded him they were meant to be a team, that there would be no question she would defend him if he needed to be defended. She wanted to know if she could count on him to defend her.

She asked him how he would feel if she had sought promotion for one of his factional enemies from New South Wales hell-bent on killing him politically. 'Oh, well,' Morrison replied, 'what happens in Victoria is in Victoria. I expect in Canberra it will be professional.'

Morrison was taken aback by O'Dwyer's reaction. Not only was O'Dwyer angry, but she had expressed her anger in no uncertain terms. Next thing she knew, she got a phone call from David Gazard. She and Gazard had worked together in Costello's office, but he was/is one of Morrison's closest friends, and at that stage was a highly successful lobbyist.

She told Gazard they needed to understand what Sukkar's

elevation meant for her in Victoria. Gazard was as unsympathetic as Morrison. *You have to get on with Scott*, he told her. That was what Morrison wanted. She had to get with the program.

O'Dwyer realised she now also had to be careful that Morrison did not set out to dispense with her. She later asked Morrison for an undertaking that if Sukkar sought to import Victoria's factionalism to Canberra, she could count on Morrison to support her. It won't come to that, was his response.

O'Dwyer was convinced that Morrison was out to ingratiate himself with Kroger and Sukkar.

One thing about Morrison that those who worked with him were sure of was that whatever he did was with an eye on how he could benefit from it. 'It's always about Scott,' they would say.

Morrison was not easy to work with. Whatever job he was in, he wanted to control everything, to restrict the flow of information, and to micro-manage everyone in his orbit. So when the time came for O'Dwyer to go on maternity leave in April 2017, she arranged directly with prime minister Turnbull's office for her work to be undertaken by the finance minister, Mathias Cormann. She knew that her staff and Cormann's would work well together, and that she would be able to keep track of what was happening.

Once Morrison found out, his chief of staff, Phil Gaetjens—who had also worked with O'Dwyer in Costello's office—demanded she change the arrangement and hand everything over to his office. She refused. She was the first cabinet minister to have a baby while serving, and Turnbull wanted to make it work for her.

Her second child, Edward, was born on 21 April. Lo and behold, on 24 April, ABC's *7.30* program ran an item on the unrest over superannuation changes in her electorate of Higgins, featuring two wealthy factional opponents, Jack Hammond and John McMurrick, who just happened to be Kroger allies.

Coincidentally, the *Herald Sun* ran a front-page story saying that Tony Abbott's former chief of staff, Peta Credlin, was being courted to run against O'Dwyer for preselection in Higgins.

Kroger went on Sky to say he couldn't possibly comment, while Credlin allowed the story to run for days before ruling it out. It was tawdry, cruel, and entirely within character for O'Dwyer's enemies and their backers, and completely unsurprising that they embarked on the campaign to damage her while she was on maternity leave.

O'Dwyer was fully committed to her job, and rightly proud of her achievements as minister for women. They were hard-won. She had argued in the Expenditure Review Committee of cabinet, the so-called razor gang, for the budget to include a separate economic-security statement for women.

There was a collective groan from the men, including Morrison, when she raised it. They had to be convinced. Morrison, particularly, wanted proof that the proposal would be popular beyond women like her. That is, outside of her electorate of Higgins, because, of course, as the working mother of two children in a leafy suburb, how could she possibly know what women wanted? And, God forbid, it might turn off men. What would tradies make of it?

O'Dwyer knew there was only one way to convince Morrison. She commissioned polling from Crosby Textor. The research was incredibly positive. People were actually interested in and supportive of the economic security of women. Who knew?

Her package was whittled down to $110 million, and it was decided not to include it in the budget. It would be saved for release in the spring. She also fought tooth and nail for $500,000 to go towards the inquiry into sexual harassment in the workplace being conducted by the sex discrimination commissioner, Kate Jenkins. It was announced on 18 June.

Before spring arrived, Turnbull was toppled as prime minister.

O'Dwyer did not want to reward Peter Dutton for initiating the spill against Turnbull; so, despite her familiarity with his faults, she voted for Morrison.

After his ascension, Morrison rang O'Dwyer to tell her he was offering her the stand-alone ministry of jobs and industrial relations.

'You are not offering me minister for women?,' she asked.

'No,' he said.

'Scott, I really appreciate your offer of jobs and industrial relations, but if you are not also offering minister for women, I cannot accept.'

An angry Morrison told her he had not expected the conversation to go like that, and hung up.

O'Dwyer was now something of a marked woman. She was forceful, and she was determined not to put up with any nonsense from the men. The head of Treasury, John Fraser, would address her as 'Kelly' during meetings. She called him 'Secretary'. He referred to the male portfolio holders as 'Minister'. It infuriated her.

She called Fraser aside after one meeting, pointing out that she treated him with respect in front of colleagues by not calling him John, and that she would prefer it if he showed her the same respect. She told Morrison what she had done, telling him that that kind of behaviour was 'not on'.

She knew they thought she was difficult. Bad luck. After the debacle of the 2018 Victorian state election, when the Liberals were decimated, O'Dwyer warned the party room that the Liberals were seen as homophobic, anti-women climate-change deniers. 'It has to stop,' she said, regretting the demise of the-live-and-let-live philosophy of the Liberal Party she had joined as a teenager. She demanded Kroger's immediate resignation as state president.

So she was not about to let the women's portfolio slip away, and the package she had fought so hard for to be forgotten. She had determined after the coup that she was going to row her own boat. Morrison called her back after a few minutes to say that, yes, she could be minister for women as well.

On 19 November 2018, she released the economic-security package for women, which became a life raft for Morrison in the swirl of bullying accusations that followed the coup against Turnbull.

O'Dwyer gives Morrison credit for wanting to solve problems, but notes that he always had to be in control of the agenda. The problem was he was not always sure what the agenda should be.

O'Dwyer is desperate for her party to recommit to the agenda that she and others tried so hard to get accepted, and to declare zero tolerance for branch-stackers with no interest in policies. Those who stand by and watch bullies in the playground attacking other children are as bad as the bullies themselves, she reckons, and she is right.

'If you look at our performance in Victoria, we have no organised structure that can fight campaigns,' she told me. 'We have so denuded our party of talent, campaign experience, and volunteers.'

A women's WhatsApp group was set up to try to build a support structure, but MPs such as Nicole Flint and Amanda Stoker resisted it because they were sick of women casting themselves as victims. That was until Flint cast herself as a victim of a hateful campaign in her seat of Boothby in 2019, and announced her retirement from parliament.

If the Liberals want to know what went gone wrong in the Teal seats, and in O'Dwyer's old seat of Higgins, they should listen to O'Dwyer and talk to women such as Kristen Lock, a former nurse and public health researcher who lives in North Sydney.

Lock joined the Liberal Party when she was 15, and worked briefly for the former New South Wales Liberal senator Bill Heffernan, around 1996, when she was doing her Masters of Public Health at the University of Sydney. She had been on an exchange program in Germany, and had wanted to rejoin the Liberal Party. Her father had been mates with Heffernan from their younger days in Wagga.

Lock handed out how-to-vote cards for Joe Hockey in Hunters Hill in 2013. Their children were good friends, as were they. She had been hoping that Hockey and Malcolm Turnbull would bring the new 'forward-looking, innovative, and constructive Liberal generation to the fore'.

She was disappointed. She told Hockey's successor in North Sydney, Trent Zimmerman, that she was worried about the party's apparent slide to the right with the loss of its centrists and moderates.

'All the more reason to vote for me,' Zimmerman told her.

Lock says now: 'I saw the logic, but hadn't seen evidence that that approach was working.'

Then along came Cathy McGowan, who as an independent had won the seat of Indi from conservative Liberal Sophie Mirabella in 2013. The model used for that campaign was put together by McGowan with others, including a lot of input from Mary Crooks of the Victorian Women's Trust, devoted since 1985 to advocating for gender equality. The community-based formula was replicated to ensure that another independent, Helen Haines, replaced McGowan when she retired in 2019. That had never happened before.

McGowan decided to go national. After her book *Cathy Goes to Canberra* came out in November 2020, detailing how the campaign energised and enthused locals to defeat Mirabella, she received calls and emails from people wanting to know more.

So, in February 2021, she organised the Community Independent Project conference, on Zoom. Around 300 people dialled in, including Simon Holmes à Court. He was as inspired as Lock. He had met McGowan, but did not know her well. He read her book, and felt motivated. The fact that he had had a major falling-out with Josh Frydenberg was added incentive.

Lock says she grabbed the opportunity with both hands.

'I knew I could not look my kids in the eyes and say I had done everything I could to save our country's democratic integrity and the survival of our very planet as we know it,' Lock says.

'Throw in the gender shit that blew up last year [2021], and a whole lot of women and men started standing up. Critically, people who had never politically stood up in their lives before. Of course, the Morrison Boyz Club was an extra gift.

'Almost every time they opened their mouths, they were sending more and more volunteers to us.'

Eight of them formed a group they called the North Sydney Independents. They held weekly meetings to get a community indie movement going.

'As absurd as our chances seemed, we had to try as a form of therapy, if nothing else. Otherwise we all would have kept breaking our TV screens throwing convenient household items at the news every night in fury,' Lock says.

My first contact with Lock came in early spring 2021, a fitting time for a revolution to begin, after Kate Baillieu called me out of the blue to alert me to the growing Voices movement that was sprouting in interesting places.

Baillieu, a former journalist and longtime campaigner to save the Port Nepean National Park in the Flinders electorate, where others like her were desperate for change, urged me to ring McGowan.

After resigning from *The Australian*, one of my early columns for *The Age* and *The Sydney Morning Herald* was about the Voices movement. Thanks to Kate, it was great timing. A few days later, Kylea Tink was unveiled as the candidate for North Sydney to challenge Zimmerman. Incidentally, Tink's colour was a peachy pink, so, while inaccurate, Teal became the shorthand moniker for the independents because it had been used by Zali Steggall.

A few Liberals chided me for being naïve about the movement—as if they could possibly be threatened by a bunch of women, given the margins they held. Before the announcement, the North Sydney Independents had between 700 and 800 people signing in to read the weekly newsletters. That swelled to more than 1,000 active volunteers and around 2,000 supporters. Liberals struggled to find people to hand out at booths.

Tony Burke said that if there had been such a burgeoning of members in his electorate, he would have been accused of branch-stacking.

Even McGowan was staggered by the success of the independents. She offered up three reasons for it. The first was Morrison's unpopularity, which she believes would have declined as an issue if he had put up even a 'crappy' integrity commission and done a little more on climate change.

'You need a unifying motivation,' McGowan says. And that was dislike of Morrison. 'He was nasty,' she said. At least he came across that way, although not to her personally in the six months they had overlapped in parliament when he was prime minister.

The second reason was that Helen Haines and Zali Steggall had shown that independents could be effective with their work on integrity and climate.

'You don't have to have the balance of power to raise issues and get things done,' McGowan says. This is an important consideration for those hoping that the independents will now fade into the background, doomed by irrelevance or political naivety to be one-termers.

The third reason was the 'generosity of spirit' evident in all the campaigns, run mainly by volunteers.

The three circles within those three outer intersecting circles was the community, the campaign, and the candidates. They all had to work together.

She says that the candidates were exceptional leaders who, while they had no real experience in politics, had track records elsewhere in medicine or business.

McGowan says that Climate 200 added value; however, money wasn't 'the be all and end all'.

After that first Zoom call, she and Holmes à Court spoke a few times. He invited her to sit on his advisory council. She thought about it, then declined. She wanted to be completely separate and to be seen to be completely independent from his fund-raising operation.

'I was disappointed for a minute by the rejection, but she was right. She always is right,' Holmes à Court said in an interview for this book.

He based his operation on the May Day super PAC (political action committee) founded by American lawyer and activist Lawrence Lessig. Climate 200 funded polling and strategic communications to help the Teals. They consulted a pollster for Joe Biden to help develop a reliable seat-polling method with Redbridge.

They could also afford to pay for social media tools, including BVOD (broadcast video on demand), a form of advertising not as sophisticated as Facebook in reaching desired demographics, but more targeted than free to air or print, and cheaper.

All of which was valuable, indispensable even; however, McGowan believes the most important factor was the community organisation. The volunteers, many of whom had drifted away from the major parties, provided vital on-the-ground work, including doorknocking. As valuable as social media is as a tool these days, there is nothing like personal contact.

Doorknocking not only enables voters to meet or hear about the candidate, but it also provides vital feedback, unfiltered by pollsters, directly from people about their mood and the issues that matter to them.

Kooyong, where Dr Monique Ryan unseated Josh Frydenberg, had more than 2,000 volunteers, 3,000 donors, and 4,000 signs in people's yards. Volunteers knocked on 55,000 doors. Around 12,000 homes were doorknocked in North Sydney. Tink raised almost $1.4 million, which included a $550,000 donation from Climate 200.

It is also worth noting that Labor's Fiona Phillips withstood an almighty challenge from former New South Wales government transport minister Andrew Constance in Gilmore, partly because she had burrowed down into her electorate. Despite bushfires, floods, and Covid, she and her team knocked on 13,672 doors around the election campaign, and 25,346 overall in the three years after she snatched the seat from the Liberals.

How Labor managed to wrest the Victorian seat of Higgins from the Liberals, pitting one talented woman against another to fight off the Greens in what was once a blue-ribbon seat—the preserve of party leaders, potential leaders, and cabinet ministers—is also instructive.

Higgins was not targeted by the Teals. That may come, and

if the Liberals want to regain it, they will have to run the right candidate with the right campaign—someone separate from the herd, prepared to buck the establishment in the party. Which may or may not be Josh Frydenberg.

Higgins was held by a woman who did not use her voice as well as she might have, and who ended up paying a price. Katie Allen, a medical researcher and paediatrician, had succeeded O'Dwyer in the once ultra-blue-ribbon seat whose margin was whittled down to 3.7 per cent in 2019.

Allen was ambitious, appeared regularly on political panels on TV, and seemed destined for cabinet. She was a good performer. But, too often, she stuck too rigidly to the talking points issued from central command.

In one memorable interview on ABC 24, on 16 January 2021, when quackery about Covid was rife, Allen was given four opportunities by host Fauzia Ibrahim to distance herself from Craig Kelly, still comfortably ensconced in the Liberal Party at the time, thanks to serial interventions by Malcolm Turnbull and then Scott Morrison to rescue him from the preselectors of Hughes.

Despite Kelly using social media to argue that mask-wearing was akin to child abuse, and to advocate highly controversial 'cures' such as hydrochloroquine, Allen, a doctor, refused to offer even the mildest criticism of Kelly's views.

Six months later, Labor identified Higgins as vulnerable. Soon after that, in October, polling by Redbridge for Climate 200 also found it was vulnerable to an independent. For whatever reason, the Voices movement never took off there.

Many Melburnians felt that Morrison had played politics with the lockdowns during 2020. Resentment grew when he talked up the New South Wales Covid response as being the 'gold standard'. Combined with the slow vaccine rollout, and the hands-off approach on quarantine, people got angrier.

It was made worse for Allen after Joyce returned as deputy prime minister, and after the Nationals appeared to be holding the government hostage over a net-zero emissions target in the lead-up to Glasgow.

Even so, there was strong resistance in Labor to making Higgins a target seat. Labor had campaigned hard there in 2019, which was later regarded by many in Labor as a mistake. Going there again invited too many comparisons with the 2019 campaign, when Labor targeted Chisholm, Deakin, Casey, and Higgins, and missed out on all four.

The challenge for Labor in Higgins was two-fold—to beat the Greens and finish in the top two, and then to win the two-party-preferred count. In 2016, when Turnbull was leader, Labor came third in Higgins with a primary vote of only 15 per cent.

Labor's national secretary, Paul Erickson, believed the party had to find someone to run who was not a typical Labor candidate, who would make people in the electorate take notice and realise that the party was serious about winning them over.

Josh Burns, the first-term Labor MP in the neighbouring electorate of Macnamara, first began talking about Dr Michelle Ananda-Rajah as a potential candidate in late June 2021, after a Supreme Court order preventing the national executive from conducting Victorian preselections was lifted.

Ananda-Rajah was one of a group of doctors who had briefed shadow health minister Mark Butler and himself during the pandemic. Burns was impressed by her subsequent performance on the ABC's *Q&A*. He remembers thinking, *This is a serious person and someone of talent.*

He contacted her, then visited her home for a cup of tea. He planted the seed, then put her in touch with Richard Marles and

Erickson. Erickson first spoke to her in July 2021.

'We all felt Michelle was exactly the type of candidate Labor would need to appeal to voters in an electorate that had never elected a Labor MP before—an accomplished, professional woman who had achieved great success in medicine and was an articulate media performer,' Erickson said later.

After Ananda-Rajah was announced as the candidate, Erickson believes that the Liberals erred in attacking her for comments she'd made earlier that year about AstraZeneca. It misread the mood in Victoria, and it raised her profile, setting her up as Allen's key opponent, and any arguments over vaccines only reminded people of Morrison's failures.

In late July, Labor's polling showed that, across the country—in cities, suburbs, and regions, among all age groups, and with both men and women—Barnaby Joyce stunk. His approval ratings ranged from a net negative of minus 29 in New South Wales to minus 50 in Western Australia. With men, it was minus 37; with women, minus 39. In inner-metropolitan areas, it was minus 46; in outer metros, minus 36; in regional areas, minus 35; and rural areas, minus 30.

In the third week of October, Labor's polling in Higgins, before the government committed to a net-zero emissions target by 2050, showed that the seat was within reach. Allen's vote had dropped 6 per cent to 41 per cent, Labor's had gone up 1 per cent to 26 per cent, the Greens were down 4 per cent to 19 per cent, Clive Palmer's UAP was at 5 per cent, and independents were around 4 per cent. After the notional distribution of preferences, it was 50–50.

More people were dissatisfied with the Morrison government's handling of the pandemic (56 per cent) than satisfied (30 per cent). And the Joyce factor was huge, with 63 per cent of voters in

Higgins holding an unfavourable opinion of him. His net rating among women was minus 53 per cent.

Another interesting finding was that Palmer, thanks to lockdowns and mandates, was strongest in Victoria, increasing the dilemma for Morrison about which way to jump —whether to get on board the freedom bandwagon or not, whether to cosy up to the Palmerites to try to secure their preferences or keep his distance. That level of Palmer's support would be reflected at the election, too.

On 29 October, David Crowe reported in *The Sydney Morning Herald* and *The Age* that Liberal MPs, including Katie Allen, Jason Falinski, Dave Sharma, and Trent Zimmerman, were so concerned federal cabinet would cave in to demands from the Nationals on climate change that they had formed a secret group to push Morrison on the issue, even threatening to cross the floor in parliament.

'Worried the Nationals would block a crucial pledge to cut greenhouse gas emissions to net zero by 2050, the Liberals mobilised in a meeting with Mr Morrison on 28 September to make it clear they could not accept a climate plan without the target,' Crowe reported.

One MP said later that they were also worried that the energy minister, Angus Taylor, was not supportive. Concerned that he would leak the details if he knew them, they did not invite him to participate.

By operating 'secretly', unlike a few Nationals who revelled in open sabotage, it all sounded too little, too late from the Liberal moderates. Labor and the Voices juggernaut had mobilised, and they were using Barnaby Joyce as a recruitment tool. The loudest voices that inner-urban voters heard speaking for the Coalition were Matt Canavan, George Christensen, and Craig Kelly, with barely a peep of rebuke from Liberals.

The moderates should have been screaming from the rooftops long before, forcing Morrison to act sooner, rather than keep looking like he was waiting for Joyce to tell him what he could and couldn't do.

As Morrison grew more and more unpopular, the combination of him and Joyce was deadly in those seats.

One threatened Liberal, still hoping he could hang on, who was confident all the way through that Allen would hold in Higgins, predicted even during the campaign that: 'People will win in these seats in spite of the prime minister, not because of him.'

Despite more favourable polling for Labor, there was still some reluctance to throw resources into another campaign in Higgins. Josh Burns took the lead to work with Ananda-Rajah to build an effective campaign team, with input over summer from national headquarters.

After Albanese and Chris Bowen announced Labor's climate policy in early December, Erickson began to believe that Labor could pick up the seat, and sought to convince others.

In early February 2022, at a fundraising dinner at the National Press Club, Albanese had to step outside to take a phone call. When the MC asked Erickson to fill in for a bit, someone asked him which seats he would recommend people place a bet on. He looked up Higgins on Sportsbet, and saw that it was paying around $3.80 for a Labor win.

'I haven't bet on an election in more than 10 years, but I gave the room a big tip, which was to put their money on Michelle Ananda-Rajah,' he recalled.

In the final week of February, a union poll in Higgins, as part of a sweep of potential target seats across the country, put Labor on a two-party-preferred figure of 54 per cent. That made it hard for people to argue that the seat wasn't winnable. Another poll by

Labor in March showed the Liberal primary vote down by 9 per cent to 39 per cent, and the Labor primary vote up by 8 per cent to 33 per cent. Those figures translated into Labor receiving 51 per cent of the vote on a two-party-preferred basis.

Key reasons given for the big swing to Labor were dislike of Morrison, dissatisfaction with his performance as prime minister, the federal Coalition mismanagement of Covid, and Morrison's failure to take climate change seriously.

After that March poll, Erickson and the Victorian ALP state secretary, Chris Ford, decided to 'throw the kitchen sink at winning Higgins'. It was added to the national target-seats list. Dee Madigan, the owner and CEO of Campaign Edge, which was running Labor's advertising campaign, went there to make some digital advertisements with Ananda-Rajah, and the Victorian ALP committed extra resources and organisers to the seat.

'It's impossible for me to know what the other side was thinking about the threat, but we noticed during the campaign that there didn't appear to be any Liberal Party digital advertising active in Higgins,' Erickson said after the campaign was over.

'I couldn't believe this at first, and kept asking our team to double-check that they weren't missing something. As far as we can tell, the Liberal Party didn't start advertising on Google and YouTube until Sunday 8 May, two weeks before polling day.'

Katie Allen suffered an almost a 6 per cent swing against her on primaries, while Labor's Michelle Ananda-Rajah picked up 2.4 per cent. After preferences, she won the seat by 52 to 48 per cent. Labor's polling had been accurate.

Depending on what happens, Higgins will be another must-watch seat in 2025.

McGowan does not see her job as finished. Not by a long shot. She was disappointed that independent Rob Priestley did not win the seat of Nicholls and that the independent candidate fell short in Bradfield. But the Voices movement is already planning for 2025.

McGowan organised another Zoom meeting in August 2022 called 'Next Steps'. There were 450 people who registered, from 103 electorates around the country. The enthusiasm was unabated. All six new independents took part, and Holmes à Court also dialled in.

The discussions revolved around making sure that those who had been elected to parliament stayed there, plus how to win the seats where they came second or made inroads.

It was too early to nominate which seats the Voices would target next, but likely options include Wannon, Aston, Nicholls, Monash, and Casey in Victoria, Groom in Queensland, and Bradfield, Cowper, Page, and Calare in New South Wales.

CHAPTER NINE

A Better Future with Climate Change

Two important events for Anthony Albanese and for Labor occurred in early December 2021. The first was on 3 December, when he released the party's climate change policy, and the second was soon after on 5 December, when he unveiled his slogan for the election, 'A Better Future', at a jaunty rally in Ashfield.

Both had taken a long time to maturate.

Mark Butler had held the climate change portfolio for seven years. Butler and perennial rabble-rouser Joel Fitzgibbon had been at loggerheads over the policy and the future of coal for months. In 2020, Fitzgibbon warned that the issue could split the party. By then, the climate wars had taken their toll on Butler. He decided it was time to get out of that portfolio.

A reshuffle was being mooted towards the end of that year. Butler told the health spokesman, Chris Bowen, that he was 'lucky' to have health. They discussed swapping. Penny Wong had also been thinking the same thing, so the three of them put the idea to Albanese. There was an amicable agreement. Bowen took over climate, and Butler health, on 28 January 2021.

It was critical to the landing of a policy that would later establish an important point of difference with Morrison. Despite resistance from key shadow ministers who wanted Labor to mirror Morrison, Bowen succeeded in landing a more ambitious target.

Bowen set about trying to heal the rift between the left and the right inside his party, while holding at bay the much greater threat from the left outside it, using his experience in economic portfolios to swing the focus of emissions reductions to job creation and economic reform.

There had definitely been a change in the electoral mood as a result of Covid lingering. The sense of togetherness was wearing thin. There was a growing impatience with Morrison over the slowness of the vaccine rollout, and his attempt to quell the unease on 11 March, when he said 'It's not a race', failed spectacularly to capture the public mood. Bipartisanship was drawing to a close. Labor's goal was to wreck the advantage of incumbency for Morrison.

On 8 April, Morrison and medical experts recommended that people under 50 take Pfizer rather than Astrazeneca. Butler zeroed in on Morrison's perceived failures. 'Scott Morrison had two jobs this year: a speedy, effective rollout of the vaccine, and a safe national quarantine system to secure our borders in the meantime, and he's failing Australians on both counts,' Butler said on 23 April. It struck home.

Bowen's task of finalising Labor's climate policy was made easier by Morrison's success in getting the Coalition to agree on 26 October 2021 to a net-zero emissions target by 2050.

Although it was the barest acceptable minimum target, it still hadn't been easy to get the Nationals on board. They were seriously split between net zero and never zero, as Bridget McKenzie put it. Ministers had to decide if they were prepared to walk if the decision went against them.

People close to Morrison grumbled later that Frydenberg 'hadn't lifted a finger' to help secure the change. That was unfair. Frydenberg had pushed it along in a speech in September—which he did not clear in advance with Morrison—in which he warned of an investment freeze if Australia didn't move to net zero.

Former Nationals' leader Michael McCormack disputed the mean-spirited claims from Morrison's inner circle, saying that Frydenberg had played a critical role in getting to net zero. 'We would have been in a far worse position without Josh Frydenberg working behind the scenes to make it a reality,' he said.

He said that Frydenberg's interventions had been critical in securing the support of National MPs who were wavering, such as Michelle Landry and Ken O'Dowd, who eventually supported net zero, helping to deliver narrow majority support in the Nationals' party room.

Frydenberg's speech had earned him a touch-up at the time from the Nationals' deputy leader, Bridget McKenzie, who said it was easy for him to advocate for net zero because his 'affluent constituents' would not be impacted. Which is kind of funny, in retrospect.

Anyway, McKenzie wasn't speaking as a climate denier, and she says that Frydenberg's speech was important because of its warnings on international capital. She was pointing out sharply where she thought the burden would fall, and how tough it was to resolve internally. She was upfront about the divisions in the National Party over the issue, and also about Morrison's failure, initially, to take account of that.

'Morrison had packed the kilt, he was off to Glasgow, come hell or high water with a net-zero 2050 proposition, but he had forgotten a fundamental part of the working partnership in our government—that there were two parties of government in the

Coalition, and he hadn't checked with the Nationals,' she told me.

'We had no friends—our usual allies were with the PM. All News Ltd tabloid papers came out to back the PM. And then we had front pages led by the Minerals Council, the NFF [National Farmers' Federation], and the BCA [Business Council of Australia]. By the end of that week, there were stories about the Pope backing net zero in Glasgow. We had everybody, every single major partner who had been with us as a political movement, going in the opposite direction to the Nationals.

'And internally we were divided. We had net-zero-now MPs, we had net-zero-never MPs, and a majority of us in between.

'The question for me was how were we—as a party that had opposed flawed policies to address climate change over several elections—to authentically address the reality we were facing?

'But we did.

'We forced Morrison to rewrite the Nationally Determined Contributions to include a five-yearly Productivity Commission review into the socio-economic impact of the climate policy on rural and regional Australia. We made sure there was a lot of investment in the regions into the future to make sure these regions could seize the opportunities of a net-zero economy over the next two decades, but just as importantly to safeguard them against the coming challenges.

'What had previously been denied was accepted—that there will be a price, and it will not be paid by those in affluent suburbs.

'Practically all the significant challenges that lie ahead in this massive economic transformation will occur in regional Australia—a concept that is woefully misunderstood by the Teals and the Greens. This is an issue of social justice.

'Our MPs represent the poorest, the most marginalised, and the most disenfranchised communities in the country.

'I believe the Nationals' position on net zero was vindicated at the election.

'We backed our communities' economic well-being — with significant caveats on the Liberal Party's ambition.'

With the Nationals having only narrowly voted for net zero, and despite having squeezed a good deal out of Morrison in the process, Barnaby Joyce voted against it. His closest allies, such as Matt Canavan, would not accept it, and undermined it publicly.

The decision was late coming, and it was far from enough to satisfy an increasingly disillusioned small-l Liberal constituency. All of which shows how difficult it will be for Dutton to present a more ambitious climate policy at the next election.

Karen Andrews was in the too-little, too-late camp. She believes the party needs to 'look at our collective behaviours' and wear the consequences of the perception that Morrison waited too long and didn't do enough.

She says that one of the Liberal Party's core values, as spelled out in its constitution, is its duty to preserve the environment for future generations.

Still, the Coalition's target provided some cover for Labor, as did the New South Wales environment minister and treasurer Matt Kean's announcement at the end of September that his government — with the full backing of the Nationals' leader and deputy premier, John Barilaro — would halve emissions by 2030.

The greater cover for Labor and the spur to resolution with a more ambitious target came from the Business Council of Australia, which in 2018 had attacked Labor's proposal of a 45 per cent emissions-reduction target for 2030 as 'economy wrecking'.

In early October 2021, the BCA opted for a much more ambitious cut of between 46 per cent and 50 per cent on 2005 levels by 2030. Singing a vastly different tune, the BCA said the higher target was needed to catch up on climate change and to drive investment.

With only a few weeks to go until the COP26 climate talks were due to begin in Glasgow, there were conflicting positions inside Labor over where to land.

Albanese's frontbench was split. Those arguing for a risk-averse position included Richard Marles, Tony Burke, and Don Farrell. They wanted to keep the focus on Morrison; they did not want to open up a point of difference. They argued that Labor would do better politically to adopt net zero by 2050, to promise that once in government they could look at going further. Before the BCA came out with its revised stance, it looked like their views might prevail. 'They were still carrying the scars of 2019,' one frontbencher said later.

Albanese's Sunday-night dinner group, which included members of the leadership team plus key portfolio holders, met several times during the week. Chris Bowen, Jim Chalmers (the shadow treasurer), Penny Wong (the Senate leader), Katy Gallagher (the finance spokeswoman), and Kristina Keneally (the home affairs shadow minister) argued forcefully for a higher target. Butler, because he had held the portfolio previously, was described as 'dark green', but kept his interventions to a minimum.

Marles, Burke, and Farrell argued that Labor was well placed, so they should avoid rocking the boat. They argued that they should concentrate on keeping the blowtorch on Morrison and his failings, rather than on providing him with a weapon to use against them.

Burke was concerned that Labor would be attacked over its planned use of what was known as the safeguard mechanism, which set carbon dioxide limits on Australia's 215 biggest emitters. He feared that Labor would be accused of introducing a carbon tax by stealth, even though the Abbott government had established the mechanism. Burke also feared that business would wilt. It didn't, and he was happy to be proved wrong.

The background noise around this time was that Albanese was too timid, that people didn't know what he stood for, and that he wasn't giving people a good-enough reason to vote for Labor.

Albanese, who did favour a more ambitious approach, allowed his frontbenchers to duke it out. The stronger arguments that held sway were that Labor had to go further, and that this was the issue where there had to be differentiation after two years of the party cosying up to the Coalition. The only question was how far to go.

Bowen decided it was best to work out the route to arrive at the destination, to devise the policies, model them, and then arrive at the emissions-reduction figure that the policies would achieve—which, in the end, was 43 per cent by 2030. RepuTex did the modelling, which never came under serious challenge until after the election.

Colleagues later praised Bowen for his perseverance and for his carriage of the arguments with his economic hat on, but also spoke highly of the way that Albanese allowed the debate to be conducted.

'He was good because he took responsibility for the final decision, and he didn't try to railroad it. People were respectful, but robust. There were times when I thought we were going to lose,' one shadow minister who had advocated the higher target said later.

It wasn't just that they needed a climate policy, another frontbencher said. They had to show they had a core and a spine.

Bowen, who later played down the differences as part of the normal 'argy-bargy' of discussion, conceded that the more ambitious targets set by the New South Wales government and the BCA were helpful.

'We recognised we could argue it brought us into line with every state and territory government in the country, three of them being Liberal governments,' he told me.

'It was one of the more significant decisions we made that established a difference between us and the government after two years of being constructive and bipartisan.'

Climate policy was important to voters, and its electoral fallout was hard to assess, even after the election. While a weaker position than Labor adopted might have garnered seats in regional Queensland such as Flynn or Capricornia, an even braver stance might have got them across the line in Brisbane and Ryan, and helped them hold on to Griffith, which were won by the Greens.

A few days later, when Albanese released his slogan, it was a study of contrasts. 'A Better Future' resonated with voters. It had taken months to land. There were any number of formulations, all road-tested.

The slogan was a collaborative effort between Albanese, Tim Gartrell, his chief of staff and the master campaigner from Kevin 07, and Paul Erickson. A few variations had been tossed around, including 'Time for a Change' and 'A New Approach', but they all liked 'A Better Future' best.

It was meant to invoke an optimistic vibe, and to put both Morrison and the pandemic in the past. They sensed that people wanted a sense of stability and certainty, and that they were also looking for hope and something positive to hold on to.

'We had to give people a sense of what would be better under us,' Erickson said later.

The other thing that looked better and sounded better in early December was Albanese himself. Much better. He had lost a lot of weight. He was wearing a new suit and new glasses. He played down the stylistic differences, telling people he had lost weight after a serious road accident at the beginning of the year had led him to take better care of himself. As for the glasses, he reckoned they'd broken when he'd trodden on them, so he'd had to zip around to his local optometrist for a new pair. No big deal. A five-minute exercise.

His speech was sharper, and so was his delivery. The TV packages that night, all playing up 'the new Albo', were favourable for him. Not so much for Morrison. Labor beating Morrison on the pictures was a rare thing.

That same day, Morrison had gone to Mt Panorama. Not only did he get booed, which a few people found surprising, because they were seen to be his people, but he had to pour himself into the Ford Mustang supercar driven by five-time Bathurst 1000 champion Mark Skaife for a lap around the circuit.

Although he looked uncomfortable, he had a snappy line ready.

'It's absolutely magnificent,' he said. 'The fact that there'll be people beaming in from all over the world and what they're going to see is Australia is open — we're double-vaxxed, people are back, they're in their trailers, they're together again.

'It's just showing where we're heading — looking out the front windscreen, not in the rearview mirror.' He couldn't resist his signature seal of approval. 'How good is Bathurst?' That went down about as well as a flat tyre on the final lap.

Even his colleagues were tiring of the stunts. Dutton was despairing. 'There's a reason they call him Scotty from marketing,' he told people.

Morrison appeared to value pictures and slogans above all else, even though they eroded his authority and left him open to ridicule.

When the Omicron variant hit in late 2021, it robbed Australians of what they hoped would be their first drama-free Christmas in three years. Families were separated, supply lines were disrupted, and Morrison's action-man plan was to get Alex Hawke to deport tennis star Novak Djokovic because he was unvaccinated. It not only smelled of a diversion, but it was yet another U-turn.

Morrison had gone from anti-closures to pro-closures and back again, from anti-lockdowns to pro-lockdowns and back again, from pro-mandates to anti-mandates for vaccination, from government interventions to whistling up the freedom fighters.

The election year began as badly as the others that had preceded it.

On 13 February, Morrison and his family participated in a *60 Minutes* special with Karl Stefanovic. Albanese's turn came on 13 March. That was a study in contrasts, too. The Albanese profile focussed on the new, svelte Albo.

Two nights later, Morrison appeared with Paul Murray on Sky. Morrison poked fun at Albanese, and tried to make a virtue of his own unpopularity.

'I'm not pretending to be anyone else,' Morrison said. 'We're still wearing the same glasses. Sadly, the same suits, and I … and I weigh about the same, and I don't mind a bit of Italian cake either.

'So I'm happy in my own skin, and I'm not pretending to be anyone else. And when you, when you're prime minister, you can't pretend to be anyone else. You've got to know who you are, because if you don't know who you are, then how on earth are other people going to know? And I think that's what the choice is at this election.

'You know, not everybody agrees with everything, every call I've made over the last three and a half years. That's the lot of any prime minister. But I think Australians know that I've been the one who's stood up for Australia in some of the most significant challenges we've faced.'

Two months later, Morrison promised he could change, too. By then it was too late.

On Thursday 31 March, Tony Smith gave his valedictory speech. Smith had been Speaker since 2015. He had been re-elected Speaker unanimously three times by the House of Representatives, and if he had remained as the member for Casey, Labor in government was prepared to make him the first truly independent Speaker of the Australian parliament.

Morrison was not there to hear it. That was unfortunate. Let's say it was because it was the same day that Ukrainian President Zelenskiy was scheduled to address the parliament by video, and Morrison was working on his speech — not because Smith had sat him down in parliament.

Worried about the low opinion that voters had of politicians, Smith offered them some advice, including the fact that it was possible to have robust debate while remaining civil.

'In recent decades, the relative decline in the combined primary vote share of the major parties in House elections, from a little over 95 per cent in 1975 to a little under 75 per cent at the last election, is often cited as one key indicator of dissatisfaction with the way politics is conducted,' Smith said.

'The major parties need to consider how to address this, because they have been vital in giving stability and certainty in the formation and the conduct of government in our parliamentary democracy.

'I don't say this out of any disrespect at all to the crossbench, who need to be congratulated for overcoming enormous obstacles to get elected.

'I simply make the point that I don't believe, if there were 151 independents in this House, we would have stable, predictable, or workable government. These are just some ideas for reflection.'

Sitting beside him while he made that speech was his friend and fellow Carlton tragic, Josh Frydenberg.

CHAPTER TEN

Rebels with Causes

A few weeks after the election, having won her seat with an increased majority, then being ignored for promotion to the frontbench, Bridget Archer was wondering whether she had any future at all in Liberal Party.

Archer, the resolute rebel with an embarrassment of causes during the Morrison era, was waiting, hoping she would see that her party had learned the lessons of the election. She wanted to assess how effectively the new parliament was working, how the women independents were faring, and whether she felt she could achieve more by sitting somewhere else.

Initially, the signs were not good. A few colleagues seemed to be in denial about the reasons for the loss. She knew that Morrison had been a huge factor. She wishes she had a dollar for every voter who had told her they would love to vote for her but couldn't bring themselves to do it because it risked another three years of him as prime minister.

Also, a number of colleagues resented her for having spoken out on the issues she was prepared to fight for regardless. Such as the cashless welfare card, when she abstained from voting, withholding her support from the government; and the integrity commission, when she seconded the bill from independent Helen Haines because she wanted the parliament to debate it; then over the religious discrimination bill, when she crossed the floor because it failed to provide the promised protections for vulnerable kids.

After the election, there was a brief flurry of speculation about her running for the deputy leadership, but it soon became clear that some colleagues would not cop her because she refused to toe the line. They saw her as trouble with a capital T. It had never hurt Barnaby Joyce that he had made a career out of crossing the floor, but uppity women were another matter. In fact, she would have made a great contrast to Peter Dutton as his deputy. It would have signalled to all those who had deserted the Liberals that there was a place for people like her and like them in the party.

Then it seemed she might get a position in Dutton's shadow ministry. That didn't happen, either. If Dutton had wanted to send a signal to the thousands of women, former Liberals, who had voted for the Teal independents that he 'got it', that he understood why, that he was listening to them and was determined to get them back, he would have selected Archer. She was standing up for all the things they cared about, well before the Teals became such a force.

But other Liberal MPs were threatening to mutiny if he appointed her ahead of them, so angry were they with her for rebelling while they behaved themselves, so he didn't dare. Instead, Dutton chose another Tasmanian, Senator Claire Chandler, who in February 2022 had distinguished herself by putting forward the Save Women's Sports bill, supposedly to clarify that clubs could not be sued for discriminating against transgender women, but also as a siren call to conservatives to sign up for a culture war.

It seemed to have become a thing among conservative Liberals to want to discriminate against transgender women or gay kids.

Archer was forced to navigate that issue every time Morrison visited her electorate — which was way too often for her liking — and even when he wasn't.

Fearful that she would speak out against Chandler's bill, the Tasmanian division delayed the scheduled announcement by Archer in the first week of the election campaign of government money for a hockey field, after Morrison had lavishly endorsed both Chandler and Katherine Deves in Warringah.

So, after the election, Archer remained on the backbench while Dutton promoted Chandler.

But there were other things that had improved. Archer watched as many of the first speeches of the Teal candidates that she could. She wanted to know what they were like and what drove them.

She listened to Kate Chaney, who had won the blue-ribbon Liberal seat of Curtin in the west. She was a granddaughter of Fred senior, a former federal Liberal MP; a niece of former Fraser government minister Fred; and a daughter of the prominent businessman Michael. Archer thought she was excellent. Not long after, she got a call to go around to see Dutton. He had also been in the chamber for Chaney's speech.

'I saw you looking wistfully at the crossbenches,' Dutton said to her. Archer thought for a second, and agreed. Yes she was, she said, but the reason she was wistful was because she wished that Chaney and some of the other independents were sitting over where she was.

She and Dutton have since talked often. She has found it reassuring that she can talk openly with him about what she thinks and what she is planning, without fearing that someone will try to bully her out of it. She sat with the independents to vote for Labor's climate change legislation, and will vote with them again if she feels her party is not standing up for things that she believes are right.

The traditional, highly prized Liberal prerogatives of speaking out or crossing the floor were actively and aggressively discouraged by Morrison and his staff.

In October 2020, Archer, who held the seat of Bass on a margin of 0.4 per cent—the tightest in the country—informed the prime minister's office that she held grave concerns over the cashless debit card, and was considering voting against the government's proposed extension of its use.

She says that soon after, two of the most senior members of Morrison's staff, Yaron Finkelstein and Bronwyn Morris, were literally standing over her in her office.

Archer says that she felt bullied, threatened, and intimidated for weeks by the staffers, both of whom had been around politics a long time, seeking to persuade her to vote with the government. They told her that she had to be more collegiate, that she had to think of her other colleagues who might be affected, and that she and her constituents were not affected by the legislation. In short, she was being selfish.

Finkelstein denied that they bullied Archer, but said they did try to talk her out of crossing the floor. He said the reason they 'stood over' her was because there were no chairs for them to sit on.

Morris also denied bullying Archer. She said they were not asked to sit down. She said they had *asked* Archer to consider her colleagues, at least two of whom had cashless debit card trial sites in their electorates, which they considered were working well.

'We did not *tell* her what she had to do,' Morris said. 'We were trying to ascertain Bridget's concerns, because she had not articulated them to us. I had previously arranged a briefing for Bridget with the relevant minister.'

In early December, Archer spoke against the legislation, then abstained from voting for it. Her decision triggered a campaign of online abuse, threatening her and her kids. Archer has five children, who were aged six, eight, 10, 12, and 18 at the time. She jokes that there are times when her home looks as if it has been burgled, but there was nothing remotely funny about what happened to her. It was a terrible time for her and her family.

She recalled that the pressure exerted on her was so intense, including from the prime minister's office, that at one point she had to ring her doctor from a booth outside the chamber to ask for a prescription to help her cope.

Almost exactly a year later, she detected a mood-shift in her electorate. Constituents were stopping her on the street to say they liked her, but … . The big 'but' was Morrison. That sentiment would reverberate at polling booths around the country.

On Thursday 25 November 2021, Archer crossed the floor to second Haines' motion for a national commission against corruption. At the time, Archer told me that the right to stand up for a principle, even if it meant going against the government and the prime minister, was the defining feature of the party. It was what had made people like her become a Liberal.

To avoid a repeat of her experience the previous year, the only people she told in advance of her intention were her staff and Haines. She did not even tell the treasurer, Josh Frydenberg, two nights before, when she and other MPs ate takeaway pizza and pasta in his office.

After the vote, there were pictures published of Frydenberg standing over her in the chamber, looking as if he was threatening her. He wasn't. She regarded him as a friend. He invited her to go around to his office so they could discuss what happened.

But when she got there, Frydenberg told her they had to go to the prime minister's office, because Morrison wanted to talk to her. Archer was furious. She felt that Frydenberg had ambushed her.

Soon after, at Christmas drinks at The Lodge, she says she 'growled' at him for tricking her into going round to Morrison's office.

'We are adults, and we are friends,' she said to him. 'You didn't have to do that. You should have said the prime minister wants to talk to you, not [tell me to] come to my office and have a quiet conversation.

'You know, you should be the next prime minister of the country, and that's not the way leaders should conduct themselves.' She says he accepted what she said.

When Frydenberg walked her into Morrison's office like an errant schoolgirl, Archer cried. It was an emotional release, not a sign of weakness. Archer had no problem with Morrison expressing his displeasure. He said his piece. After composing herself, she said hers. She owned her actions. She did not apologise for supporting Haines, and she did not take a single backward step.

He asked her why she had not said something beforehand. She told him she had decided that after the way she had been treated over the cashless debit card, she would not go through that again. She told him his staff had sought to bully her. He didn't seem to understand, so she warned him: 'Keep them away from me. Just keep them away from me.' She didn't hear from them again.

She told Morrison she was neither a 'drone' nor a 'warm body'—words that he later appropriated to describe rebellious backbenchers and to convey to the media a tolerance of them that he never felt. They were words that Archer had heard Christian Porter use in the House. She heard him say to Garth Hamilton, the new member for Groom, that he had 'never been so happy to have a warm body on the floor of the chamber'. Archer took that to mean that Porter welcomed a compliant backbencher who did as he was told.

Later that day, Morrison doubled down in parliament, making

it clear that he was dead opposed to a federal anti-corruption commission similar to the one in New South Wales, which had forced Gladys Berejiklian's departure from politics.

Morrison said that the state's Independent Commission Against Corruption 'should be looking at criminal conduct, not who your boyfriend is'.

'The premier of New South Wales was done over by a bad process, an abuse … I'm not going to have a kangaroo court taken into this parliament.'

Archer believed that her government had got its priorities all wrong. Although she empathised with Berejiklian, she thought the ICAC had done its job, and that the setting-up of such a body, rather than the passage of a religious discrimination bill, was essential to help restore peoples' faith in politicians.

One was dealing with a problem that had to be fixed; the other looked like a fix for a problem that didn't exist. Even the deeply religious New South Wales premier, Dominic Perrottet, could see this when he asked 'Why now?' about the religious discrimination bill, which had been on the backburner for years, only to be revived as the federal election approached.

On this issue, Archer had company inside the Liberal Party. Prominent New South Wales moderate Senator Andrew Bragg threatened to cross the floor against Morrison's bill because it would allow discrimination against trans kids. This helped scuttle the bill, ensuring it never made it into the Senate.

Bragg's threat was known at the time, and on its own was enough to kill the bill; however, not so well known is that three other Coalition senators were prepared to cross the floor with him. They were Perin Davey, who was voted in as deputy National Party leader after the election; and Andrew McLachlan, a Liberal from South Australia.

Davey had been prepared to support the bill even in its original form because she believed it was necessary. She was satisfied with the assurances that had been given by the leadership that there would be changes later to include protections for transgender children. However, once the bill was amended in the House to strengthen protections, she felt even more obliged to vote for it, despite Morrison wanting it passed unaltered.

Davey, who lives in Deniliquin, had received representations from people in the regions anxious to ensure that transgender children were protected. Davey points out that these kids do not just exist in the cities and suburbs; they are in remote places, too, in towns where there might be only one high school, where they have no choice but to transition before their schoolfriends, their neighbours, and their community. They did not have the option of appearing somewhere else as someone else.

Davey felt she owed it to the people who had approached her to vote for the amended bill. That is what she told the Nationals' leader in the Senate, Bridget McKenzie. Davey says that McKenzie respected her decision, and passed it on to others in the leadership group. Morrison would have known that the Senate vote would have been as humiliating as the one in the House of Representatives.

And yet Morrison had stubbornly wanted to keep going, to put the bill up in the Senate in order to overturn the changes made in the House. He was forced to confront reality—that he would have faced further embarrassment—and eventually withdrew the bill. It was a rare thing.

Andrew Bragg, Dave Sharma, and Fiona Martin had given Morrison fair warning in the party room on 23 November the previous year when the bill was presented, even though it had not been provided to the backbench committee, as was usual practice.

They made it clear that they wanted the problem of discrimination against students and teachers fixed in the bill. Others also said they wanted the bill to go through a proper review process.

Sharma, who had promised the change to his electors, said he 'could not stomach' anything that allowed discrimination to continue. Asked by Morrison at the time whether he would support the bill if he made the changes, Sharma told him: 'Yes, I will.'

Morrison introduced the bill, which was then sent to the Joint Human Rights Committee for a review.

On 1 December, with the approval of the prime minister's office, Sharma, Fiona Martin, Angie Bell, and Katie Allen put out a press release welcoming 'proposed amendments to the *Sex Discrimination Act 1984* that will remove the right of religious schools to discriminate against students on the basis of sexual orientation or gender identity. These amendments were negotiated as part of discussions related to the Religious Discrimination Bill, currently before the Parliament.'

On the same day, Morrison wrote to Albanese, thanking him for the opposition's constructive approach and undertaking to include the amendment.

Everyone thought they had a deal. Morrison had given verbal and written undertakings to include the protections. Except, it transpired—or so some of his conservative colleagues said later—he didn't fully understand what he had committed to do.

Conservatives who spoke to Michaelia Cash back then say she was horrified by what Morrison had agreed to. He had done the deal with a small group that had not included his attorney-general.

During the Wentworth by-election in October 2018, Morrison had promised to act to prevent the expulsion of gay kids; now, according to conservative MPs, he was promising to end the right of religious schools to 'discriminate', which opened up all sorts of other areas that most of them tried to manage sensitively without government diktat.

Once the implications of what he had done were explained to Morrison, he is said to have responded by saying: 'I didn't mean that, that's not what I had in mind.' One MP paraphrased his excuse thus: 'He stuffed up, but couldn't bring himself to say it.'

Everyone felt dudded. The moderates were furious; the conservatives were incredulous.

On 7 February, the Coalition's legal affairs backbench committee met to consider new amendments that Cash wanted to add to the bill that would have addressed discrimination against gay students, but not trans students and not teachers. Allen told Cash she would not support it, and therefore the bill and the amendments did not have the full support of the backbench committee.

The next day, 8 February, there were two party meetings on the bill, at which several MPs — including Zimmerman, Archer, Bragg, and Warren Entsch — complained that their concerns had not been addressed. No concessions were offered. Morrison declared that he believed he had the support of the room, and would proceed.

Bragg alerted Morrison to the fact that he was unhappy with the bill, and asked him if they should speak or if he wanted him to speak to Cash about it. Morrison told him to speak to Cash. Bragg told her he had 'deep reservations' about the bill. That night, over a dinner with Olympian Ian Thorpe organised by Equality Australia CEO Anna Brown, Bragg told them it was going to be difficult to fix the bill.

It turned into a disaster for Morrison.

'The prime minister reneged on the deal,' Sharma told me later.

Archer also rejects claims that Morrison had been blindsided by some of them, and assertions by Dutton that they had misled the prime minister.

'I always said I wouldn't trade my reputation, my brand, my integrity, and my views,' she told me during a long interview for this book. She had expressed those same sentiments to Morrison before the vote.

Archer had been summonsed — again — to a meeting in his office with attorney-general Cash to see if they could convince her to change her mind.

'I am not moving,' she told them. 'I can't do what you want me to do, and if that is insurmountable to you, I will resign.'

She said she offered her resignation two or three times. Morrison refused it each time. While he didn't like a lot of what she said, he knew full well what the consequences would be if she followed through.

Morrison behaved himself around her. It would be safe to assume he had judged, rightly, that if he had tried to push her around, she would have made sure the world got to know about it. Archer also believes that, ultimately, he respected her for holding true to her beliefs.

Morrison and those close to him felt he had been betrayed by Fiona Martin, who ended up voting with the others against his bill. Archer says, yeah, maybe so, but the problem often with them was that they could not see what was right in front of their faces.

Martin was a child psychologist who had to deal with kids suffering from bullying and discrimination. Archer says that Martin and the others believed they had an agreement in December that kids would be protected by amendments to the bill. They went to the media saying that, which would not have happened without permission, and then in February the amendments were off the table again.

'So who was betrayed by who?' Archer asks. Good point. So was her other point that it was the job of Finkelstein and Morris, or the whip, Bert van Manem, to take the temperature of the backbench.

Archer says that Sharma came to her office to tell her that he had been 'monstered' by the prime minister's office.

Sharma says he had meetings with Morrison and his staff, and then later with Frydenberg and Birmingham. He said he made clear to Morrison that he could not support the bill, and told the prime minister he needed to figure out whether he had the numbers to get it passed or not.

'If you put it to a vote, you will lose,' Sharma warned Morrison. Morrison said that would be a disaster, and told Sharma he was making life very difficult.

'A lot of pressure was put on me to change my position,' Sharma said later. He says he told Morrison that the issue was existential for him, and the best thing the prime minister could do would be to go with the amendment to abolish the right of religious schools to discriminate against gay and transgender students, moved by independent MP Rebekah Sharkie. It would not provide him with everything he wanted, but he would be able to claim a victory nonetheless.

He says that Morrison was exasperated and frustrated by the resistance. He had promised to legislate for religious freedom, but they were blocking him.

'They were very tough conversations. I didn't believe he was inappropriate.'

And the prime minister's staff? 'They probably went a bit further,' Sharma said.

Birmingham, Cash, and Frydenberg were also used to try to persuade the rebels, stressing the importance of unity and the need to stick together.

'The leadership of the moderates within the party didn't do us any favours,' Sharma told me later. 'It shouldn't have reached the point where the backbenchers were having to go to this extent.

'Birmingham and Marise [Payne] should have been making clear there were danger signals. They should have been debated in cabinet and tactics. They often weren't, because the prime minister steamrolled them.'

Karen Andrews described the whole thing as a 'debacle'. She says the moderates missed the 'charismatic' leadership of Christopher Pyne, who would have struck a deal and then made sure everybody stuck to it.

Sharma believed that the Australian Christian Lobby had got to Morrison over the summer, hence his reluctance to remove the discrimination clause.

David Hughes, Morrison's director of strategy, who was involved in the negotiations with backbenchers, says this was not the case, but said that the prime minister did meet with faith leaders, including representatives of the Jewish, Islamic, and Greek Orthodox communities.

Morrison was also being pressured by conservative MPs, including James Paterson and David Fawcett, to press ahead. Paterson would have preferred it if the legislation had been introduced much earlier in the term, but in his view it would have been an even bigger breach of faith with supporters if the government had not even tried to bring it on.

By the end, Hughes agreed that the differences were irreconcilable.

Birmingham left the building at 2.30 on the morning of 10 February as the bill was being debated in the House. At that stage, he believed that only Archer and Zimmerman were going to cross the floor, which would have ensured passage of the bill. Sharma and Allen had given a commitment they would not be the ones to make the bill fail. But they had also told him that if it looked like Sharkie's amendment would get up, they would vote for it.

Throughout the night and morning, while the leadership and staff were exerting pressure to stop the backbenchers crossing the floor, the backbenchers were talking to one another, trying to stay strong. Archer spoke to Martin inside the chamber and in the annex.

It was around 3.00 or 4.00 am. Archer said that Martin was stressed, in pieces, but holding firm. Martin kept saying to her: 'I have to protect kids. I have to do this.' Martin felt it was not only morally and ethically right to oppose the bill, but that her professional reputation was at stake.

Bragg, who also objected to elements of the statement of belief in the legislation, because it gave greater privilege to religious speech, was coming under intense pressure to conform.

'Cash told me Morrison wouldn't move on the statement of belief and on the students or teachers, except to accelerate a review by the Australian Law Reform Commission,' Bragg says.

The bill was due to go to the Senate the next day. He told her and Birmingham that he would cross the floor in the Senate, if need be, to address those issues.

'I didn't want to blindside anyone,' he said later. 'Frydenberg called me around 8.00 pm to tell me that if I crossed the floor on this, we'd lose government. I told him I didn't agree with that analysis, and that the government had bigger problems. I wasn't for turning.'

An important contribution came from Labor frontbencher Stephen Jones. Jones revealed that his gay nephew had suicided, and that he feared for the safety of his own son.

In a compelling speech, he said he worried himself sick every time his 14-year-old son left the house. 'He wears heels that give me vertigo and has more handbags than his sister,' he said. 'He has more courage than any boy I have met. He swims against the tide.

'I know that the love and protection that he enjoys with his mother, with his friends and family is very different to the reception he may receive in the world outside.

'Could this be the day when we get a call telling us that something has happened? That he has been attacked just for being who he is?'

Jones urged Morrison to step into his son's heels. 'Earlier today, the prime minister said we should exercise our power with love,' he said.

'It's so easy to giggle and dismiss a phrase like that ... But I agree.

'I'd ask the prime minister and every other member in this place to put themselves in the shoes of the parents or the heels of their kids as they step out in public.'

Around 5.00 am, the House, with the support of the rebel Liberals — Archer, Zimmerman, Allen, Martin, and Sharma — passed the bill with Sharkie's amendment to protect vulnerable kids.

Sharma and Allen had seen Martin moving with Archer and Zimmerman to support the amendment, so they also moved to vote for it.

Birmingham woke around 5.45 am after a couple of hours' sleep to a string of messages on his phone. *Oh fuck*, he thought.

Birmingham spoke to Bragg at 7.30 am to tell him that Morrison and Cash wanted to get the bill through the Senate without the amendment passed by the House. Bragg was flabbergasted. He told Birmingham that he wouldn't support it and that he couldn't believe they wanted to spend more capital on the issue.

At 8.30 am, at the usual leadership meeting with Morrison, Birmingham told the prime minister that the bill would not make it through the Senate with the House's amendment removed, because Coalition senators would not support it. Morrison persisted for a while, and then realised around mid-morning that he had been defeated.

'He [Birmingham] told me it would put a big black mark against my name,' Bragg said later. 'I said I understood that, but that I couldn't go back to where I lived in East Sydney and look the community in the eye if we singled out these students.

'I also felt the weight of the many teachers who had been sacked in New South Wales just for being gay who we were letting down, including a member of the Liberal Party, councillor Nathan Zamprogno, who had been sacked.

'My decision meant the bill was shelved. It was over.

'I could tell that Birmingham shared my frustration about the handling of these sensitive matters. It was clear to me that he was relieved that we wouldn't have to go through another day in parliament bashing up a vulnerable minority group. The calls to mental-health support groups hit record levels that week as the parliament discussed the ins and outs of transgender issues.

'It was unseemly and way out of alignment with the priorities of Australians. Years before, Birmingham and I had worked together on Liberals for Yes [for same-sex marriage], so I knew his strong support for that community.'

Morrison pretended it was no big deal having so many members of his own party vote against him, and what a grand old party he led that allowed members to express themselves freely.

Stuart Robert knew differently. He was not worried about a challenge to Morrison's leadership, but he was worried about the structural defects in the government that had been exposed.

'I was worried about the fracturing of left and right. My concern was we were not holding the party together. It was broken,' he said.

'Antic and Rennick said they would withhold their vote—the hard right saying unless you give us what we want, we won't be voting for government legislation—and the left was not happy with the religious discrimination bill. The left and right were fraying.'

Robert thought Morrison had left it too late.

'We should have progressed it; we should have tried to do it earlier,' he told me.

Archer always felt that the moderates had left it too late to take a stand. They did manage to get Morrison to move on climate change, but Barnaby Joyce took all the credit for that, bragging about how much he had squeezed out of the government for the Nationals.

Archer had also taken an early decision to stand with the women marching for justice in March 2021. She had received an emailed invitation, and responded almost immediately to say she would attend. She never considered for a moment that would also be controversial.

When it became public, another of Morrison's female advisers rang to reproach her, saying it probably wasn't a good idea. The spiel was something to the effect that: 'You fought so hard as a woman to be elected, why would you want to leave the building to support a protest.'

It was silly. Archer had been furious with Morrison over his handling of the Brittany Higgins allegations, particularly when he said that Jenny had counselled him, and was doubly glad that she had gone to talk to the women outside when she heard him say in parliament that they were lucky they weren't being shot.

Martin ended up losing her seat of Reid. Morrison rang a few other backbenchers to commiserate, but he did not ring Martin. Sharma suffered almost an almost 7 per cent swing against him on primaries, and lost to independent Allegra Spender. Zimmerman lost to independent Kylea Tink, and Katie Allen to Labor's Michelle Ananda Rajah. At the first party meeting after the election, Morrison congratulated Archer on her win. She had increased her margin, gaining a swing of 1.5 per cent.

Archer says that there have been a lot of times when she has looked at situations and thought: *Excuse the language, this is fucked.*

'You do have to choose the hill you are prepared to die on. I know I am seen as difficult and troublesome, I knew there were going to be consequences,' she said. She hopes the party will change, because she won't.

Bragg also missed out on a frontbench position after the election. He was told it was because he wasn't a woman. Archer was, but she was a troublesome one.

CHAPTER ELEVEN

No Way to Reset the Reset

The night before Morrison's fateful 1 February 2022 appearance at the National Press Club, Tony Abbott christened his new office at 25 Martin Place in Sydney. The blessing was delivered by his friend and father confessor, George Pell, with guests including luminaries such as the New South Wales premier, Dominic Perrottet, former prime minister John Howard, Brian Loughnane, Dallas McInerney, and Piers Akerman.

Abbott told his friends that night that Morrison's problem was that he was not giving people a compelling reason to re-elect him. It was impossible to argue with that. There was a sense of impending doom. Omicron had wrecked the summer, wrecked any chance that an election would be called on Australia Day for March, and almost certainly wrecked Morrison's re-election prospects.

Morrison was in deep trouble, with no clear way of getting himself out of it. He did not have a a single policy to bless himself with.

Around the same time, Labor's national secretary, Paul Erickson, who never allowed himself to dream of victory, surveyed the polls — public and private were aligned — saying that if the Coalition was still as far behind by the time of the budget, scheduled for 29 March, it would be carrying such a heavy load it would be unlikely to get lift-off.

His counterpart, the Liberals' federal director, Andrew Hirst, could read the polls as well as Erickson. He knew how tough it was going to be, as did Morrison, who was telling colleagues what was happening was 'existential'.

There was no proper explanation for the shortage of rapid antigen tests. Apart from the fact that the Australian Medical Association had advised a national strategy was needed, the government itself knew how vital they would be. On 14 September 2021, the health minister, Greg Hunt, was gung-ho about RATs, promising they would be available soon:

> Rapid antigen testing will play a big part in Australia's pathway out of lockdown, and so I have asked the TGA [Therapeutic Goods Administration] to rapidly consider the role of rapid antigen tests, and they will be going through that process.
>
> They are already assessing and approving the rapid antigen tests themselves, and now on the basis of their medical advice, I'm hopeful that these tests will be available at the earliest possible time for workplaces and then subsequently, once we have the support of AHPPC [Australian Health Protection Principal Committee], within the home.
>
> But rapid antigen tests will be available in workplaces and soon enough in the home environment.

They weren't. So, in January 2022, Morrison said it was up to the states to secure supplies for their needs—which, strictly speaking, was true, but he was the national leader of the national cabinet. Again, it sounded like blame-shifting.

His first real opportunity to claw back some ground after

being dragged down again, to reset his agenda — or indeed to set one — was at the National Press Club on 1 February.

First up, he refused to accept Laura Tingle's invitation to make a clean breast of things and to apologise unequivocally for his mistakes, including the Hawaiian holiday, the shortage of RATs, and funding cuts for the National Disability Insurance Scheme.

With the cost of living climbing, Sky's Andrew Clennell cornered him by asking him if he knew the price of bread, petrol, and a rapid antigen test. Of course, he didn't. Then Ten's Peter van Onselen sucker-punched him by reading out a text exchange between Gladys Berejiklian and a federal cabinet minister, where she called him a 'horrible, horrible person' and the minister responded by saying he was a 'psycho'.

Berejiklian would later say she could not remember this exchange, which was a convenient memory lapse, but not a denial. One senior New South Wales Liberal, claiming he had seen a screen shot of the exchange, later told me that the minister was Paul Fletcher. Fletcher denied it at the time through a spokesman.

Fletcher either inhabited a world of his own, or was putting on a show, but he told people after the election that he had no idea how unpopular Morrison was until election day, when he was out at polling booths.

Fletcher held onto his seat of Bradfield. Just. The independent candidate, Nicolette Boele, secured a 15.3 per cent swing against him on primaries — the biggest against any sitting Liberal. Worried, as he should be, that he will lose the seat at the next election, after converting it from the bluest of blue-ribbon to marginal, Fletcher was contemplating quitting parliament.

Boele was not as high-profile as the other independents, and didn't get the same attention or support as the other Teals. Perhaps, with a bit more help, she might have won, but the seat has been left vulnerable to a full-throttle assault in 2025.

The Press Club disaster left Morrison looking for a reset for his reset. It never came. Three days later, Brittany Higgins released the text messages that Barnaby Joyce had sent to a third party almost a year before, on 22 March 2021, which he had asked to be sent on to her, saying that he believed her and describing Morrison as a 'hypocrite and a liar'.

Morrison and Joyce went into overdrive, saying that the highly damaging messages had been sent before Joyce returned to the Nationals' leadership and therefore the deputy prime ministership. Joyce unreservedly apologised, saying Morrison was a 'person of high integrity and honesty'. Morrison accepted the apology in good faith, and, of course, they trusted one another now and got along swimmingly. Of course. And, of course, no one believed a word of it, especially as they avoided one another like the plague during the election campaign.

Soon after, on 10 March, tragedy struck, threatening to derail Labor. It also threw the government completely off track.

The untimely death of Labor Senator Kimberley Kitching, at the age of 52 from a heart attack, triggered a flood of recriminations that led to three of Labor's most effective advocates being sidelined for weeks by a concerted campaign to damage them as well as Albanese and his deputy, Richard Marles.

Their enemies, both in the Coalition and inside Labor, jumped onto a narrative that Kitching had been bullied and ostracised by Penny Wong, Kristina Keneally, and Katy Gallagher, that they had unfairly removed her from Labor's tactics committee, and that Kitching's preselection had been threatened. The insinuation was that all this had contributed to her early demise.

Wong, Keneally, and Gallagher were incredibly tight. After Keneally and Gallagher had bought her trendy designer sneakers for her birthday, Wong called the other two her 'Senate sisters'. They were regular attendees at Albanese's pre-parliamentary Sunday-night dinners for members of his leadership group and key tacticians.

Keneally, who was ketogenic, regularly baked cakes for the dinner, where dietary requirements were as diverse as the personalities of the participants. Katy Gallagher was vegetarian, Mark Butler pescatorian, and Tony Burke coeliac.

As well as providing insights into Albanese's management style, because all the shadow ministers ended up giving him free advice about where he was going wrong, and he responded in kind, the dinners strengthened the bonds and increased the trust between his frontbenchers and with him. They also fostered unity.

There was something else that bound the three women. All of them had experienced devastating personal tragedies: Keneally had given birth to a stillborn daughter; Gallagher's first husband had died in an accident when she was pregnant with their first child; and Wong's brother had taken his own life.

So, for those who knew them and knew about their experiences, the notion that they were callous or would act out of spite towards Kitching was ridiculous. They were tough operators. They were not cruel or selfish, and they knew that if they all stuck together they might just be able to bring Morrison down.

Kitching had her friends inside Labor, particularly Bill Shorten, but she had as many on the other side of politics, and had cultivated numerous senior journalists. Everyone was genuinely shocked and saddened by the untimely death of someone clearly talented.

That didn't stop a few from seizing the opportunity to settle scores or weaponise it against their opponents. Albanese's enemies inside Labor and the media busily orchestrated days of damaging headlines.

Instead of hoping for clear air for in the lead-up to his all-important pre-election budget, Morrison dived head-first into the muck surrounding Kitching's death, ignoring the time-honoured tradition that when your opponents are tearing themselves to pieces, your best option is to step back and leave them to it.

There was something curious as well as unseemly about a prime minister who was facing so many critical problems getting embroiled in a brutal fight ignited by the death of an opposition politician — particularly as one of his cabinet ministers was central to her removal from the tactics committee, and suspicions abounded about the close connections between her and people close to Morrison.

Full of grief and guilt for having convinced her to go into politics, Shorten was interviewed on radio about Kitching the morning after she died. His tears were understandable following the shock.

Quickly, however, sadness morphed darkly into anger, revenge, and murky power plays for control of the bedevilled Victorian Labor Party. Day after day, there were accusations of bullying and about the impact of the stress caused by her unresolved Senate preselection.

Suggestions persisted that the stress of the uncertainty had contributed to her demise, even though she had a thyroid condition, and despite the fact that one of her great friends, Senator Don Farrell, insisted there had been 'no prospect at all' that she would have lost her preselection.

Constrained by the knowledge of widespread grief for her family and friends, Albanese's initial responses, while standing by Wong, Keneally, and Gallagher — who copped accusations for days on end that they had bullied Kitching—sounded a bit lame. He also got a bit stroppy with the media.

That encouraged members of the government to believe that he would fold under pressure in a campaign.

The bullying accusations were not taken seriously by insiders who knew what had happened, but the legitimate grief around her death meant that the three senators could not publicly go into the details of why Kitching had been isolated and dropped from the tactics committee while still being kept in Albanese's shadow ministry, albeit in a junior portfolio. The saga had a significant psychological impact on the three women.

Kitching had been a clever, ambitious, and a tough player who revelled in political intrigue, making enemies as easily as she made friends.

She loved the nickname 'Mata Hari' bestowed on her by one of her mates, Joel Fitzgibbon, who admired her for not toeing the line—something he was also very good at.

Fitzgibbon would also simultaneously warn her to be careful she did not cross that line. Fitzgibbon reckoned she never complained to him about her treatment, except that she wanted to be restored to the tactics committee. 'She was tough, she didn't want people holding her hand,' he told me at the time. 'She didn't ask anyone to feel sorry for her.'

Kitching had lost the trust of many on her own side because she was suspected of leaking and undermining colleagues, and not only by briefing members of the media. The Nine Network's Chris Uhlmann and News Corps' Andrew Bolt confirmed that she briefed against colleagues when they revealed publicly after her death that Kitching had told them she was concerned that Wong would be weak on China.

She was also accused of briefing Coalition MPs, former Liberal

Party officials, and even senior staff in the prime minister's office.

I spoke to Kitching on 16 February, a few weeks before she died, the day after she had tried to inveigle the head of ASIO, Mike Burgess, to confirm to a Senate committee that Chau Chak Wing was the mysterious Chinese donor 'puppeteer' behind a thwarted foreign-interference plot to back political candidates at the election.

'I am reliably informed that the puppeteer mentioned in your case study in your annual threat-assessment speech given last week is Chau Chak Wing,' Senator Kitching put to Burgess.

'I believe it to be Chau Chak Wing. Are you able to confirm that it is Chau Chak Wing?' she insisted.

Burgess told the committee he would not discuss the matter publicly.

Clearly irritated, Burgess addressed himself to Kitching. 'Senator, as I said before, I will not comment on speculation of who is and who isn't targets, in general or in specific, as you are asking me there. I think it's unfair that you ask me that question in public.'

The exchange ran prominently on all the news bulletins that night, with footage of Chau Chak Wing alongside senior Labor figures.

It seemed to me that Kitching had dropped her own side in it by pursuing Burgess so vigorously. At that time, blissfully unaware of all the behind-the-scenes intrigue involving her and her suspicious colleagues, I was curious to know why she had pressed Burgess so hard, to the point where he rebuked her.

When I told Kitching what I was calling about, she said 'they' — meaning her colleagues — thought she had been put up to it by the prime minister's office. She laughed, and dismissed it. I pressed her on why she had done it, and, after pausing, she said: 'For transparency.'

None of her colleagues had said any such thing to me then, and in fact were wary about responding to queries about her. The most they said was that her intervention had cut across their attacks on the government in the House.

The 'puppeteer' story was soon overtaken by Morrison calling Marles the Manchurian candidate in Question Time, then being publicly rebuked by Burgess and former ASIO chief Dennis Richardson for politicising national security.

That was another shocking moment for Morrison. Over in the west, where Labor was eyeing off a clutch of seats, its focus groups were alive with observations from people that Morrison was using national security to try to score points off the opposition. Whatever else they thought about Albanese, they did not believe he was disloyal or weak on China. They thought that Morrison was running a desperate scare campaign. One woman said that the prime minister was behaving 'like a toddler having a tantrum'.

Of course politicians leak, and they do have friends across the aisle, but the breadth and depth of Kitching's friends and connections was shown in the outpouring of emotions over her death.

The rupture that led to her dumping from the tactics committee came in June 2021 when the defence minister, Linda Reynolds, told Senate Estimates that she had been forewarned by a Labor senator that she would face questioning over the alleged rape of former government staffer Brittany Higgins.

There was an outcry from Labor senators, including Penny Wong.

In private meetings later, to prove she was telling the truth, Reynolds provided information for Wong, Gallagher, and Keneally. First was video footage from the Senate chamber showing Kitching approaching her months before, on 2 February before prayers, two weeks before the Higgins allegations were revealed.

As referred to previously, Reynolds says that she also told

Yaron Finkelstein, Morrison's senior political adviser, about her conversation with Kitching that morning.

In June, Reynolds told Wong and Gallagher, who later informed Keneally, that this was when Kitching first told her that Labor's tactics committee had discussed it and were planning to weaponise the alleged rape.

Second, Reynolds showed them text messages she had received from Kitching, effectively confirming their initial conversation.

Lastly, Wong, Gallagher, and Keneally discovered that Reynolds had made sworn statements to authorities investigating the rape allegations, detailing her conversation with Kitching on the matter.

Reynolds accepted Labor's assurances that the rape allegations had not been discussed in tactics, and therefore that Kitching's 'leak' was not true. The three frontbenchers found that the three pieces of supporting evidence from Reynolds made a compelling case against Kitching. So did their male colleagues.

Kitching was dropped from tactics. Fearing continuing leaks to their opponents or the media, they had no choice but to restrict her access and to limit their contact with her.

Wong, Keneally, and Gallagher, who were shattered by the accusations and by the way some sections of the media lapped them up, had deep wells of support inside the party. They were all close to Albanese, and were seen as indispensable to his frontbench team.

Coincidentally, not long before all this broke, Wong, after weeks of absence on medical leave, had appeared on *Insiders*, where David Speers put her through her paces. Close to a million viewers saw Wong provide a masterful defence of the opposition's positioning on China, the Russian invasion of Ukraine, and national security generally.

Her critique of the government's record on defence capability and Australia's self-sufficiency gaps was persuasive, and was described by one Labor man as one of the best performances he had seen. Even coming from a different state and a different faction, he enthused that she was probably the best of them. There was no way they were going to allow her, Gallagher, and Keneally to be torn down, and also no way that Kitching's accusations she would be weak on China were sustainable.

There were mutterings that if the attacks continued and damaged Labor's election prospects, Shorten and his allies would be held responsible. Other Labor frontbenchers privately accused them of using Kitching's death to cut down deputy leader Marles in an attempt to preserve Shorten's powerbroker status.

There was no prospect that Shorten would ever make it back to the leadership. According to one of Shorten's colleagues, a frontbencher from Victoria, Arthur Calwell had been given three goes at winning an election, and Labor was never going to make that mistake again. Ouch.

When you think about it, though, if Labor had been knocked out of the race then, and subsequently lost the election, it would have been chalked up as a third defeat for Shorten. But I digress.

In his eulogy for Kitching, Shorten appealed to everyone to work for a Labor victory. His furious colleagues waited to see if he meant it. The attacks ceased.

Not everyone on the government side had enjoyed the sordid spectacle. Liberal backbencher Russell Broadbent, first elected to parliament in 1990, who lost in 1993, was re-elected in 1996, defeated again in 1998, and then came back in 2004, knows how brutal politics can be, particularly for people like himself who go against the leader or the party line on policy issues—in his case, on refugees.

Broadbent knew and liked Kitching, but was dismayed that such odious imputations flowed from her death.

'Politics breaks peoples' hearts. It doesn't stop their hearts from beating,' he said.

Soon after this, Morrison caught Covid. The floods in northern New South Wales brought misery to thousands of Australians, Morrison was accused of playing politics with financial assistance, victims complained about the rescue efforts, and he barred cameras from filming when he visited a flood-affected property. He wasn't going to risk another Cobargo-style event. When he did let them film, he was pushing a mop inside, pretending to clean an already clean timber floor.

By the time of the budget, Morrison was sinking.

Frydenberg put in his usual polished performance delivering the budget. It was short on policy, but brimming with handouts. The cost of living was the economic and political problem that needed to be addressed. Frydenberg announced $8.6 billion in spending, $3 billion of which was for a temporary cut in the fuel excise, cash payments of $250 for pensioners and other welfare recipients, and tax cuts for low- and middle-income earners.

It went down well, but Albanese neutralised it by adopting all the measures, and then added more of his own, including an aged-care package.

The budget disappeared without trace, amid a welter of damaging character assessments of Morrison — first from Connie Fierravanti-Wells in the Senate, then from Michael Towke, who had been preselected initially as the Liberal candidate for Cook back in 2007, only to be replaced by Morrison after an especially dirty campaign.

Senator Fierravanti-Wells launched her torpedoes on budget night. Responding to accusations later that she had chosen that night deliberately to inflict maximum damage on Morrison, Fierravanti-Wells said there was no other night she could have made her speech. She knew Morrison was about to call the election and that parliament would be prorogued.

She also did not regret that she had done it. Not one little bit. She felt vindicated by the election result, as she said in a note to supporters on 17 June, headlined 'Thank You and Farewell'.

Fierravanti-Wells, who had been relegated to an unwinnable spot on the party's New South Wales Senate ticket, told the Senate on 29 March that Morrison was 'not fit to be prime minister'. She said his interventions on preselection processes had destroyed the party, and accused him and Hawke of 'corrupt antics'.

'In my public life, I have met ruthless people. Morrison tops the list, followed closely by Hawke,' Fierravanti-Wells said. 'Morrison is not interested in rules-based order. It is his way or the highway. An autocrat, a bully who has no moral compass.'

She said Morrison's actions conflicted with his 'portrayal as a man of faith'.

'He has used his so-called faith as a marketing advantage,' she said.

Claiming that she had received 'hundreds if not thousands of emails' from Liberals outlining their disgust, she said they had lost faith in the party.

'They don't like Morrison and they don't trust him. They continue to despair at our prospects at the next federal election. And they blame Morrison for this. Our members do not want to help in the upcoming election. Morrison is not fit to be prime minister. And Hawke certainly is not fit to be a minister.'

In her post-election farewell email to members and supporters in June, she said it was 'noteworthy' that two out of three eligible Australian voters had not voted for the Liberal Party.

'Against this background, the result of the election was as inevitable as it was predictable,' she wrote.

On 29 March 2022, I made certain comments in a speech to the Senate. A multitude of people contacted me after that speech, including Liberals, to congratulate me. Only a few were negative—a portent of things to come.

There is no doubt that in conjunction with the 'captain's picks', the deliberate orchestration of delays to select candidates coupled with preselection skulduggery contributed to an even worse result in New South Wales. The denial of plebiscites and democratic processes set out in our constitution will hang heavily on the heads of the cabal of so-called 'factional negotiators' and their puppets. The wheels of justice turn slowly, but eventually justice is served.

Although he denied acting in concert with Fierravanti-Wells, her speech spurred Towke to provide his version of events surrounding the original Cook preselection, which he had won resoundingly by 82 votes to eight against Morrison, which had immediately prompted a campaign to overturn the result.

Towke had been accused of branch-stacking. Supported by statutory declarations, Towke, a Christian, also claimed that Morrison and his supporters had used his Lebanese heritage against him, telling preselectors he was a Muslim.

Towke said that the toxic campaign against him and his family had forced him to withdraw from the contest. Morrison emphatically denied Towke's allegations.

Fifteen years later, Towke's allegations, combined with Fierrevanti-Wells' speech, dominated the media for days. Towke claimed he had received text messages from a serving federal cabinet minister saying, 'I believe you', and urging him to do what he needed to do, but to be careful.

It was a foetid atmosphere in which to launch an election campaign. Morrison had no choice. He had run out of time.

CHAPTER TWELVE

Trans-gressions

Scott Morrison couldn't wait to take credit for choosing Katherine Deves as the Liberal candidate for Warringah, and couldn't wait to make her views on transgender women a focal point of his election campaign.

On 11 April, the first day of the campaign, in an interview on 2GB, a radio station that, as one local Liberal observed, no one on the northern beaches listened to, Morrison described Deves as 'an outstanding individual' who stood up for 'something really important'.

That something really important was to 'ensure that, you know, when it comes to girls playing sport and women playing sport, that they're playing against people of the same sex'.

'And she's standing up for things that she believes in, and I share her views on those topics,' he said on radio. 'And, and I think it's important that they're raised, and it's got nothing to do with, you know, the broad agenda debates. This is just about, you know, common sense and what's right. And I think Katherine's right on the money there.'

Later that same day, at a press conference at Culburra Beach in the marginal New South Wales seat of Gilmore, Morrison was asked about those remarks. Again, he was effusive in his praise, eagerly claiming credit for her candidacy.

'I welcome Katherine Deves' selection, and I'm very pleased to play a role in that,' he enthused.

'I think she raises very important issues, and I think Claire Chandler has also been very outspoken and brave on these issues.

'And I share their views, and I'll have more to say about that at another time.'

And so it came to pass. It was biblical. Morrison ended up reaping what he had sown. He gained nothing and lost a lot from a pointless, unedifying fight that further trashed the Liberal brand and ensured that the spotlight stayed on him and his appalling judgement.

Publicly, his comments that day were overtaken by Anthony Albanese's bloopers when he could not nominate the unemployment rate or the Reserve Bank cash rate.

Internally, Morrison's elevation of Deves did not go unnoticed. There was a lot of disquiet. Few disagreed with the substantive issue that rules were needed to govern transgender women competing in sporting events. What disturbed them was the voluminous, offensive, transphobic, widely known public commentary by Deves that went with it, and Morrison's effusive endorsement of her that would thrust her into prominence.

Pretty soon, the most senior Liberal officials, backbenchers, and cabinet ministers were asking him to dump her. He wouldn't. He doubled down, and so did she.

Local party members were also still burning after having been deprived of a vote to select the candidate of their choice.

If the proper processes had been followed, there was no way known that Deves would have been preselected. Jane Buncle—a bright, articulate, moderate lawyer—would have been the candidate. Buncle had all the potential to be a first-class candidate. She had the full backing of the locals, and a solid infrastructure had been put in place to support her campaign — until the continuing shenanigans led to her withdrawal in late January.

The shabby treatment of Buncle, the spurning of another local favourite, David Brady, and the choice of Deves left local Liberals in despair. Most of them withdrew their services, choosing to help out elsewhere. Only 96 of 880 members turned out to support Deves during the campaign.

Morrison asserted on 13 April at a press conference that he had not been aware of Deves' more offensive posts, which by then were saturating mainstream media. He also claimed when he had said two days before that 'she was right on the money', he was referring to Chandler's bill, which he most definitely was not.

In fact, Deves' views were well known in the Liberal Party, in the LGBTIQ community, and to Sky after Dark devotees.

The former state president Chris McDiven was asked by the federal director, Andrew Hirst, to sit on the committee with Morrison and Dominic Perrottet to sort out preselections after the federal executive decided in March to take over the New South Wales division. She reluctantly agreed. At that time, their task was to confirm the three sitting members under supposed threat — Alex Hawke, Sussan Ley, and Trent Zimmerman — which they did.

Hirst called McDiven again after that to ask her to help select candidates for other seats deemed critical to the result that were still without candidates, including Warringah, Dobell, Hughes, Parramatta, and Eden-Monaro.

Deves' name was on a list of candidates for Warringah presented by the state director, Chris Stone, to the committee of three. The other two were Lincoln Parker, an expert in defence known as a climate change denialist, whose nomination had previously been rejected, and David Brady, a disability advocate who did not live in Warringah but did have support in the electorate.

The party organisation only had a matter of days to conduct due diligence on the three candidates. Nominations for the seat opened on 10 March and closed the next day. Although having been deemed ineligible in January to nominate because she had not been a member long enough, Deves sought and gained a waiver in March.

Few knew she had even nominated. Trent Zimmerman had been discussing Warringah with Yaron Finkelstein, who led him to believe that the prime minister's office supported Brady.

Alex Hawke says he told Morrison that Brady was the best candidate, and urged him to choose him. Hawke and others knew that Deves was in the running. Claire Chandler was also asked her opinion, and even she expressed caution about going with Deves.

Deves' views and extreme language were known to those who paid attention to these things. Hawke says she was chosen because Morrison felt pressured to get more women into parliament.

'He was hoist on his own petard,' Hawke told me.

It was clear that even if Morrison sought advice, he seldom took it. Except he had been told he had a woman problem, so the answer was to choose as many women as possible. Regardless of their credentials.

Given the tight time frame after federal intervention began on 27 March, effective until 2 April, the division was hard pressed to properly collate all the information on the three people vying for Warringah, as well as all the other candidates for the other vacant seats.

Ultimately, more than 130 pages of information on Deves, including some of her social media posts, were sent by email to members of the vetting committee, the Nominations Review

Committee (NRC), by the deputy state director, Simon McInnes.

But the information was sent at 4.20 pm, only an hour before the committee was due to meet on 18 March to decide whether her name could go forward as a suitable candidate. It was a telephone hook-up, which included Hawke as the prime minister's representative.

Knowing that Morrison was readying to call the election, with no candidate in the field and the pressure on for a decision, there was little time to do anything other than skim the material. So the vetting process was a cursory flick and tick. Local Liberals were convinced that Brady—who, as previously stated, Hawke had recommended to Morrison—would be chosen. They were stunned when he wasn't.

During the meeting with Perrottet and Morrison, McDiven recognised Deves' name from a conversation she'd had with a golfing friend who had praised her as a confident person with strong views, particularly on transgender women,who would make a good candidate.

McDiven was aware generally of her views on transgender women in sport, but not of her extensive social media history. McDiven thought she would be okay. There was a discussion about the strengths and weaknesses of all three potential candidates.

Deves was also known inside the prime minister's office. Finkelstein was aware of her views, and had heard good things about her from his friend Mark Westfield—later appointed by him to run her campaign, but afterwards blamed a lack of due diligence for her selection.

Which was undoubtedly a direct result of the preselection gridlock engineered by his boss.

McDiven says now that maybe she should have asked more questions, but because Deves' name was on the list, she assumed she had been vetted and cleared by the Warringah Nominations Review Committee.

She believes she did ask at the time if Deves had been cleared. McDiven had been state president when the NRC process was instigated 20 years before, after a couple of spectacular fails, to ensure that no one who had nominated could be chosen as the candidate until they had been cleared, so she was conscious of the pitfalls.

Deves was selected for Warringah on 28 March. On 2 April, the day she was officially announced as the candidate, *Out in Perth*, a website for the LGBTIQ community with a couple of thousand subscribers, wrote about her social media history, including her likening of transgender processes to surgical mutilation.

Deves was extremely photogenic and always immaculately groomed. Without knowing anything about her, Birmingham walked past a television set soon after she was chosen. As her image came up on the screen, Birmingham thought *That's good. They've preselected someone who looks like a modern woman.* He kept walking.

Looks can be deceiving, as he quickly found out.

Morrison's remarks on the first campaign day on radio and at a press conference had set off alarm bells among members of the Liberals' campaign team, MPs, and cabinet ministers. Chris Stone asked for clarification from campaign headquarters in Brisbane about the prime minister's intentions. Stone wanted to know if Deves and her issues were going to feature in the campaign, because if they were, it would be very damaging for people under threat from independents, such as Zimmerman and Sharma in North Sydney and Wentworth, who were already anxious about her impact on their electorates.

Stone was assured that the comments were not officially sanctioned by the campaign, and that headquarters did not plan for them to feature. The message that came back was 'Don't worry.'

In fact, they were very worried. After her more offensive posts burst through to mainstream media, Birmingham and Hirst privately suggested to the prime minister that he disendorse her.

That was around 12 April, which was only a week before bulk nominations for parties officially closed on 19 April. Because of the complications of processes with bulk nominations, officials did not believe there would have been enough time if she had been disendorsed to nominate another candidate.

That was a process problem. The political problem was that she was out there as the captain's pick. Morrison refused to disendorse her. Perversely, he was worried that his reputation would suffer if he had to admit he had made a mistake. The other slight complication was that under the New South Wales division rules, the only way to remove her as the candidate during the campaign would have been to expel her from the party.

Deves had likened her push to stop transgender women from competing in women's sports to standing up to the Nazis during the Holocaust, and had referred to 'the Rainbow Reich'; claimed that surrogacy was 'a human rights violation'; that trans teenagers were 'surgically mutilated'; and that there was a link between transvestism and sexual predators or serial killers.

Deves apologised on 13 April for using 'unacceptable language'. Morrison accepted her apology, but it did little to quell the pressure for her to be dropped. Zimmerman and Sharma publicly distanced themselves from her comments. They repeatedly pressed for her disendorsement.

Meanwhile, campaign headquarters in Brisbane was trying to get Zimmerman and others to tone down their objections, because she was the prime minister's pick. Zimmerman had confided to friends that he had told the prime minister's office he would give them 24 hours to disendorse her, or he would cut loose.

The response by campaign headquarters was to ban Zimmerman from doing national media. They were worried what he would say if he was asked about Deves.

Matt Kean was the most outspoken against her, arguing that there should be no place in the Liberal Party for bigots. Lo, Perrottet soon fell victim to Morrison's leaky-text syndrome, as messages appeared from him to the prime minister agreeing that girls should play sport against girls, and women against women, while urging the issue should be handled sensitively.

On 15, 16, and 17 April, Sharma texted and called Stone and Birmingham. Sharma argued the party had sacked other candidates for offensive social media posts in 2019, so the same thing should happen to Deves. Zimmerman was putting a similar case.

'This is untenable,' Sharma told them. 'She is clearly not going to win the seat of Warringah, and she is causing huge damage to neighbouring colleagues.'

Even if you put the principle to one side, the politics were shocking, Sharma argued. He wasn't telling them anything they didn't know. They agreed it was damaging. They understood Sharma's concerns, and sympathised with him about the damage her candidacy was causing.

Birmingham was trying to calm his moderate colleagues, while pressing Morrison and Hirst to disendorse her. He believed there was still time to do it before nominations closed.

Despite recognising the difficulties this would create, Hirst was sympathetic to the calls for her to be dumped. She was a distraction that the party could ill afford. Hirst wanted the campaign focus to be on the economy and on Albanese's inexperience, not on Deves.

Morrison had wedged himself, compromised his ministers, and undermined his candidates, but he refused to back down.

He argued to those pressing him to dump her that he was in a lose-lose situation. If she was disendorsed, he would be pilloried for having chosen her in the first place, and his judgement would be questioned. If she wasn't disendorsed, he would still be pilloried for having chosen her. It was a vicious circle and a wicked problem of his own creation.

Morrison also continued to defend her to his colleagues, arguing that what Deves had posted was not as bad as the media had made out. He was confident that the issue would quieten down.

It was quintessential Morrison. Refuse to admit a mistake, stick with it, and turn it into an even bigger one. Allow a problem to become a crisis before mishandling it.

Birmingham now says that if she had been disendorsed it would not have saved a single Teal seat. But, as he volunteered, that was not the point. The point was, he believes, that she should have been disendorsed as a matter of principle. Reputations matter; brand matters; values matter.

He says she was a 'motivating' factor for people to vote against the Liberals, and it would have been 'helpful' if she were gone.

According to Sharma: 'Morrison had too much personal prestige tied up in her selection.' He says that if she had gone through the normal processes, her deselection would also have gone through the normal processes. She would have been sacked as a candidate.

Sharma says that, after their protests were ignored, he and the other moderates had no choice but to strap themselves in.

Campaign strategists dealing with her at the time were convinced she had been on the verge of quitting when her posts first became public. Deves had been subjected to a torrent of abuse. She was shocked by the reaction to her remarks. She cried when she was talking to campaign officials. Showing her naivety, she told people she thought that, once selected as the candidate for Warringah by the prime minister, there would be a reset. That the slate would be wiped clean metaphorically and literally.

She received death threats. She feared for the safety of her family. She moved to a secret location, and refused to take phone calls even from the New South Wales division. Then Morrison's office rang the division, looking for her phone number so the prime minister could call her.

In response to questions later for this book, Deves denied she had contemplated quitting.

'No, I never thought of withdrawing,' she said. 'Nothing can prepare you for the sort of media attention I was subjected to during the election campaign, and I took the threats seriously, mainly out of concern for my family.

'There were moments where it was overwhelming, but I had been selected as the candidate, and was committed to seeing it through.'

However, she did confirm that Morrison had contacted her. 'I heard directly from the prime minister to encourage me to keep going,' she said.

The campaign strategists rightly assumed that Morrison had intervened, because after that, Deves toughened up. She told state campaign headquarters she would not make any further apologies and regretted apologising in the first place. Morrison backed her even more emphatically. Deves told people they had spoken a number of times.

Morrison sought to turn it into a free-speech issue. He accused people of seeking to cancel Deves, and argued that Australians were fed up with walking on eggshells. The problem was that this didn't ring true, at least not in the places that really mattered, and not beyond the increasingly strident religious-right members of the Liberal Party.

Morrison was accustomed to controlling everything. Indeed, he insisted on it. Although they deny it, his office effectively took over Deves' campaign after Finkelstein engaged a friend, former journalist Mark Westfield, to become her media adviser–campaign manager.

Finkelstein knew that Westfield knew Deves and that he supported her. Westfield was a big rap for Deves, and had been 'vouching' for her to Finkelstein before she was preselected. He had told Finkelstein that she would be a 'great candidate'. Finkelstein dismissed suggestions he had passed on this endorsement to Morrison.

Westfield's salary was paid by the division. Security guards were also hired to protect her.

In response to my questions, Deves said she had met Morrison once before she had been chosen as the candidate. She said she had also sought assistance from him when the media attention was 'at its height with respect to a media adviser for my campaign'.

'My campaign was run through New South Wales Liberal Party headquarters, just the same as all the other candidates from my state,' she said, even though at campaign headquarters they complained they were never given advance warning.

She also said she did not alert Morrison's office in advance that she was planning to retract her apology over some of her social media posts.

'I want to clarify that I did not, and do not, resile from my position with respect to women's and girls' sex-based rights,' Deves added. 'I apologised for the language that I had previously used, as I was aware that some people found it confronting or offensive.'

Deves also claimed that the issues she had highlighted had since been 'proven to be correct'.

Usually in campaigns, candidates have to clear each and every media interview in advance with campaign headquarters. Deves did not clear any of hers, including the most controversial one with Sky in the dying days of the campaign, when she retracted her apology. The first that the campaign team in New South Wales knew of any of her interviews was when they appeared.

When Morrison held a rally for western Sydney candidates, on Sunday 1 May, the same day as the Labor launch, Deves was invited to attend.

If the media had not noticed she was there, they certainly realised after Morrison made a point of singling her out from the podium, before he even deigned to mention Zimmerman, who was also there and who was livid because he had been led to believe she would not be.

Morrison's office had pleaded with Zimmerman to attend the rally, because they were worried it would look as if inner-city Liberals were boycotting the event. He had told them he would attend, but only after he had sought and received an assurance that Deves would not be there.

Yet there she was in a prime position, being lauded by the prime minister. Morrison's staff told Zimmerman they had tried to convince her not to come, but she had insisted.

Deves made a carefully orchestrated escape from the room with her bodyguards, with cameras and journalists in hot pursuit firing questions at her as the lift doors, in a prearranged move, were held open for her. The pictures and story ran a close second on every news bulletin that night.

The circus surrounding Morrison's polarising captain's pick was a stark contrast to the lead item, a showcase of unity from Labor's official launch in Perth.

Any lingering doubts that moderate Liberals might have had that Morrison was prepared to sacrifice heartland seats to harvest votes in the regions and outer suburbs with a call to the religious right were dispelled that Sunday.

MPs and campaigners smelled a rat when, on that same day, Morrison came out defiantly pledging to proceed with his religious discrimination bill in its original form, which had been defeated by his own MPs.

Morrison's team had been trying to gather together the leaders of religious communities in the seats of Parramatta, Greenway, and Reid to discuss the future of the legislation.

A letter was sent to faith leaders promising he would continue to press for passage of the bill if he won, but the meeting was never organised:

I pursued this law in good faith, putting politics aside, as I did not wish this to divide our nation,' he said in the letter. 'This is why I agreed to reasonable concessions that would protect those of faith from discrimination without impeding on the rights, freedoms, and protections of others.

Sadly, Anthony Albanese and the Labor Party prized scoring a political victory against the government as more important than achieving laws to protect Australians of religious faith against discrimination.

Labor supported amendments from members of the cross-bench that hollowed out the protections we were seeking to make law. They also used the Bill as a device to make unacceptable changes to other laws that would further undermine the ability of religious institutions, particularly religious schools, to practice their faith.

The changes Labor supported would have ultimately rolled back protections for people of faith in Australia—one step forward, three steps back. Even further detrimental amendments were proposed by the Labor Party in the Senate.

Until a consensus can be found and the issues that have been created by these amendments can be resolved, we cannot in good conscience put at risk the existing protections that currently exist for people of religious faith.

If re-elected, we will pursue passage of the Religious Discrimination Bill as stand-alone legislation in the next Parliament and will not accept any attempts to make changes to other laws that undermine protections for religious institutions.

I want to assure you that guaranteeing Australians are safe from discrimination on the basis of their faith remains a priority for me and my Government. I will also not allow this issue to be used by Labor and the Greens to undermine existing protections.

The fact that five of his own backbenchers had doomed the legislation by voting against it in the House, and that Coalition senators were also not prepared to support it, was conveniently ignored in his letter, which pinned the blame for its failure solely on Labor.

His pledge to proceed with the legislation was quickly followed by Deves' retraction of her apology for her transphobic tweets when she was conveniently doorstopped on a street in her electorate by a Sky reporter with a camera.

Morrison had for weeks used Deves' apology to deflect questions and to excuse her repugnant assertions. He defended her retraction of that apology the next day, at a press conference that included an uncomfortable-looking Natalie Ward, the New South Wales minister for metropolitan roads, women's safety, and the prevention of domestic and sexual violence.

Morrison even supported the substance of Deves' claims about surgical mutilations. Journalists corrected him both on medical and legal facts before Morrison ended the press conference as journalists tried to ask Ward about Deves.

According to one well-connected Liberal, Deves' Sky interview recanting her apology was set up deliberately to revive the issue with the prime minister, knowing he would be asked about it at his press conference the next morning. Which he was.

Morrison's office denied it was set up by them, and also said the office was not involved in her campaign, saying that Morrison had spoken to her on Tuesday to remind her 'of the need to show sensitivity around this issue'.

Yet he endorsed her without qualification. 'I am absolutely pleased that I've been able to recruit and we've been able to appoint strong female Liberal candidates that won't just run with the pack when it comes to issues, but will actually stand up for what they believe in. That's what being a Liberal is all about,' he said.

Not everyone agreed. 'Hateful and hurtful,' was how one Liberal described it at the time, fearing for the future of the party if Frydenberg lost his seat.

Liberals from Warringah later described it as a 'hideous debacle' and 'a corruption of processes', even going so far as to accuse Morrison of treasonous behaviour. None of it would have happened if Morrison had allowed the proper processes to be followed.

Even if Buncle had not won the seat, the vote would not have been driven further down, into the teens, in booths once considered rock-solid Liberal.

Towards the end of 2021, when it appeared that Buncle would be the only nomination, Finkelstein had advised Warringah Liberals that she was 'acceptable' to the prime minister, that he had no problem with her candidacy.

A campaign committee and strategy was put together for her. It was an elaborate plan with a designated campaign chair, a campaign director, and a committee representing all interests in the branches. A fundraising plan was put in place, and Frydenberg was locked in for the campaign launch to be held just after Australia Day 2022.

Buncle was prepared to put her legal practice on hold to campaign fully from January to May. Dates had been lined up for chambers of commerce in Manly and Mosman to invite Buncle and Zali Stegall to debate issues of national and local concern. Warringah Liberals were confident that Buncle would trounce her opponent.

But soon after the locals had settled on Buncle, it emerged that Morrison was trying to get Berejiklian to run. Morrison had earlier tried to get another former premier, Mike Baird, to run. Baird was not interested, then it was made known that Morrison was courting Berejiklian, whom he had taken to describing as a dear friend—which didn't fool anybody, including her. Given the tense relationship between them, Frydenberg was acting as the go-between.

In November 2021, Frydenberg spoke to Berejiklian a number of times, encouraging her to run, saying she was needed federally and would add heft to the government. She told him and others that she would think seriously about it. She also reassured him that she had no leadership ambitions.

Berejiklian probably would have won the seat. She still had enormous respect from people in New South Wales for her leadership during the fires, and then the pandemic, but the Independent Commission Against Corruption had not yet resolved her situation, and she felt a bit burned by politics.

To a few interested onlookers, it seemed to have the air of a charade around it, that Morrison had needed another distraction. Everybody played along with it, pretending it was a serious option when it wasn't.

By the New Year, when Warringah remained unresolved, Buncle was worried. According to locals, Deves was 'waiting in the wings'.

Buncle resisted attempts by friends and members of the state executive to run as a captain's pick—with the backing of the New South Wales division—without a preselection. She knew the party in Warringah, and she knew the locals would not like it.

She had heard that candidates would not be chosen in the undecided seats until March or April. Buncle could not wait that long. There was a state executive meeting towards the end of January. After she learned that it had not discussed Warringah, she emailed Chris Stone on 29 January to tell him that if a timetable for preselection could not be set by close of business on Monday 31 January, she would have to withdraw.

She texted the federal director, Andrew Hirst, that same day to alert him to her email to Stone foreshadowing her withdrawal. Hirst responded on Monday morning, pleading with her to hang on for a few more days. At that point, Hirst was hopeful Warringah could be regained by the Liberal Party.

By 5.00 pm, when she had not heard back from Stone, Buncle withdrew her nomination.

One former Liberal MP described the appointment of the three-person committee of Morrison, Perrottet, and McDiven to sort out the contentious seats without preselections as 'constitutional corruption'. He said that McDiven had been a strong campaigner for greater representation of women in parliament, but that progressives were furious with her.

Morrison paid no heed to the concern of the locals, nor to the likely reaction to Deves' more offensive remarks. Having embraced Deves, having taken credit for choosing her, Morrison was determined that she would stay in the race and that her views, poisonous as they were in inner-urban areas, and as unpersuasive as they turned out to be elsewhere, would be at the forefront at key points.

Moderate Liberals believed that Morrison was driven by a concern that the religious right was giving up on him. In January, the head of the Australian Christian Lobby, Martin Iles, had complained on Instagram that expelling Novak Djokovic was a political tactic, something a dictatorship would do, and warned that: 'This may be the moment the Morrison Government has finally broken my last sliver of grudging support.' "But we are not as bad as the other lot" is now a hard sell.'

The ACL campaigned against Liberals in key seats, including Reid and Bass. As well as fielding complaints from moderate Liberals, campaign headquarters was getting calls from branch members saying that Morrison should go in harder on the transgender issues.

It was an insight into the great divide that may yet consume the Liberal Party.

Deves was another nail in the coffin for moderate Liberals. They reckon that, ultimately, it cost Jason Falinski his seat in Mackellar, which is ironic, given that he backed her preselection, then backed her during the election campaign. Falinski told people later that she was not a factor in his defeat.

Deves became a symbol of everything that had gone wrong with the Liberals under Morrison. It was intolerant, it was removed from the everyday concerns of voters—whether in the leafy inner suburbs or in the west—and it smelled of a wedge or a lure.

Frydenberg, who had publicly condemned Deves, would later reflect that it seemed to be bound up with the toxic relationship between Morrison and the New South Wales branch, and with senior members of the state government.

Frydenberg had passed on the concern of colleagues to Morrison when the controversy first broke around Deves; however, at that stage, he did not press for Deves' disendorsement. In his view, that would have only pushed the story along. He should have known she would keep talking and that Morrison would keep promoting her.

'It was an ugly episode in the Liberal Party,' he said later. 'What happened in New South Wales was to our huge detriment.'

Morrison was poison in so many places. He could not physically set foot in any of the seats challenged by the Teal independents. All references to and photos of him were removed from campaign material.

The Liberal logo was buried in those seats and others like them, including Kooyong, Boothby, and Higgins, then from everywhere in New South Wales. The only photos of him that appeared were negative ones produced by his opponents.

He visited Kooyong once, during Passover, when he went to a synagogue with Frydenberg. The photos said it all. Morrison was hugging Frydenberg for dear life, as if his life depended on it. Which, in a way, it did. Maybe he was hoping that some of Frydenberg's popularity would rub off on him. It actually worked in reverse. Morrison dragged Frydenberg down.

According to colleagues, during the leadership troubles of 2018, Morrison had also sought to capitalise on Frydenberg's popularity internally by asking him to run on a ticket with him. Frydenberg refused.

Frydenberg asserted that Morrison was supported on issues such as Deves because he was prime minister, not because his position was right.

'I supported him because he was the prime minister and the leader of the Liberal Party,' he told people.

Subsequently, there was no evidence indicating that the strategy with Deves had worked as Morrison had hoped. The inner-urban seats were lost, and none were gained. In a state where, the year before, Liberals could rattle off 10 possible gains, including Gilmore (where former state minister Andrew Constance was running), plus Parramatta, plus Dobell, they did not pick up a single seat.

A poll conducted by the Redbridge group on 20–21 April in the western-suburbs seat of Parramatta found that the issue of most concern to voters was the cost of living at 22.6 per cent, followed by the economy at 18.2 per cent, and climate change at 15.9 per cent. The last thing on their minds was transgender participation in women's sport, which registered at 0.8 per cent.

Redbridge strategy and campaign director, Kos Samaras, says that Deves' candidacy was 'all downside for the Coalition'.

There was a more than 6 per cent drop in the primary vote of the Liberal candidate, Maria Kovacic, in Parramatta, and while Labor's star recruit Andrew Charlton registered a swing against him on primaries of more than 4 per cent, his two-party-preferred vote was a 1 per cent improvement on 2019.

It prompted gay Liberals to question whether the driving force behind Morrison's support for Deves was, in fact, a deep-seated aversion to the LGBTIQ community.

Frydenberg was not the only one asking later: 'What was that all about?'

The former deputy state director, of the Victorian Liberals, Tony Barry, who also worked for Redbridge, predicted during the campaign that Morrison's strategy of sacrificing the Liberal heartland, including Frydenberg, to court the religious right would mark him either as a genius or as political roadkill.

'In the end, he wasn't just political roadkill—they reversed back over the body and drove over it again,' Barry told me after the election.

Deves' subsequent claim that she had only suffered a small swing compared to Liberals in Teal seats left moderate Liberals spluttering. Firstly, the adverse swing she recorded was on top of the two swings that had already been recorded against one of her most vocal supporters, the former prime minister, Tony Abbott, who had delivered Warringah in 2019 to independent Zali Steggall.

In 2022, Steggall won the seat by a margin of more than 17,000 votes. On first preferences, she scored 45.2 per cent to Deves' 33.9 per cent. Her final vote after preferences was 60.8 per cent. On top of Abbott's 2019 loss of 13.3 per cent in 2016, Deves lost another 5.6 per cent—so the Liberal Party's vote in a once-heartland seat had dropped by 18.9 per cent.

Faring even worse than Abbott, Deves lost every single booth in the electorate. In one booth at the Manly village school, where the prices of homes begin around $5 million, Deves received 24 per cent of the vote. In another, her vote dropped 13 per cent to just 10 per cent.

There had been $250,000 to begin with in the kitty, and with a decent candidate, Liberals believed they would have been able to double that during the campaign, and that they would have beaten Steggall. Deves did a fundraiser with Abbott that raised between $30,000 and $40,000.

Liberals from Warringah fanned out to other electorates, including Hughes, where Craig Kelly, who had been used ruthlessly by Abbott to destroy Turnbull's prime ministership, had deserted to run as leader of Clive Palmer's United Australia Party.

When volunteers arrived to help run the campaign of moderate Jenny Ware—whom Morrison had not wanted as the Hughes candidate—there was $92 in the kitty. Kelly had even taken with him the A-frames used to prop up posters.

Facing a stiff challenge from an independent, and suffering an almost 10 per cent swing against her on primaries, Ware nevertheless won the seat with a two-party-preferred swing against the Liberal Party of less than 3 per cent. Kelly, 'the future prime minister of Australia', got less than 5 per cent of the primary vote.

In North Sydney, just about every Liberal booth worker on election day reported that multiples of people going in to vote were refusing to take the Zimmerman how-to-vote card, saying: 'Trent's a nice guy' or 'Trent's a good member', before adding: 'But I just can't vote for Morrison.' Some of the booth workers were reduced to tears.

Zimmerman would later tell people that the combination of Deves and the shambolic preselection process was 'calamitous'.

After the election, efforts were made to drag others into what had been a debacle created and orchestrated almost entirely by Morrison. They accused Kean of having texted a journalist to ask Natalie Ward questions at the press conference with Morrison in order to embarrass Morrison — something, really, that he needed no help with — and Andrew Bragg of commissioning polling separate from Crosby Textor, which the prime minister's office reckoned was wrong, and had only succeeded in 'confusing' the candidates.

Kean had engaged in what he says was 'light-hearted banter' with Ten Network's Stela Todorovic by direct-tweeting her after she had chased Deves into the lift at the Sunday rally. They continued direct-tweeting, including on 10 May, the day that Morrison defended Deves for retracting her apology. Unwisely, Kean suggested that Todorovic 'pap' Ward [photograph her like a paparazzo would]. Todorovic responded that they had tried, but Morrison had closed down the press conference.

This exchange actually occurred after the event, while Todorovic was on the press bus.

That night, Andrew Carswell contacted Kean's press secretary,

Sean Berry, to tell him they had photos of the tweets between Kean and Todorovic. Yaron Finkelstein contacted Kean himself to tell him they had the photos. Kean asked what they were doing taking photos of journalists' phones.

Journalists said later that they suspected the prime minister's official photographer had been instructed to get photos of journalists' phones at Morrison's press conferences. Carswell later denied this.

However, one journalist noticed that Morrison's photographer appeared to be aiming his camera lens at Todorovic's phone during a press conference about a week before in Western Australia. This female journalist challenged him immediately. He denied that was what he was doing, but she was concerned enough to warn Todorovic of her suspicions.

There was a moment on the press bus after the press conference with Ward when Todorovic's phone was exposed. It happened to be when staff from the prime minister's office were boarding.

As if by magic, the communications between Kean and Todorovic made their way into a Sharri Markson news story in *The Australian*. It was clearly briefed by Morrison's staff, prompting suspicions that Todorovic had either shown the tweets to the prime minister's office, or someone else had taken a screen shot and given it to the office, or Kean had released them or showed them to someone who released them.

Todorovic, who sits in the tough-but-fair category of reporter, not afraid to take on all sides, flatly denies that she showed the text messages to the prime minister's office. Or anyone else. 'Absolutely not,' she said. Kean also denied he had passed them on.

Bragg remains unrepentant about having commissioned separate research, dismissing allegations he had muddied the waters.

Others were clear about the reasons for the debacle.

Former senator Chris Puplick told the Warringah electorate's first local conference meeting after the election: 'I really didn't believe that even the Liberal Party in its current chronic, leaderless state could find a candidate for Warringah more toxic than Tony.'

Birmingham believes that Morrison was helped to victory in 2019 by the resolution of the same-sex marriage problem. Labor had tried and failed to make his faith an issue. Three years on, according to Birmingham's analysis, the religious discrimination bill and the transgender issue made Australians, particularly in inner-urban areas, question the government's motives.

They became a distraction, and also made people look askew at the government.

'They reinforced concerns about whether we were respectfully tolerant of equality,' Birmingham told me.

'This time around, if people had lingering doubts, there were issues they could attach to those doubts.'

Sharma believed that Morrison's choice of Deves was driven by ideological conviction. He couldn't believe it had been driven by a hunt for votes, because there weren't any in it for the government.

He never saw any evidence anywhere after the election that Deves had helped in any electorate, including in western Sydney. But she had certainly damaged them.

In late June, at a meeting of the Balgowlah-Fairlight branch in Warringah, a motion was moved by the branch president, Andrew Morrison SC, seconded by Jane Buncle, condemning both the federal and state executives of the Liberal Party for not having allowed a proper preselection to occur.

The motion, which did not mention Deves or Morrison by name, said that branch members had been deprived of the right to choose their candidate because of the manipulation and intervention of the federal executive.

It said that, as a result, there was a record low turnout in Warringah, there was no candidate who represented the Warringah federal electorate conference, and the primary vote of 33 per cent was the second election in a row to record a drop for the Liberal Party.

One woman at the meeting, who said she had been a member for 45 years, burst into tears when she spoke of the number of people who had told her they could never vote Liberal again after what happened.

Deves attended that meeting. She was furious. She accused senior Liberals and moderates of 'coming after' her, of spreading misinformation and lies about her, and of ruining her reputation.

At the subsequent Warringah federal electorate conference meeting on 18 July, the motion passed unanimously. There was a lot of anger directed at Alex Hawke as a substitute for Morrison.

Deves did not attend that meeting. She said later that she had been on a skiing holiday with her family and had broken her shoulder. However, Deves had also been forewarned by the Warringah federal electorate conference president, Lee Furlong, that the meeting would get fiery, and that it might be better if she wasn't there. She was seen as fragile. He was worried about how she would react.

On election night, after one booth came in at 6.30 showing a crash in the primary vote down into the teens, Furlong, who had lost friends during the campaign, was the one who had to tell Deves that she had not won, that she would have to ring Steggall to concede, then go out to tell her 'victory' party that she had lost. She burst into tears. She was said to be almost hysterical.

She had become convinced during the campaign that she was going to win. She refused to concede, saying she wanted Frydenberg or Falinski to concede before she did. Furlong appealed to Abbott for help.

Abbott sat with her in a private room to try to calm her down. He told her that in 2019, as the former prime minister, he had lost to Steggall. He had to call his opponent to concede and to congratulate her, and then he had to do it all over again in front of nine cameras. Deves would only have to face one.

Asked later if she regretted running for the seat, Deves said: 'Not at all. It was an amazing experience, upsetting at times, given the behaviour of some journalists and Liberal politicians, but no regrets.'

And would she like to run for Warringah next time or for the Senate? 'Yes, but only if preselected, which was my preference at the last election.'

She said that her positions had proven to be correct. Deves cited the International Swimming Federation's issuing of guidelines for women's swimming; the closing of Tavistock's GIDS clinic in the UK; and the apology from SBS for their 'misreporting and decontextualising of my claim that over half of males in the UK male prison estate with gender identities were convicted sex offenders. This is a fact upheld by the UK Ministry of Justice.'

On 20 August 2022, Deves addressed the annual general meeting of the South Australian Liberal Women's Council. More than 200 people attended. Held after the twin debacles of the state election and the federal election, it was seen as part of a wider push to force the Liberal Party further to the right. Moderate Liberals accused arch-conservative senator Alex Antic of signing up Pentecostals and anti-vaxxers in an attempt to gain control of the South Australian state executive.

Seasoned Liberals worried that the party had an 'end of days' feel about it.

CHAPTER THIRTEEN

The Best of Days, the Worst of Days

The first day of the election campaign was the worst for Anthony Albanese—the worst of the campaign, and the worst in his political life. Not knowing the unemployment rate of 4 per cent, and the Reserve Bank's cash rate of 0.1 per cent, fitted perfectly with the Morrison government's narrative against Albanese. All its advertising and its messaging was designed to show that Albanese was not up to the job, that only the Coalition could be trusted to run the economy, that he was inexperienced, that he had never held an economic portfolio.

And there he was, in response to tricky but nonetheless legitimate questions from the media, apparently not even knowing the most basic, the most often-repeated, economic statistics. Labor staff, strategists, and frontbenchers felt their hearts sink to their stomachs. A few dropped f-bombs as they watched the live broadcast or the repeats. At that moment, a couple of them genuinely thought they were going to lose the election, or that the best they could hope for was a hung parliament.

Whatever Albanese imagined would happen in that first week

was shattered by the demoralising reality. He had succeeded in taking Morrison to the brink of destruction, only to then fall into a black hole himself.

This was stuff he already had in his head that he talked about all the time with his colleagues and advisers, that he heard every day, so there hadn't been any real need to check beforehand if he was across it.

Something else was different that day: the media. Sometimes only a couple of journos would turn up for his media conferences, so they would often be perfunctory or rambling. Not that day in Launceston.

Whatever cockiness or complacency he may have felt beforehand, that first day knocked it out of him. If there was any good news for him at all that Monday, that was it. It awakened him to the reality of the campaign and to the dangers that lay ahead.

He had to smarten up, or he was going to lose. It was that simple. No one had to tell him. He knew, as they all knew, that he had fix to it, then rally—or else. None of them dropped their bundles. After absorbing the shock, they knuckled down to the task.

In politics as in life, when all else fails, black humour can work. A few days later, his chief of staff, Tim Gartrell, recalled boxer Mike Tyson's famous quote that 'Everyone has a plan until they get punched in the mouth.' Gartrell and everyone else had to trust that the punch would bring out Albanese's inner street fighter.

That Monday also happened to be Paul Erickson's first day at campaign headquarters in Sydney after he had contracted Covid. He had not fully recovered, but his period of isolation was over, and there was no time to waste. He walked in just as Albanese began his doorstop.

Albanese was shattered. He kept saying over and over that he had 'let people down'. For days afterwards, he looked like he hadn't slept. Probably because he hadn't. Thanks to the saturation coverage over succeeding days, the story registered with voters. Those who liked him blamed the journos. Those who were unsure about him had their reservations confirmed.

To the surprise of many, the Liberals did not rush out a TV advertisement in response. Partly, the Liberals felt their job had been done for them with the wall-to-wall coverage on every news bulletin, plus the unflattering still photos, all highlighting Albanese's gaffes.

The Liberals' campaign team decided that the exchanges with the journos could not be easily condensed to 15-second or 30-second TV spots, which were very expensive anyway, so they forgot about free-to-air TV, concentrating instead on longer-form ads on social media. Apart from the gaffes giving Liberal campaign headquarters a morale boost, their focus groups showed what Labor's showed: Albanese's stumbles had fed the doubts about him.

With Albanese that day was his shadow finance minister, Katy Gallagher, who was also one of Labor's designated campaign spokespersons. She wasn't even supposed to be there with him. It was meant to be the health spokesman, Mark Butler, but Butler had caught Covid and was still in isolation.

Gallagher got along well with Albanese. They had bonded after she had to resign from the Senate during all the citizenship brouhahas in 2018. He had rung her when she was in tears, sitting by Lake Burley Griffin, thinking her career was finished. He wanted to make sure she was okay.

She liked him because he was a fighter who literally had to fight for everything he got from the time he was a child until the time he became leader, and because he was able to forge genuine relationships with people.

Gallagher had been told only a couple of days before Morrison called the election that she would have to spend that first week with Albanese. Gallagher was an attractive politician, competent and empathetic. She had served as chief minister in the Australian Capital Territory before entering the Senate, but never liked campaigns very much. She describes herself as a control freak, and if there was one thing about campaigns, it was that there was always so much that was outside your control.

So there she was on the Sunday afternoon, after Morrison had called the election, as the sole passenger on the RAAF VIP aircraft made available for the opposition leader, heading to Sydney from Fairbairn in Canberra to pick up Albanese and his team. They boarded, then flew straight to Launceston to position for his announcement the next morning.

They were all excited and apprehensive, feeling the full gamut of turbulent emotions that came with finally getting going with an end date in sight. Around six o'clock the next morning, Gallagher went for a walk. It was chilly and sunny, something like the weather in her own hometown of Canberra. She felt okay.

Albanese did interviews with every breakfast TV show, and Gallagher did a couple as well, before Albanese was scheduled to announce a funding package to help hearing-impaired children.

As she approached the location of the doorstop and saw the waiting press pack, Gallagher thought to herself that she would have been petrified if she had been the one to have to face them. She was picking up a different vibe from the pack, too. It wasn't the usual relaxed atmosphere there was in Canberra. She could tell the journos were edgy.

She stood a few steps away from Albanese, off to the side, listening. Albanese was expecting a question on unemployment, on the comparative rates between what the previous Labor government and the Morrison government had achieved. That wasn't what he was asked. Instead, he got a question on the Tasmanian unemployment rate, then on the national unemployment rate, then on the Reserve Bank's cash rate.

Fair enough if he didn't know the Tasmanian number, but he couldn't say what the national rate was, or recall the cash rate. Unlike the feral behaviour by some journalists that followed later in the campaign, these were basic, legitimate questions. He should have been able to spit out the answers.

Gallagher was wishing someone would wrap up the press conference by yelling out 'Last question', but she knew that was impossible. It just kept going.

She knew that Albanese knew the numbers, because she and shadow treasurer Jim Chalmers had discussed them with him any number of times before. He had simply, inexplicably, gone blank.

Talking among themselves, the journos debated asking Gallagher the same questions. A couple of them thought that would be unfair; however, Jonathon Lea from Sky persisted, and asked Albanese if they could question Gallagher. He said of course. If she had answered incorrectly, or didn't know either figure, it would be game over for Labor's campaign.

If the ground had opened before her and swallowed her up at that moment, Gallagher says she would have been grateful. In the few seconds it took her to walk slowly to the microphone, she played different scenarios through her head about how she might respond, asking herself whether she should give the wrong answer, too, so she didn't show up the leader. In the end, she decided, correctly, to play it straight, to give the answer and get out.

Gallagher answered plainly: 'The Reserve Bank current rate is 0.1. And the unemployment rate is at 4 per cent.'

With the media conference over, Albanese was distraught. He knew how damaging his brain snap was for himself and for the campaign generally. He had stuffed up badly. Over and over, he kept saying: 'I have let everybody down.' He spent most of the one-hour-and-15-minute drive from Launceston to Devonport on the phone.

His shadow ministers, his advisers—including Gartrell, who had been watching the media conference from his hotel room in Launceston and Erickson—all gave him the same piece of advice. *Fix it, and fix it as quickly as possible. Fess up, apologise, and move on.* He didn't need convincing; he knew exactly what he had to do.

One of Morrison's big mistakes was to never own up when he got something wrong. Albanese and those around him were determined not to copy that, at least, and did what they could to make a virtue out of a disaster.

One of his closest colleagues, Tony Burke, was still recuperating from a bad bout of Covid. After a staffer texted to tell him about the media conference, he watched it online, realised it was a major problem, and knew how disappointed Albanese would be in himself. Burke had no voice, and could not speak to offer him moral support, so he texted him. Burke recovered in time to be more helpful in the second week.

Penny Wong didn't call Albanese on that first day. She knew he would be beating up on himself, but in a funny kind of way thought they might look back on it not as the day he lost the election, but as the day he won it. Knowing him as well as she did, she was confident he would steel himself for the days ahead, front up to the press pack, and concentrate on his debate preparation.

Kristina Keneally called Katy Gallagher, one of her Senate 'sisters', to see how she was bearing up. Gallagher was in turmoil. She tried to call Jim Chalmers. Chalmers had not seen the conference live, as he was on the phone waiting to do a radio interview. His press secretary, Brett Mason, walked in and waved at him to turn on

Julie Bishop in December 2019 after news broke that the prime minister was holidaying in Hawaii while Australia burned. Addressing New South Wales Liberal moderates from a balcony, in what attendees described as a 'stunning' white dress, Bishop 'happily' remarked about Morrison: 'The further from the fires, the easier the solution.' *Photo supplied.*

ABOVE: Scott Morrison in Hawaii posing for a selfie with other Australian tourists. Bushfires were raging back home, but Morrison told colleagues before he left he had promised the family a holiday, somewhere they wouldn't be pestered for selfies. Morrison flew there secretly, and then was compelled to return. His decision to go and his immortal words on his return, 'I don't hold a hose, mate', effectively destroyed his prime ministership.

LEFT: Almost every poster of Scott Morrison outside polling booths was negative, put out by his opponents, including this one in the seat of North Sydney, won by independent Kylea Tink. Not even Stuart Robert would display a poster of Morrison during the campaign. The only ones Robert used at booths in his electorate were of himself. *Photo supplied.*

RIGHT: Scott Morrison with state and territory leaders taking selfies before dinner at Kirribilli House on 12 March 2020. It would be the last meeting of the Council of Australian Governments, the night before the formation of the national cabinet to handle Covid-19. *Photo supplied.*

BELOW: As the leaders were having drinks outside, two massive cruise liners, one of them the *Spectrum of the Seas*, which can carry more than 4,000 passengers, sailed past. 'There go some floating petri dishes,' Morrison joked to his guests. A week later, the *Ruby Princess* docked in Sydney, 2,700 passengers were allowed to disembark without testing, and 28 later died. *Photo supplied.*

LEFT: Frydenberg and Morrison heading out to do the rounds of breakfast TV on 7 October, the morning after the 2020 budget, which revealed a budget deficit of a staggering $213.7 billion, thanks to Covid spending. Despite the storm, Frydenberg managed to keep his umbrella up. *Photo © Alex Ellinghausen/Fairfax Media/MEAA.*

ABOVE: Scott Morrison's unpopularity was used remorselessly against Liberals in their blue-ribbon seats, including in Kooyong, held by the treasurer, Josh Frydenberg. Internal polling in September 2021 showed that Frydenberg's approval rating in his seat was plus 15. By April the following year, a month out from the election, it was still positive, but barely — it had slipped to plus four. In September, Morrison had a net approval rating of minus 18 in Kooyong, and by April it had more than doubled to minus 38. *Photo © Kym Smith/Newspix.*

ABOVE: Scott Morrison hugging Josh Frydenberg as if his life depended on it. Which it did. *Photo © Jason Edwards/Newspix.*

ABOVE: Josh Frydenberg and Monique Ryan in their one and only debate during the epic battle for Kooyong. Ryan said later if he had wiped the floor with her, it would have been over. She thought if she could hold her own, that would be a victory. She held her own. *Photo supplied.*

LEFT: When Adam Bandt delivered one of the three or four most cut-through moments of the election campaign on 13 April, telling a cheeky journalist with a gotcha question at the National Press Club to 'Google it, mate', thousands followed the advice. On election day, the Greens were the most Googled party. The fifth-most-asked question on the search engine that day was how to vote for the Greens. *Photo© Julian Meehan.*

BELOW: Bulldozer: Days before the election, Morrison promised no more bulldozer. Not long after, he crash tackled eight-year-old Luca Fauvette at the Devonport Strikers Football Club in Tasmania. It was one silly stunt too many. Albanese's chief of staff, Tim Gartrell, says it 'sealed the deal' with voters. Three days later, Australians bulldozed him and the Liberal Party. *Photo © Mick Tsikas/AAP images.*

ABOVE: 12.15 am in the boardroom of the Canterbury-Hurlstone Park RSL Club after Anthony Albanese delivered his victory speech, with two of the people who helped make it happen — Labor's national secretary Paul Erickson (left) and Albanese's chief of staff, Tim Gartrell (right). *Photo supplied.*

RIGHT: Six days after the election, as acting immigration minister, and with the full blessing and authority of Anthony Albanese, Jim Chalmers announced the Murugappan family — Nades, his wife, Priya, and their daughters, Kopika and Tharnicaa — would be removed from detention and allowed to return to Biloela after five years in detention. They travelled to Gladstone to personally thank the new prime minister. *Photo supplied.*

The first photo of a very relaxed prime minister-elect Anthony Albanese in ugg boots and footy jumper, with his great friend Penny Wong on the couch at his Marrickville home on election night. The photo was taken just after Scott Morrison rang him to concede defeat. *Photo supplied.*

the television, using sign language to indicate that something really bad had happened. Chalmers turned it on, but couldn't tell what had gone wrong. Fortunately, the interviewer about to question him didn't know either. Chalmers' phone was immediately flooded with messages. When the interview was over, the first person he rang was Gallagher, who is probably his best mate in parliament.

She was worried she had done the wrong thing by showing up the boss. Chalmers reassured her she had done exactly the right thing, told her not to worry, then rang Albanese. Chalmers sought to comfort him, and then, like the others, told him to use it to make a point of difference with Morrison: to own the mistake and apologise for it.

Gallagher, who had promised herself before she set off on the trail that she would have a dry campaign, downed a glass of white wine at the end of that day. She said later that she suffered PTSD for weeks afterwards.

Keneally also texted Albanese, saying he should 'shake it off', reassuring him that everybody made mistakes and that he needed to fix it. While some believed that it had happened because Albanese was cocky, or complacent, and that he needed the journos to slap him around a bit so he could get his head straight, Keneally had a different theory.

Two years of Covid with little to say, except to support the government or urge everyone to follow the medical advice, had left him out of practice. He had grown unused to handling hostile or tricky questions from the media. He would bowl up, deliver his lines to the few journos who bothered to turn up, and then clear off.

Little did she know that her text would trigger a tune for Albanese, the former DJ with an encyclopaedic knowledge of pop music, to use at his doorstop the next day when journalists asked if he had less chance of winning the election 'today than two days ago'.

Albanese repeated that he had made a mistake and had confessed to it. 'From time to time, if ever I make a mistake, I'll own it. And I'll accept responsibility,' he said.

'But as I quoted The Ramones on day one of the campaign, so here's a Taylor Swift comment for you. My theory is, shake it off.'

That day shook him out of his complacency, but it also affected his confidence. It wasn't the only mistake he made that week. He wrongly stated that the Parliamentary Budget Office had costed his policy on emergency-care centres. The PBO demanded a retraction, which Gallagher had to deliver, but Albanese had to confront it himself again with the media on Good Friday.

There was another muck-up on boats policy, when he wrongly said that Labor supported temporary protection visas, when in fact it was going to abolish them. It was raining heavily during that doorstop, and he complained later that he hadn't heard the full question. He thought he was being asked if he supported boat turnbacks.

The first mistake was a brain snap. After a bit of concerted framing from Labor, people understood how that could happen; he had apologised quickly, people were nodding, saying it was the media, and anyway, Morrison never admitted to any mistakes. For some, it made a good contrast between the two of them.

There was a dip in the tracking poll after that first day. The encouraging aspect, though, was that the focus groups didn't just hear the mistake; they heard him take responsibility for it, too. But the blunders fed into the coverage and the media pack's behaviour all that week.

Labor had a conference call every morning to plan tactics for the day, and usually another at the end of the week to take stock, to review what had happened and to look ahead. On those calls was Albanese, the leadership group — including Marles, Wong, and Keneally — plus Gallagher, Clare, Chalmers, and Butler. Also on the calls were Gartrell, Erickson, and other campaign staff.

There was a hook-up on the first Sunday, after the week of saturation coverage of unforced errors. By then, there had been a slight change in the focus-group feedback. According to one person familiar with it: 'People started to go, "Oh, is he up to it?" They weren't writing him off; they were asking the question.'

The group decided, partly as a form of inoculation, to kickstart the negative advertising a week earlier than they had planned. Bookings for ads had already been made in expectation of a 14 May election, so they pressed the button to begin the ads on the Thursday after the first debate, and before anyone knew that Albanese had Covid.

The devastating ad, using Morrison's own words — 'It's not my job' — ran in every capital city (except Canberra) and regional television market. It ran as heavily as the Liberals had run their negative ad in 2019 warning about Shorten being the bill that Australians could not afford.

Labor had worked out that the best ads — the most effective, the most potent — were the ones that quoted Morrison himself, such as him protesting repeatedly (14 times) that it wasn't his job, that it wasn't a race, and that he didn't hold a hose. His political suicide notes.

His words played into peoples' main gripes about him: he nicked off to Hawaii during the fires; he had failed on vaccines; and he politicised Covid by criticising the states.

Jim Chalmers also appeared more frequently at news conferences with Albanese. It was a dangerous period. Labor strategists said at the time that the election was 'still there for the taking'. Liberals sniffed the possibility of a hung parliament.

More mistakes would completely unravel his campaign and destroy any chance of victory. It was as serious as that. Everything was riding on the first debate, which had already been locked in — a people's forum in Brisbane on 20 April organised by Sky, with 100 undecided voters.

Albanese knew that his early near-death experience meant he was never going to be allowed to skate through the campaign, that another mistake could prove fatal, and that he had to win the debate outright. Not being Morrison was not enough.

The person who helped make sure that Albanese performed, who was charged with running the debate rehearsals, was Katie Connolly, who had joined Albanese's staff a year before.

Connolly, an Australian from Queensland, had spent 16 years in the US and worked as an online journalist for the BBC, where she covered John McCain's ill-fated campaign against Barack Obama in 2008. She then branched out as a consultant, working for the Democrats, including Obama, Hillary Clinton, and presidential aspirant Pete Buttigieg. She moved back to Australia with her New York born husband and two children during Covid.

Albanese has Murray Watt to thank for finding — or rediscovering — Connolly. Watt had recruited her for Young Labor when she was a 17-year-old student at the University of Queensland. He had maintained casual contact with her during her time in the US, so was familiar with her career achievements. She and her sister, Julie, caught up with Watt for a coffee when she migrated back. He knew there was an opening in Albanese's office, and thought she would fit in well there. He asked her if she was interested in working in Albanese's office in the strategic-communications role. She told him she was, so he put her in touch with Tim Gartrell.

She signed up for what she thought would be a four-month gig. There were high expectations of an early election; then, when that didn't happen, she stayed on.

Connolly's colleagues have been lavish in their praise of her work and her temperament, which in politics is as vital as talent. She was described as ultra-smart, calm, understated. She understood the party hierarchy. She was focussed and humble. She stayed out of the limelight, much preferring to operate under the radar. Few people even knew she was there.

Her preparation for the debates was regarded by everyone involved as the best and most thorough they had seen. And it showed in Albanese's debate performances. Albanese was judged to have won all three.

Regardless of how many people — or how few — watched them, the debates infected coverage for days after. Just as in the US, debates have become a critical part of the fabric of Australian elections. No leader would dare squib them. They can change perceptions or embed them. If they are uneventful, they might not change a vote. But there is always the potential that they might, particularly if one of the leaders makes a mistake.

Albanese understood that completely, and, given her experience in the US with the presidential debates, Connolly was exactly the right person to help him prepare.

The preparations began early, before the election was called, sketching out what the likely issues would be, what the formats would be, and how they would be conducted. Debates were different from media conferences, from parliamentary Question Time, from every other kind of television interview or media performance.

They had their own character and rhythm. They were an opportunity for the leader to have an extended conversation with the audience, and for the audience to draw a comparison with the other leader. In many ways, the moderator didn't matter, and nor did the questions, although it was important not to fumble the answers. It was the highest political performance art, with piercing pressure on the two participants.

Connolly watched tapes of the 2019 debates between Morrison and Bill Shorten. Although Shorten was judged at the time to have won, she could see that Morrison was a very good debater, on message with impressive discipline. Despite the fact that he was prime minister, he acted like an insurgent, with a clear understanding of his mission. He took everything back to his central arguments that things were going well under him and that Labor couldn't be trusted. He would talk in a way that made him the stand-in for ordinary Australians. He would include people in the conversation by saying that Australians understood this or knew that, or they agreed with him on the point he was making.

He would begin with assertive statements, sounding confident and informed. He was good. He could not be underestimated. It was imperative that they not allow him to occupy the arena.

Albanese didn't need convincing about the importance of the debates. He was conscientious, took on board all of the advice, and didn't lose his cool when he was corrected.

They had a bit of a trial run with the shadow treasurer, Jim Chalmers, playing Morrison, in March at the Commonwealth Parliamentary Offices (CPO) in Sydney. Connolly and Kristina Keneally put Chalmers and Albanese through their paces. Obviously, the economy was the key issue.

Chalmers knew his stuff backwards, and knew Morrison's lines backwards, too. His select audience was knocked out by his performance. It was uncanny how Chalmers morphed into

Morrison, down to the heavy-footed walk, with a bit of a sway, his hand in his pocket.

Everyone was pleased with the way the first trial had gone. They went home drawing up plans for the next meeting. That night, Senator Kimberley Kitching died suddenly of a heart attack, aged 52.

The extraordinary aftermath, which featured largely baseless and tasteless accusations against Wong, Keneally, and Gallagher, in particular, but also against Albanese and Marles, consumed the media, the Labor Party, and the prime minister and his government, who paid glowing tributes to Kitching while they levelled claims of bullying by their opponents against her.

It was impossible to set aside time for more debate prep. The South Australian election on 19 March wiped out Stephen Marshall and his party, there was a memorial service for Kitching on 21 March, and the federal budget was on 29 March. In his budget-reply speech on 31 March, Albanese pledged an extra $2.5 billion for aged care. On 10 April, Morrison announced the election for 21 May.

If they had set aside more time, maybe they might have avoided what happened on the first day on 11 April. When he was opposition leader, his allies would say that Albanese hated prepping because he thought it robbed him of his authenticity. His critics would say if it was a subject he wasn't interested in, he couldn't be bothered.

That changed after the end of his horrible week, with the first debate looming and so much riding on it. Between then and the third and final debate on 8 May, practice sessions became a priority—in their hotels, in the Sydney CPO, on the plane, and at his home in Marrickville.

Preparation began in earnest after Albanese arrived in Cairns on

Saturday 16 April. He had to reset. He had to reintroduce himself to people. It had to be a comeback story because, hey, who doesn't love a comeback story?

Albanese and his team — Gartrell, press secretary Liz Fitch, Connolly, and Chalmers — gathered in a meeting room at the Crystalbrook hotel in Cairns. The economy was obviously going to be important. Connolly listed around 10 of the most difficult questions she thought he might be asked or criticisms that Morrison might make: Labor taxed too much; Labor spent too much; Albanese was too inexperienced, he had never held an economic portfolio, he was each-way Albo.

Chalmers was fully across Morrison's mannerisms and arguments. Connolly had set them all homework to do, had sent them video clips to watch and notes to read. Morrison would dismiss accusations as Canberra-bubble stuff; he would reference Jenny, or what quiet Australians said at the football, about the issues that really mattered.

The first debate would be more free form than usual, with no standing at lecterns. The two leaders would have a live audience, and would interact.

That was why Chalmers was both aggressive and offensive, standing in front of Albanese, insulting and belittling him, challenging his lack of experience and economic expertise.

'He used all those BS alpha male moves from Morrison,' one of them said later. Chalmers found it weird and unsettling to get into the Morrison character, to attack his boss, and then to have to step out of the role.

Tony Burke would critique Albanese's performance, and former foreign minister Stephen Smith would make suggestions on improved responses. Connolly and Fitch alternated as moderators. Keneally was in isolation with Covid.

They decided that if Morrison moved into his space during the debate, Albanese would tell him to back off; he was not going to talk to him, he was going to talk to the audience. Asking to not be interrupted could make him sound weak. Nor was he going to copy Bill Shorten's line from 2019 when he called Morrison a 'space invader'.

Albanese had to look and sound strong. There could be no whingeing or complaining. There were lines that were used as anchor points, such as 'Going missing' or 'It's not my job', but Burke saw little point in trying to get him to memorise lines or be too rehearsed. 'The lines need to come from him,' he said. Whatever he said had to sound like him or be like him.

It was incredibly tough, but Albanese never complained, never lost his cool. They could see that Connolly's aim was to 'let Albo be Albo', but also to put a structure around his thinking.

There was no need for Albanese to labour the point about Morrison's unpopularity. Everybody was well aware of it, so Albanese's job was to grab those who didn't like the prime minister but were unsure about him, to present himself in a positive way, to show what drove him and what he would do to deliver that better future. He had to make the case for himself rather than against Morrison; to talk about the future, not the past. He was prepared to say: 'I want the job, and I am ready to do the job.'

They put a lot of work into the opening statement. Wong and Burke offered advice, helping workshop his remarks. It was important that Albanese felt comfortable with the opening, because once he got through that, he could ease into the remaining hour. He had to speak directly to the people in the room and those watching at home.

They discussed what Albanese would call Morrison. If he called him 'prime minister', Morrison might respond by calling him

'Anthony', and that would not be good. They would not be on a level playing field.

They continued rehearsing for a couple of hours a day after they flew to Brisbane for the debate, which would be moderated by Kieran Gilbert and would feature questions from 100 undecided voters.

When they arrived in the green room before it began, they were relieved to see Marles there. While the others had spent days criticising Albanese, or beating up on him, Marles was the friendly, conspicuously supportive face he needed to see. Marles sat in the room for the debate, and occasionally Albanese would look across to him for reassurance.

Albanese performed better than Morrison. Despite the preparation, or maybe as a result of it having lifted his confidence, he came across as natural, whereas Morrison seemed contrived. Morrison dived straight into his spiel, with no foreplay, whereas Albanese was more affable, thanking everyone, including 'Scott', for having come along. It sounded friendly enough, but it put them on an equal footing. Morrison then had to acknowledge 'Anthony'.

There were a number of interesting moments during the debate. In response to a question from the mother of an autistic child, Morrison said that he and Jenny were 'blessed' with their kids. He was trying to empathise, but didn't quite make it.

The audience audibly groaned after Morrison sought to politicise national security by implying that Labor was weak on China. This was a big hint to cut out the wedging and game playing. People were sick of it.

'People saw it for what it was. It was a "reds under the beds" style campaign, and it smacked of desperation,' Albanese said later.

Hint number two: they were sick of the dodgem games that Morrison was playing on the establishment of an integrity commission — calling ICAC a kangaroo court, looking like he was avoiding scrutiny, or seeking to blame Labor for the fact that he had failed to even introduce his own legislation.

There were three questions from the audience that went to the issue of trust in government. At that point, it was obvious it was no fringe issue, and that Morrison had been wrong to treat it like one, just as he was wrong to try to blame Labor for preventing him from legislating an anti-corruption commission.

Albanese was judged the winner by 40 votes to 35, with the rest undecided. That was another big hint.

The next day, Albanese was diagnosed with Covid, and was taken out of the campaign. It was a logistical nightmare for his campaign team, but it would have gone very badly for him if he had lost that debate. It's not hard to imagine the calls it would have prompted for him to be kept in isolation.

He bounced back after a week, and then flew to Perth for Labor's official launch on 1 May. Albanese rightly judged the west — where they hoped to pick up Pearce, Hasluck, and Swan — to be critical for Labor's prospects. Labor even managed to keep the location of the launch secret until invitations went out a fortnight before the due date.

Before the start of the campaign, Albanese had also caught the red-eye special from Sydney to land in Perth after midnight on 3 March as soon as the state's borders reopened so that he could resume campaigning in Pearce and Hasluck.

Launching in Perth was a masterstroke. It went without a hitch. The reaction to the event itself, to Albanese and to his policies, was as good as could be expected.

Albanese had first floated the idea of launching there just after Easter 2021. At that stage, Labor was contemplating the four possible federal election periods that theoretically were open to Morrison — the first in August–September 2021, before the COP26 conference in Glasgow; the second at the end of 2021; then in March 2022; and finally in May 2022.

Albanese raised Perth with Erickson during a meeting at his electorate office in Marrickville the day after the nation's technical advisory group on immunisation changed its advice on the AstraZeneca vaccine and recommended that under-50s take Pfizer instead.

He had good reasons to head west. In the Western Australia state election held a month before, McGowan had wiped out the Liberals, securing a primary vote of 59.9 per cent and an extraordinary two-party-preferred vote of 69.7 per cent. He remained incredibly popular.

Albanese wanted the launch to be early in the campaign. He also figured that if it was in a place where there had not been a launch for a long time, it would have a big impact, unlike in a capital city on the eastern seaboard, where it might not even get noticed.

Labor had never launched a federal election campaign in Perth in modern times. John Curtin had delivered his policy speeches for the 1937 and 1940 elections from Western Australia, but they were broadcast around the country on radio.

Campaign staff worked out scenarios to cover the next 12 months, each one launching in Perth, whether for an election in September, November–December 2021, or March or May 2022.

For instance, during the Delta outbreak, they figured that if Morrison had called a late November/early December election after New South Wales passed the 80 per cent double-dosed vaccination threshold, Albanese would have quarantined in Canberra for a fortnight at the end of October, campaigned remotely from his hotel room, flown to Perth, launched the campaign, and then travelled through every state and territory in blocks of a few days each until election day.

Because Labor's special platform conference in March was a combination of Zoom and in-person, and because of all the remote work that Covid had imposed, they were confident they could pull it off. They paid close attention to the Canadian election in August and September 2021, which occurred in the middle of their Delta outbreak, where both sides did a lot of remote campaigning.

The launch came at the end of the week that Albanese had spent in isolation, when Morrison had been in full focus, and when Albanese's shadow ministers had capitalised adroitly on events such as the China-Solomon Islands security deal and the 5.1 per cent jump in inflation.

The second debate was held a week later, on 8 May, hosted by the Nine Network, with Sarah Abo as moderator and three journalists — Chris Uhlmann from Nine, Deb Knight from 2GB, and David Crowe from *The Sydney Morning Herald* and *The Age* — asking the questions.

Albanese's team rehearsed before that as well. Keneally helped draft the questions and acted as moderator. Keneally had presented a TV show, and she had dealt with the media for years as a New South Wales premier and then senator. She garnered high praise from her colleagues later, because she predicted almost every question the three journalists asked.

'She was fantastic,' one of the key participants said.

There was also another actor in one of the lead roles. Chalmers had engagements elsewhere, so another of Labor's stars of the campaign, Jason Clare, played Morrison. Clare had done his homework, too. He had the expected questions, and he read Morrison's transcripts to help formulate his answers.

He leaned heavily on Morrison's remarks at his media conference after visiting the governor-general to call the election — the one where he framed his narrative for the campaign.

'This election is about you, no one else. It's about our country, and it's about its future. And, above all, this election, as all elections are, this election is a choice,' Morrison said. 'It's a choice between a strong economy and a Labor opposition that would weaken it.' Morrison's spiel was well framed and persuasive.

Clare, who knew Morrison well, figured that Morrison would be more aggressive in this debate than in the first one, that he would construct his opening and his answers around choice. Clare was brilliant in the role.

They knew this debate would be different. They knew that Nine would want to ginger things up. They figured that Morrison would want to be more assertive this time, to either draw Albanese into a fight — which would mean they both got covered in mud — or to make Albanese look weak if he didn't fight back.

Albanese had to go into the debate with backbone, showing he was not going to be pushed around. It was a character test.

The format and the stage set was engineered for a clash. The two leaders would stand quite close to one another, with the moderator to the side, slightly behind them. From there, it would be impossible for her to moderate anything. That seemed to be the point.

Albanese and his team did their preparation in the Sydney CPO. Nine had told them how it would be staged, so they fashioned a mock set. Keneally stood where Abo would be, with Albanese and Clare at the lecterns. Clare took it up aggressively to Albanese, to prepare him for what lay ahead. But he couldn't go full-bore Morrison. It was Mothers' Day, coming up to the anniversary of the death of Albanese's mother, and Albanese was feeling a bit tender.

They would pause if it became too intense, or after Albanese gave his responses, and then either Burke, Clare, or Keneally would offer their critiques and suggestions of how he might do better.

The Nine debate turned into a slugfest. Morrison was in full flight, at one stage stretching his arm out and turning his palm to Abo, in a clear sign to the moderator to be quiet and butt out. Liberal campaign strategists winced. He had gone too far. Instead of looking strong, he was way too aggressive. He looked and sounded like a bully. Rather than come across as puny, Albanese retaliated.

He landed a blow in the final stages with a question to Morrison, when he asked him why he had said the vaccination rollout was not a race. 'It was a race, Anthony,' Morrison conceded, getting dangerously close to admitting he had made a mistake, before swerving rapidly to add: 'We shouldn't have said that.' Not I. We. Meaning, of course, that Brendan Murphy started it.

Nine's voting system was curious, but Albanese appeared to win that one as well. In the end, it mattered little what either of them said that night; the story was the fight. Importantly, no one cast Albanese as the loser.

Labor figures reckoned that one of Albanese's best moments of the campaign came when he was asked about wage increases at a doorstop on 10 May, the day before the third debate.

'Just back to wages. You said you don't want people to go backwards. Does that mean you would support a wage hike of at least 5.1 per cent just to keep up with inflation?' the ABC's Tom Lowery asked.

Albanese, who has been known to use six words when one will do, responded with one: 'Absolutely.'

No one was more surprised by his answer than the journos. It took them a while to process, because Albanese had been dancing around the issue—although, to be fair, no one had asked the question as precisely as Lowery just had. He had been thinking about how to frame it while on the press bus on the way to the event, after having listened to Albanese that morning talking with Patricia Karvelas on Radio National.

Karvelas pressed Albanese to say whether he backed the ACTU's slightly higher claim for a 5.5 per cent increase. He hedged, sticking to his formula that he did not want people to go backwards.

Albanese was already planning to back a wage increase, and he had discussed Labor's approach with Burke and Chalmers. They had essentially agreed that Labor would come out publicly for it; the only question was when, but most likely it would be later that week.

When the question came, rather than continuing to hedge or dodge, or qualify his answer, as he had before, Albanese went with it. 'It was a completely instinctive moment, from complete conviction,' Burke told me later, declaring it as 'the turning point of the campaign'.

It was a rare moment on several levels. It was spontaneous, it was unqualified, and it set up a key point of difference with the government. Albanese had ensured that the campaign focus would stay on the economy, and that Morrison would have to respond to him. With one word, Labor had dragged Morrison into a fight on Labor's territory.

It was a decisive day, probably his best in the campaign.

Chalmers said at the time that if Labor won the election, that moment, with that one word, and two other events — the Reserve Bank increasing the cash rate by 0.25 per cent after inflation shot up to 5.1 per cent, and Morrison promising he would stop being a bulldozer — would prove to have been decisive.

The next day, Morrison derided Albanese's answer, and ridiculed him as a 'loose unit'. Morrison argued that the way to get wages up was to get unemployment down and to ensure that businesses could perform strongly.

'Now, what we saw from Anthony Albanese yesterday was reckless, was incredibly reckless. We all want to see wages go up. And indeed the Reserve Bank governor has made it very clear that we are seeing wages starting to go up,' he said. He went on:

> But the way you engage in economic policy is not in the loose way we saw from Anthony Albanese yesterday. Anthony Albanese is a loose unit on the economy. We saw that right at the start of the campaign. He didn't know what unemployment was. He didn't know what the cash rate was. He said his policies are costed, but they're not costed. And when it comes to what he said yesterday, ill-thought-through, not understanding the potential consequences of what he was saying. I mean, yesterday, in what he said yesterday, it's like throwing fuel on the fire of rising interest rates and rising costs of living.

With Frydenberg locked in the fight of his political life in Kooyong, Morrison, a former treasurer, was largely flying solo in the economic debate. Albanese struck out on his own, but he had Chalmers and Gallagher as backup.

Although the release of the March-quarter figures showing the huge 5.1 per cent increase in inflation switched the debate to the cost of living and to wages, Albanese's commitment still needed to be boiled down, to reduce it to its simplest level so that Albanese's promise would continue to register with ordinary Australians.

Connolly had been wondering what her American friend David Axelrod, the master Democrat strategist, would have done in this situation. Then she had a lightbulb moment. She texted press secretary Liz Fitch to ask her how she thought it would go if Albanese referred to the wage rise he was supporting as a $1-an-hour increase, rather than using the percentage figure all the time. Fitch liked it, and so did Albanese.

He came up with the idea of holding up a dollar coin to reinforce the point. The picture was just what was needed to tell the story. 'It was pure genius,' Chalmers would later tell people.

Who could possibly object to the lowest-paid people in the land, doing the toughest jobs, getting a $1-an-hour increase? As it turned out, Morrison did. Albanese kept holding up his dollar coin for the cameras, and Morrison kept sounding like he was opposed to a pay increase, not only for the poorest workers, but for the ones who had helped get Australia through the pandemic.

It played out that way in the third and final debate on the Seven Network on 11 May, a much more civilised affair, with Mark Riley as the moderator and chief inquisitor. Selected punters in pubs awarded it to Albanese.

Journalists had tested Albanese every day during the campaign. That was fair enough, as with Lowery's question and the questions Albanese was asked on the first day about the economy. However, a few journalists crossed the line, particularly on the day Albanese was asked to name the six elements of the National Disability Insurance Scheme package. The questioning was feral, hysterical. Reporters had cameras trained on themselves and on him, making themselves the story, desperate for a notch on the belt. It infected the coverage, all designed to make Albanese appear that he wasn't across his stuff.

On another occasion, they made it look as if he had stormed away from questioning, by following him with cameras when a lengthy press conference had ended without them getting the answer they wanted.

Campaign strategists later claimed their research showed that the savage NDIS press conference had worked in Albanese's favour. 'During Covid, people got to see through the daily press conferences how the media operated, and they were shocked at how rude and how belligerent some of them were,' one said.

Albanese did not complain; instead, he took a tougher line in the dying days of the campaign, choosing who could ask questions and telling them firmly when to back off.

Mark McGowan, who witnessed some of the behaviour, cut loose afterwards, accusing members of the federal parliamentary press gallery of insulting, bullying, and unethical behaviour, the kind that would get them sacked in the workplace.

'I have never seen anything like it,' McGowan said.

Importantly, however, Albanese did not drop his bundle after he had mucked up so badly on that first day. He showed his determination and his resilience. He kept his cool under pressure. He had also surrounded himself with smart people in his office and on his frontbench, and he was smart enough to take their advice.

Morrison had left his launch late. Again. He needed to do something to get the story off wages and on to something else. But, again, he made it all about himself.

The daggy dad was gone, Scotty from marketing had passed his use-by date, and his bully-boy tactics had worn thin.

His efforts to empathise had often missed the mark, whether in response to Brittany Higgins' rape allegations or when confronted by a mother with an autistic child.

He was weakened or exposed on almost every front. He had begun by wearing his unpopularity as a badge of honour, pleading with people to set aside their feelings and to vote for him anyway, as if their dislike was ephemeral, unrelated to his trustworthiness or competence.

Morrison had started the campaign telling people, including those whose votes he was courting, that they mightn't like him, but at least he got things done. It wasn't working.

Andrew Hirst and others in Morrison's office, including Carswell, had workshopped a possible recasting of that narrative, suggesting different ways and wording that he could use to explain how he would change from a Covid style of governing to a more normal style. The idea sounded good in theory, but of course there was no way to control its execution once he stood in front of the cameras.

He went about it like a bulldozer. Literally. No one had suggested that word to him — it was all his own work. In the interview in January with Deborah Snow in *The Sydney Morning Herald* and *The Age*, the one where he had said he wasn't interested in leaving a legacy, he had described himself as 'a bit of a bulldozer'.

Morrison decided to recycle it on 13 May.

'Over the last three years, and particularly the last two, what Australians have needed from me going through this pandemic has been strength and resilience,' he said.

'Now, I admit that hasn't enabled Australians to see a lot of other gears in the way I work.

'And I know Australians know that I can be a bit of a bulldozer when it comes to issues.

'But over the last few years that's been pretty important, to ensure we've been able to get through some of the most important things that we've had to do and land some really big security agreements.'

He promised he could change: 'I know there are things that are going to have to change with the way I do things.'

Albanese had a brilliant cut-through response to this for voters: 'If you want change, change the government.'

At this point, Chalmers was confident that Labor was going to win, telling people that Morrison playing that gambit was a last roll of the dice for him. He believed that it showed 'their polling is worse than ours'.

Morrison couldn't believe everyone was latching onto 'bulldozer'. It wasn't like he hadn't said it before.

As always, timing and context are everything. Unfortunately for Morrison, he not only could not adequately explain what he meant, but when journalists asked him if that meant he would stop lying—or words to that effect—he said they had misunderstood what he was trying to say.

Then, to the delight of a few and the mortification of many, he offered visual proof of what he meant by 'bulldozer'. He had his very own Mark Latham moment, when Latham gripped John Howard's hand so viciously to shake it in the 2004 campaign that he reminded voters at a critical time of everything they didn't like about him.

Three days out from the election, on Wednesday 18 May, Morrison crash-tackled eight-year-old Luca Fauvette at the Devonport Strikers Football Club in Tasmania. He tried to say later that he had come off worse than the little boy, because he had tried to cushion the boy's fall.

Much as he might have tried to do that, as the awful realisation of what he had done penetrated in that split second, young Luca's head could be seen bouncing off the ground. A big, boofy, competitive bloke who had been using the issue of transgender women playing sport with other women as one of the centrepieces of his bid for re-election, who had promised no more bulldozing, had bulldozed a little kid into the ground.

His staff could be heard agonising over how the media would treat it. They were relieved at first that the journalists seemed to think it was funny, and were laughing. But that was a reflex response to an extraordinary moment. It wasn't funny. It was incredibly damaging, and the pictures told the story. The video went viral the moment it was posted.

It was one stupid stunt too many, on top of so many stupid ones that preceded it, like washing a woman's hair in a salon, or welding by lifting the protective mask with sparks flying, or playing the ukelele. No one had dared tell him to stop. They kept feeding his addiction for prearranged acts of self-parody.

One rare, spontaneous appearance replete with unsolicited feedback had come shortly before he called the election. It was at the Edgeworth Tavern, west of Newcastle, on Thursday 7 April, when Ray Drury, a pensioner, accosted him on a range of issues. The complete encounter was captured by the media like an X-rated version of *Candid Camera*. Drury finished up by telling the prime minister: 'You better fucking do something … I am sick of your bullshit.'

Morrison's once very good friend Stuart Robert, in an interview with Patricia Karvelas on Radio National the morning after the crash-tackle, reassured everyone that young Luca was OK.

'Poor little boy,' Robert said. 'I think he was pretty good. There was a high-five afterwards, so it was just an error from both of them.'

Of course. An error from both of them. It was Luca's fault that he had got in the way of a two-legged bulldozer.

The attempted rebranding had come very late, in the few days before his official launch, which also came late, on the final Sunday of the campaign, 15 May.

Labor strategists reckoned that in 2019, Labor had believed its own hype by effectively rerunning the 2016 campaign that Shorten had come close to winning; yet here was Morrison in 2022, thinking he could run 2019 all over again, down to having his launch late, and using it to announce a housing policy.

In 2022, the policy was to allow people to use part of their superannuation to buy a house. It was generally seen as too little, too late, but it might have helped if it had come sooner and been explained better. Tim Wilson had put it forward almost two years before, in his book *The New Social Contract*, released in 2020 and launched by Frydenberg.

As chair of the House of Representatives Standing Committee on Economics, Wilson had asked for a referral from the treasurer to allow a public inquiry to be conducted into the proposal. Frydenberg had refused, even though he was supportive of the idea. Morrison wasn't keen to take it up at that stage, and Mathias Cormann as finance minister was dead opposed to it.

However, in the run-up to the 2022 budget and the election campaign, the Expenditure Review Committee of cabinet ticked off on the super-for-housing idea. It was decided not to include it in the budget, but to wait until a few weeks later to announce it. There was some concern, particularly from Morrison, that industry superannuation funds would attack the idea. The point was to have something out there to fight for that would differentiate the government from the opposition.

The other two options ticked off by the ERC were an expansion of the cashless debit card, and allowing pensioners to earn more while still keeping their pension.

Anne Ruston, the minister for families and social services, argued that the best form of defence is offence. In Ruston's view, the answer to Labor's attack on the card was to extend it. She was convinced it was working to help people in areas where it was being trialled: in the Ceduna region of South Australia; the Goldfields and East Kimberley regions of Western Australia; the Bundaberg and Hervey Bay region; selected Cape York communities, including Doomadgee in Queensland; and in the Northern Territory.

Morrison was concerned that Bridget Archer would come out against it. Frydenberg was also reluctant to expand it. It came with a big price tag, and there was also the worry that it would add to Morrison's unpopularity.

'The leader was not seen as warm, caring, and fuzzy, so the question was whether this would add to the impression that these guys are mean and nasty,' one member of the ERC said later.

Eventually, everyone — including Peter Dutton, Dan Tehan, and Simon Birmingham — got on board. It was agreed that it would be released after the budget, again as another point of difference, and again as something else to fight for.

But that policy never saw the light of day, nor did the pension idea (one of the first policies announced by Dutton as opposition leader), which had only lukewarm support from Treasury and from Morrison himself, although Frydenberg strongly supported it, particularly after Omicron hit and triggered widespread staff shortages.

Morrison was said to be concerned that pensioners would see it as a threat rather than as a reward, that they might interpret it as the government pushing them into working longer, instead of providing them with an incentive to do it.

Treasury argued that it would cost more than it was worth in terms of its impact on work behaviour. However, it also would have appealed to the Liberals' support base.

Morrison waited until launch day — deliberately kept late, in the hope it would provide some momentum in the final week — to release the housing policy, which would have enabled first-home buyers to withdraw $50,000 from their superannuation.

There was little time left to explain it, and Labor had already stolen a march with its alternative scheme announced two weeks before to allow for up to 40 per cent equity from the government, with a minimum deposit of only 2 per cent required from eligible first-home buyers.

Until Morrison's launch, Labor had decided to match the government on economic measures. On their regular Sunday hook-up, they decided to oppose this one. They had heard whispers that the government would head down this track.

Morrison's suspicions about industry super funds opposing it were correct, and some Liberals apparently were concerned that, while the policy might have superficial appeal initially, it would not withstand scrutiny—which was another reason for the late announcement.

According to Labor's focus groups, the idea was friendless. People could not see how it would make housing more affordable. In fact, they were worried that it would push prices up. They also didn't like the idea of using superannuation, because it was meant to see them through retirement.

Liberal MPs believed otherwise. Tim Wilson said on the Victorian Liberals' chat group that night that it was 'outstanding'. The next day, there was great enthusiasm from his colleagues.

Greg Hunt, who was not running again, said he thought it was 'the best election policy I have seen'.

Jason Wood thought it was 'fabulous' and a 'game-changer'.

Katie Allen said it had neutralised key policies from Labor and UAP in one hit. 'As well as appealing to BOTH under 35 and over 55,' she wrote. 'It's genius.'

They were trying to keep each other up, but it sounded like they were clutching at straws.

By then, Frydenberg knew he was headed for defeat.

CHAPTER FOURTEEN

JoshKeeper

Josh Frydenberg's loss in Kooyong left him unable to fulfil — for the time being at least — what seemed predestined. That he would lead the Liberal Party. That he would become the first Jewish prime minister of Australia. That he would be the first prime minister from Victoria since Malcolm Fraser in 1975.

Frydenberg has not completely given up on his dream. But he has been forced to put it on hold. The day after the election, he was 'philosophical'; a few weeks later, he described himself as 'super-well'.

Frydenberg suffers the occasional glass-jaw fracture, but generally he is an ebullient, confident, optimistic kind of character. Losing his seat was probably the first serious setback of his life. Apart from the moment he realised he would never win the Australian Open tennis tournament.

The outpouring of support for him after his loss provided succour. Frydenberg prided himself on his ability to make friends across the aisle. Ed Husic, the first Muslim elected to parliament, was one of them. In a gracious move, Frydenberg rang Albanese the day after the election to congratulate him. Albanese had taken the trouble to call him during the campaign to apologise and to tell him he had ordered a photo to be removed from a Labor supporter's social media website showing Frydenberg in a Nazi uniform.

Frydenberg had been in a deadly serious contest with his shadow, Jim Chalmers, for the entire term. It had seemed certain to continue—and it may yet—with one or both eventually leading their respective parties. They were young, highly intelligent, personable, ambitious, and very good at their jobs. On a personal level, Chalmers found Frydenberg's loss jarring, never thinking he would lose his seat.

Chalmers texted him on election night to ask if he was okay, and to wish him and his family all the best. Frydenberg called him the next day. Frydenberg also rang Kristina Keneally to commiserate over her defeat in Fowler.

Peter Dutton rang him. Even though they were rivals, Dutton reckoned he still regarded Frydenberg as a friend, and considers him a big loss to the party. 'We never had a terse conversation, we are not bitter factional enemies,' he says.

Three weeks after the election, one of Frydenberg's many mentors, John Howard, called to comfort him, to tell him that, as the architect of the economic response, he had been the 'stand-out' performer in the government.

'You must come back,' Howard told him. Howard was far from alone.

It had been suggested to Frydenberg that he might run for state parliament to become premier. He wasn't interested. Or that he might bid for a Senate spot. He wasn't interested in that either.

Frydenberg was determined that if he made a comeback, it would be into the House.

It was not certain he would try to reclaim Kooyong, or try for the neighbouring seat of Higgins (where his parents live), which on the surface seems a more straightforward contest against Labor.

It's not as if that would be a parachute into a safe seat. He would be stepping across the border to another marginal that has to be reclaimed if there is to be any hope of the Coalition regaining government.

There is no doubt that Morrison's unpopularity cost Frydenberg his seat. With Morrison now eliminated, and depending on what else is happening and how Monique Ryan is going, Kooyong remains Frydenberg's most likely option, assuming there is a drift back to the Liberals—which is not guaranteed.

Josh Burns, who suffered a near-death experience in neighbouring Macnamara, and who 'discovered' Labor's winning candidate for Higgins, Michelle Ananda-Rajah, thinks that Frydenberg would struggle, even without Morrison dragging him down, to win Higgins. Burns reckons that the Liberals could run with Mother Theresa there, and they still wouldn't win if they kept their same climate change policies.

The pollster for Climate 200, which funded the Teals, Kos Samaras, believes that Frydenberg wouldn't stand a chance in Higgins. 'He would get slaughtered,' Samaras predicts. He believes that the demographics have changed so much—just as they have in the state seats—that it would be impossible for him to win.

Other Liberals tend to agree with this, and believe that if Frydenberg does run again, it has to be to reclaim Kooyong—partly because he built his brand on commitment to the electorate. Not that they think it will be easy for him to win next time, unless there is a recession that Labor mishandles, and Frydenberg can present himself as the person to help fix it.

Frydenberg says that during the campaign, many people, including a woman wearing a T-shirt supporting Monique Ryan, told him that they loved him but couldn't vote for Morrison—and, by the way, he did not lose by much.

At the party's state assembly a fortnight after the election, on Friday 3 June, Frydenberg received a standing ovation. The state director, Sam McQuestin, said in his speech that Morrison was 'a big factor' in the defeat.

Tim Wilson, who was defeated in Goldstein by former ABC journalist Zoe Daniel, also refused to take his defeat personally.

'The so-called "Teal" movement created the artifice of legitimacy through community campaigns fronted by local campaign amateurs, but cleverly hid a far more sophisticated and connected back-end operation that was closely tied to GetUp and US-linked campaign operations,' Wilson said.

'The thing that stood out about the local "Teal" campaigns was that they never targeted or mentioned the local MP.

'Instead, the local "Teal" candidate was squared up against the prime minister and deputy prime minister, which was clearly informed by research showing it was the best method to move votes and hence why there was a significant shift in all their targeted seats all at once.'

Wilson wrote about the demographic challenge facing the party in his 2020 book, *The New Social Contract: renewing the Liberal vision for Australia*. He warned at the time of a 'soft revolution at the ballot box'.

That shift on its own wasn't enough after the 2019 election to deliver the 2022 result, but he believes that the success of his campaign against the retiree tax in 2019 helped mask how far it had progressed. Morrison's deep unpopularity sped it up.

The Teals' use of integrity, climate change, and gender equity wreaked havoc in the heartland seats. Gender was added after the March for Justice protests by women, on the advice of former Liberal MP turned independent Julia Banks, then on the advisory board of Climate 200.

Her book, *Power Play: breaking through bias barriers and boys' clubs*, released in July 2021, detailing allegations of bullying against Morrison and sexually predatory behaviour by a cabinet minister, reinforced the already strong sentiments that the Morrison government was anti-women.

The night before the 2019 election, Morrison had texted Frydenberg to thank him for his hard work and for his loyalty. They had done everything they could, Morrison said; now it was in God's hands.

In 2022, he did not text him or call him until late on Saturday night, and only then to tell him he was going to concede the election. He advised Frydenberg to wait until more counting had been done in Kooyong. Maybe the pre-polls or the postals would fall his way, and he could hang on.

Perhaps Morrison was trying to offer him some hope to cling to, but it had a perfunctory air to it. Frydenberg knew it was over and that Morrison's unpopularity had smashed his vote.

Frydenberg had lost every which way. He had been led to believe by Morrison that if he won the election, he would only serve part of the next term, leaving Frydenberg as his logical successor. Frydenberg never believed for one minute that Dutton could beat him in a leadership ballot, and bristled at any suggestion that he might. He always regarded himself as the natural successor, and was encouraged by Morrison to believe that he would clear the way for him.

This was another piece of insurance taken out by Morrison. It kept Frydenberg tethered. One of the arguments running against him as Liberals despaired about Morrison was that Frydenberg was too close to Morrison, that he didn't push him hard enough on policy or seek to moderate his more extreme views.

Frydenberg had stood up to him a few times, but he never

advertised it. When Morrison tried to insist he deliver the delayed budget the day after Yom Kippur, Frydenberg refused. 'No way,' Frydenberg told him. He forced Morrison to agree to a childcare package in 2021, and he did not clear with him his speech warning of an investment freeze if the government did not adopt net-zero emissions by 2050, which played a big part in convincing wavering Nationals.

But the notion persisted that he had not done enough to separate himself or to push him harder on reform. Certainly, his enemies inside and outside the party used that against him.

Morrison deliberately played on Frydenberg's instincts to be loyal to the leader. He kept him so close that he would find it impossible to break free, encouraging him to believe he would be rewarded later for his good behaviour. Maybe he meant it. Maybe he meant it as much as Bob Hawke did when he signed the Kirribilli agreement to hand over to Paul Keating, or as much as John Howard meant it when he said he would retire when he was 64, which had kept Peter Costello hoping. Or maybe he was straight-out playing him.

Morrison's invitation to Frydenberg to stay at The Lodge with him during Covid helped Morrison and damaged Frydenberg. Frydenberg couldn't see it then, although he did later, even before he knew about Morrison's secret takeover.

'Loyal to a fault,' was how he would describe himself, and he was right. Later, he would say that if he got back, he would be different.

Before the campaign began, Frydenberg was confident he could hold on. He thought he had withstood everything that could be thrown at him in 2019 when independent Oliver Yates stripped away more than 8 per cent of his vote, and The Greens' candidate, Julian Burnside, took another 2.7 per cent.

When Cathy McGowan looked at those same figures as the Voices movement began to gear up, she had a different take. McGowan thought that Frydenberg was vulnerable. She thought that if such a disorganised effort could reduce his primary vote to 49.4 per cent, a better-organised, better-funded one could do a lot better.

This was the argument that the Kooyong Voices, including Yates, put to Monique Ryan, a paediatric neurologist at Melbourne's Royal Children's Hospital who was prepared to leave her dream job to take on Frydenberg in what looked like — to her friends, colleagues, and so-called experts — a futile mission.

Ann Capling, a professor of politics at the University of Melbourne, missed the initial Zoom meeting in February 2021 with McGowan, so she and others asked the Voices of Indi to train them in Kooyong on how to run Kitchen Table conversations. She says she always found Morrison objectionable, dating from his time at the Australian Tourism Commission. She had hoped Turnbull would do well, and was horrified when he was deposed.

They were a bit slow to get going in Kooyong, only placing their ads in *The Age* and the *Australian Financial Review* on Saturday 30 October. A friend of Ryan's sent her the ad in *The Age*, which prompted her application.

As soon as Ryan applied, the group immediately thought Ryan was the 'dark horse' they were searching for. She had submitted a 26-page CV. She was fully embedded in the community. She played hockey, and was an ocean swimmer.

Capling says now the fact that Ryan was a political novice frightened all of them to begin with, but that reservation disappeared as they got to know her. 'She was courageous, values-aligned, warm, and funny. Incapable of lying. Authentic,' Capling says.

'In her job, she had to deal with children at the end of their lives and their traumatised parents. She connects with people.'

If there was a moment that convinced Ryan she had to do it, it was when her then 12-year-old son, Patrick, was watching David Attenborough's final documentary, *A Life on Our Planet*, charting the changes to Earth since he was born in 1926, warning what could happen if humans did not change their ways.

Patrick was physically distressed. She hugged him, but she could not tell him that everything would be alright, that climate change would be fixed and that the planet would heal.

When she travelled overseas for her job, she was embarrassed by the way Australia was seen on climate change. She felt that the country's reputation had been trashed. It was not only Scott Morrison who made her mad. Marise Payne did, too.

There were other things that drove her, such as the disrespect for Grace Tame and Brittany Higgins shown by members of the government. It reached the point where she could no longer watch *Q&A* and couldn't read about politics. 'It was visceral,' she said.

During her first interview with the selection panel, she told them she was probably not the right person for the job. She admits she felt conflicted. She had a job she loved, and she thought they would look for someone better known, a Kerryn Phelps or Maxine McKew type, or somebody like Zoe Daniel, who had already been preselected in Goldstein.

Then she would look at a lot of the people already in parliament, and think how unimpressive they were.

Australia was coming out of a difficult period with Covid, which, she hastened to add, was not over yet, there was so much to be done with health and the NDIS. She had been involved in acute health care for 30 years.

'I thought, these nongs aren't going to do anything about it,'

Ryan says, freely admitting that sometimes she can be a bit full of herself.

When she told colleagues at the hospital that she was running against Frydenberg, they laughed and said they would see her back at work on 1 June.

'I said, "Possibly, probably, but someone needs to do it."'

Ryan is confident, direct, occasionally disarmingly frank, assertive, with a sharp sense of humour. Far from a programmed politician, her reflexive reactions occasionally got her into trouble.

She encountered pockets of hostility to her candidacy. After all, she was challenging the heir apparent in the seat held by the founder of the party and the longest-serving prime minister in Australian history.

Rusted-on Libs would say to her face, 'How dare you?' A man at a community forum told her she was a 'silly girl who should go back to the job you were given'. Ryan told him she wasn't a girl, she was 55, she wasn't given her job, she had earned it, she had every right to change careers if she wanted to, and that he would not have said that to Katie Allen (the sitting Liberal in neighbouring Higgins) or to a man. Take that.

Frydenberg made a tactical mistake in agreeing to debate her. She says now that if he had wiped the floor with her in their only direct contest, it would have been over. She thought if she could hold her own, that would be a victory. She held her own.

Another tactical mistake he made was to insert her elderly mother-in-law into the campaign, by revealing she had told him she was going to vote for him. Initially, it sounded like a bit of a joke; however, when he was questioned about it by Michael Rowland on ABC TV's *News Breakfast*, he doubled down instead of saying it had been a mistake, or it was regrettable, or even that it was meant to be funny.

Frydenberg was angered by the intervention of Rob Baillieu, a son of his good friend the former premier Ted, who had written an opinion piece for *The Age* revealing he was helping Ryan in Kooyong and why.

The difference was that Rob was a young adult who had volunteered, whereas Ryan's elderly, fragile mother-in-law had bumped into Frydenberg, her near neighbour, and told him she was backing him, perhaps not thinking he would use it in his campaign-launch speech.

It was a tough campaign. Frydenberg and Ryan stood a metre apart at a pre-poll booth for 11 days in freezing-cold rain. It was brutal being so close. She had her volunteers, and he would have his special guests, like Alexander Downer or Ted Baillieu or Peter Costello, helping him hand out how-to-vote cards.

'He looked like a hunted animal at the end,' she said. 'We all got PTSD after that.'

Did she feel sorry that in one night she had wiped out Frydenberg's dreams? She said she did, although not for long. Ultimately, she felt justified. She says she never regarded him as a particularly good economic manager, nor as a moderate, and that if he had been really engaged with climate change, he would have done more.

Anyway, any sympathy she and her supporters felt for him in those latter stages, because they knew by then he would either be opposition leader or lose his seat, was tempered by the trucks circling with attack ads and being called by him or his supporters a Labor stooge, or a fake independent, or an anti-Semite.

They called the giant 'Keep Josh' billboards 'JoshKeepers', a clever play on what he regards as his proudest achievement, JobKeeper.

Once they got going, it became a juggernaut.

Capling says: 'I always said that Mon was our secret weapon and that if she could meet everyone in Kooyong, she would win. She spent hundreds of hours literally on the street talking to people, doorknocking, and making phone calls.'

The objective of the Voices groups was to strip all the targeted Liberal members down to a primary vote of around 40 per cent in their seats. If they could do that, they knew they would be in with a chance. At the election, they managed to get Frydenberg's primary vote down to 42.7 per cent—and that was enough.

There were only a few thousand votes in it, Frydenberg would say to people later. He was right.

In September 2021, polling in Kooyong showed that Frydenberg's net approval rating in his seat was plus 15. By April the following year, it was still positive, but had dropped to plus four. In September, his two-party-preferred vote was 57 per cent to 43 per cent in his favour against Labor, and 59 per cent to 41 per cent against the Greens. By April, against Ryan, he was in negative territory, at 47 per cent to 53 per cent.

There were other factors running against him, including the changed demographics in his seat. A younger population had moved in, comprising more students and more renters, but the biggest negative was Morrison.

In September 2021, Morrison had a net approval rating of minus 18 in Kooyong; by April 2022, it had more than doubled to minus 38.

In neighbouring Goldstein, as measured by Redbridge, in April it was minus 9. Zoe Daniel's campaign had begun towards the end of 2021 by using Joyce as the bogeyman. By February, she had switched to using Morrison.

Zimmerman saw the same thing happen in North Sydney. The Voices' campaign began by saying that Zimmerman voted the same as Joyce, then that he did what he was told by Morrison.

Evidence of the devastating impact of the Morrison factor in Kooyong came after the election in July, when polling in state seats that covered Kooyong, in preparation for the Victorian election in November, showed that Frydenberg's approval had gone back up to plus 15.

Frydenberg devoted his life to networking, to collecting 'friends' and allies. Some of the people he collected, or stayed close to, no matter what, were not good for him, and in the end not only could not help him, but damaged him.

He aligned himself with Michael Sukkar, who faced repeated allegations of branch-stacking and of trying to bully women MPs, including Julia Banks, either into submission or out of the party. As well, there were the allegations that Sukkar was playing a double game on the leadership in 2021.

Sometimes, though, Frydenberg fell out badly with people who might have been useful or helpful—such as, fatefully, Simon Holmes à Court.

In 2018, Holmes à Court had written an article criticising the Coalition's energy policies, which Frydenberg as energy minister was running. A day later, Holmes à Court got a message from Kooyong 200, Frydenberg's fabulously successful fundraising vehicle, saying that his membership was being declined, and that he would be refunded the fees plus a four-figure donation he had made.

When Holmes à Court tackled Frydenberg about this subsequently, Frydenberg said that Kooyong 200 was only for 'unconditional supporters'. Holmes à Court's money was refunded in April 2018.

On 30 October 2018, warning of what was to follow, Holmes à Court tweeted:

oliver yates: the only way an MP will move their position is if their seat is threatened. Why do we have to have a fiscally conservative liberal who doesn't care about climate represent us federally?

Yates was readying to run against Frydenberg in 2019. He announced his candidacy in January.

In March 2019, in the run-up to the election, Holmes à Court was invited by a friend to accompany her to a meet-and-greet with Frydenberg at a local hotel. Frydenberg was working the room. He got to them, it was all hail-fellow-well-met, there was no sign of tension or aggro, and Frydenberg moved on to the next group.

But Frydenberg saw their presence as a deliberately provocative act, given that Holmes à Court was supporting Yates. Soon after Frydenberg had moved away from them, Holmes à Court and his friend were approached by the woman hosting the event, and were asked to leave. When they asked why, the woman said it was because Frydenberg had asked that they be told to leave. They did.

That night, Holmes à Court pretty much conceived Climate 200, the fundraising vehicle that in 2022 raised $13 million, helped win six seats from the Liberals, gutted the party, and thwarted Frydenberg's political career.

Frydenberg spent around $2 million trying to save his seat. His campaign team estimated that his cashed-up opponent spent at least that.

Ryan celebrated her victory with more than 1,000 volunteers in the Auburn Hotel in Hawthorn. It was the same hotel from which Holmes à Court had been ejected in 2019. He was mightily pleased to walk in through the same door from which he had been thrown out three years before.

The two men make no secret of their mutual dislike. Frydenberg says that Holmes à Court can't be trusted. Frydenberg was infuriated when reports appeared in February 2020 that Holmes à Court had sat in the gallery to observe the full bench of the Federal Court dealing with the challenge by Michael Staindl to Frydenberg's eligibility to sit in parliament. He was quoted as saying he was offering 'moral' support to Staindl.

Frydenberg also viewed that as a provocative act. And it was.

Holmes à Court responds by saying of Frydenberg: 'He is a talented politician, but a hollow man.'

Whether or not the Voices decide to contest Higgins next time with an independent candidate is not up to Holmes à Court, but it will be for him to decide which candidates to fund. He will most certainly continue to fund Ryan.

Unlike Ryan, Allegra Spender had a pretty good idea what she would be getting into. Growing up as the daughter of a politician, and the granddaughter of one, she knew how tough politics can be, so she felt some sympathy for Frydenberg and for Dave Sharma, the man she went on to beat in Wentworth.

There was also a family history involving independents.

Her grandfather, Percy, was elected to parliament in 1937, initially as an 'independent United Australia Party candidate' for the seat of Warringah, which was held by the serving defence minister. A year later, he formally joined the UAP. Prime minister Robert Menzies made him treasurer in 1940.

Spender, who says she will stay an independent and has 'no intention ever' of joining the Liberals, remembers sitting around the breakfast table with her father, John, the morning after he had lost North Sydney, the seat he had held for the Liberals for a decade, to an independent, Ted Mack, in 1990.

They tried to make the best of it, but it was heartbreaking.

She had to think long and hard about running for parliament. Initially, her father was lukewarm about the idea. He had become increasingly disillusioned with the Liberal Party, believing it had left him, rather than the other way around.

But he was conscious of the burdens that political life would place on his daughter. He worried about the personal cost, the potential public humiliations, how she would go from nothing to having to build up finances, and the challenge of finding the personnel needed to run a campaign. 'Going from zero to an army' was how she put it. He didn't want to say anything that would push her into it.

'He was really excited when I said yes,' she said. After that, it didn't take long for him to get on board.

Along with all the cheap shots from the Liberals about fakes and stooges, there were other cruel remarks, even though she had studied at Cambridge, was a businesswoman and renewable-energy expert in her own right, and had a rich history of working for the UK Treasury and volunteering in Kenya. She says that opponents mocked her as the 'superficial daughter of a fashion designer'.

In fact, Spender found great inspiration from her late mother, Carla Zampatti, one of Australia's most admired women, who had built a fashion empire and who believed 'absolutely that women should have the power to do anything'. Spender looked at the percentage of female Liberal MPs in parliament, and saw that it had barely moved in 25 years.

Climate change was the main driver for Spender's candidacy. She said that Morrison's refusal to increase the 2030 target for greenhouse-gas emissions beyond that set by Tony Abbott, and to stick with net zero by 2050, was 'the straw that broke the camel's back'. Even with that, she never believed Morrison was sincere.

Spender says that of all the sitting members, she believed

Frydenberg would be the most difficult to dislodge. When she thought about it, though, he was the treasurer and the deputy leader. He was someone with power and influence who should have used such assets to better represent the interests of his community.

She agrees with Sharma when he says there was a lot of anti-Morrison sentiment, but she believes it went beyond that to disaffection with the party and its policies.

Nick Minchin says the Liberal Party can take some heart that there wasn't a massive transfer of votes from Liberals to independents. He says there was a lot of tactical voting in those seats, pointing to the final results in Kooyong and Goldstein to back his assertion.

According to the Australian Electoral Commission, Monique Ryan received 40.4 per cent of the primary vote, the highest of any of the independents

Frydenberg received 43,736 votes and Ryan 41,303. His primary vote dropped 6.5 per cent to 42.7 per cent, while Labor's went down from 10.6 per cent to 6.9 per cent, and the Greens' crashed from 14.8 per cent to 6.3 per cent. In Goldstein, Labor dropped a massive 17.3 per cent, and the Greens 6.2 per cent. Tim Wilson's vote fell by 12.3 per cent to 40.4 per cent—almost exactly the Voice's target level.

Frydenberg agreed with those who thought that Dutton's anti-China rhetoric was too aggressive and was another contributing factor in his defeat. Liberals later claimed it cost them votes in seats such as Chisholm, Bennelong, Reid, Menzies, and Kooyong that had high populations of Chinese Australians.

According to the 2016 census, people of Chinese ancestry living in Kooyong comprised 11 per cent of the population; by the 2021 census, that figure had almost doubled to 19 per cent.

Morrison never slapped Dutton down over his rhetoric. In

fact, he matched or exceeded him. Former New South Wales Liberal president Philip Ruddock said later that the government did not make it clear enough that its remarks were directed at the communist regime in China, not at Chinese Australians, and that the failure to distinguish between the two cost the party dearly at the election.

'There was a collective responsibility. It was not done well,' he said.

Ruddock said he had picked up on the problem with Chinese Australians when he was campaigning for re-election in local government elections. He was at a booth in Epping, in the electorate of Bennelong, and noticed they were 'seriously unwilling' to engage, which was a marked change from previous occasions.

He passed this observation on to candidates in electorates with high concentrations of Chinese Australians, including Frydenberg.

Dutton later held firm.

'My concern was always to fight for our national interest,' he said. He believed that China was upset by the decision to ban the Chinese-owned Huawei from Australia's 5G telecommunications network. 'The alternative was to allow the infiltration of our telecommunications system. That was completely untenable,' Dutton said. He defended his criticisms by saying they were informed by the briefings of Australian intelligence agencies.

After the election, Liberal MPs did not press for a change in policy on China; they wanted more nuanced language and new policies on small business and tax that would draw Chinese Australians back to the party.

In the Victorian seat of Menzies, where the Teals' messaging also resonated, Chinese Australians voted strongly against Keith Wolahan, who was running for the first time to replace long-serving MP Kevin Andrews. In one booth, at the Box Hill Town

Hall, Wolahan's vote plummeted 16.7 per cent.

Picking up early on the disaffection, Wolahan's campaign team made more than 2,000 calls to Chinese Australians. They were extremely upset by the government's language, particularly the use of the expression 'drums of war', which originated with the home affairs head, Mike Pezzullo.

That, combined with Morrison's unpopularity, reduced a once-safe seat to a marginal.

Minchin, who was surprised by the level of hostility to Morrison at the booths in Queensland, where he spent two weeks handing out how-to-vote cards, accepts that Morrison's unpopularity was a big factor.

But he said the independents won't have an unpopular Coalition government to vote against next time, so their call to arms might not resonate as well. 'They did run very professional, well-orchestrated grassroots campaigns with significant on-the-ground presence, and very good digital campaigns,' Minchin said.

He is also not sure how well some of the new independents will adapt to life as MPs, having to cope with the demands of constituents to fix potholes or quieten noisy neighbours.

Other Liberal campaign strategists echoed Minchin's views that, come the next election, if the Teals haven't been seen to deliver much and the economy is tanking, voters will have second thoughts about re-electing them.

Albanese will play as tactically with the crossbenchers as Labor voters did in the electorates where they succeeded. The early unpleasantness over his cuts to their staff entitlements passed. The crossbenchers were never going to win that one, and it was a mistake for them to even try. They realised that later. They have to keep the aura that sets them apart, or even slightly above, other politicians.

They should take their lead from Ted Mack, who retired prematurely from the New South Wales parliament, and then from the federal parliament. He was making a point by not staying long enough to qualify for a parliamentary pension because he didn't want to take even more money from long-suffering taxpayers.

Albanese made sure that the Teals were included in the debate on climate change. Amendments that they had proposed were made to the bill, and the attorney-general, Mark Dreyfus, also consulted them on the National Anti-Corruption Commission.

While Cathy McGowan is right to say that you don't have to have the balance of power to have influence, or even to be seen to have influence, Albanese's challenge is to ensure that the crossbench remains relevant and therefore a continuing threat to the Liberals—but, as with the Greens, not too powerful. He needs to be seen to be consultative, conciliatory, and all the while in control.

CHAPTER FIFTEEN

Google It, Mate

On election day, it was probably not a coincidence that the Greens were the most googled party, or that the fifth-most-asked question on the search engine that day was how to vote for them.

When the party's leader, Adam Bandt, delivered one of the three or four most cut-through lines of the campaign on 13 April, telling a cheeky journalist with a gotcha question at the National Press Club to 'Google it, mate', plenty of people followed the advice. They not only googled the Greens, but they also voted for the Greens. Almost 1.8 million of them did, or 12.3 per cent—an increase of 1.9 per cent—to deliver the party's best result ever.

By the end of the campaign, when a lot of voters couldn't decide between the major parties, young people worked out that they could vote Greens or vote Teal, and get change. They could, if they wanted, get Anthony Albanese as prime minister. That was like a fringe benefit. The main objective was to be rid of Morrison.

The joint ANU poll/Comparative Study of Electoral Systems survey released after the election, which compared Australians' voting intentions between April and May 2022, as well as how people voted in the 2022 federal election compared to the 2019 election, showed that the two most critical factors in deciding the result were age and education.

The report's co-author, Professor Nicholas Biddle, said they were the two key demographics 'driving Labor's path to victory' at the ballot box. 'We found age and education were the two key areas where the Coalition government lost the most support in this year's election,' Biddle said.

The survey showed that women were less likely to have voted for the Coalition compared to men, but the biggest difference in voting patterns by gender was for the Greens, where 22.5 per cent of women voted for them compared to 16.4 per cent of men.

Young Australians were more likely to have voted for Labor, and substantially more likely to have voted for the Greens. Coalition voters tended to be older, non-Indigenous, with a low education, living outside capital cities, and with a household income that put them outside the bottom-income quintile. Labor voters tended to have high levels of education, and lived in capital cities.

Greens voters tended to be female, young, born in Australia or another English-speaking country, and without a trade qualification.

As good as the result was, and as much as the Greens sought to parlay it into a mandate later to force Labor to bend on its climate change or tax policies, their leverage was diluted by the Teals. Still, they remain as much of a threat to Labor as the Teals do now to the Liberals. And once the Teals have exhausted their run on Liberal seats, they could easily zero in on Labor.

Albanese has to smother the Greens and support the Teals so they keep the Liberals out, but not so much that they threaten him.

Labor's majority in the lower house, along with the election of the six new Teals, left the Greens with no bargaining power there. Even if that hadn't been the case, Albanese was never going to repeat Gillard's mistake of a mock marriage with Bob Brown after the 2010 election.

While the Greens—and the Coalition, thanks to the support of denialists—had profited mightily from the climate wars, a repeat of 2009, when they voted down Kevin Rudd's carbon pollution-reduction scheme, was never going to work for them a second time around.

Bandt was smart enough to know that the political climate had changed. The Greens' actions in 2009 might have kept the debate going, might have increased their membership and fired up the enthusiasm for a fight, but it led to more than a decade of missed opportunities on investment in renewables and other emission-reduction measures. Australia fell behind a lot of other countries.

Apart from the moral case for action, there would have been a serious political cost for the Greens if they had again opted for all or nothing on Labor's climate change policy. People wanted action, not conflict; something, rather than nothing. The key message from their increased vote and the success of the Teals was that people wanted a different brand of politics. Bandt knew, then managed to convince his party, that this time allowing the perfect to be the enemy of the good would damage, not enhance, their reputation.

It was a strategic decision, neither surrender nor retreat. It was an advance. Everybody won. As he put it when he announced the decision at another Press Club appearance the day before the Greens voted for Labor's bill in the House on 4 August 2022, it was round one. Bandt, sounding more pragmatist than ideologue, said that one of the lessons he had learned from 2009 was that 'everyone has to give a bit'.

Bandt is determined to build on the Greens' election result, which was more than a protest vote that all happened on one day thanks to his one line, as good as it was. The planning and activity that went into delivering three seats in the House of Representatives, making it four in the lower house, including Bandt's, and another three senators, taking the party's representation in the upper house to 12, was meticulous and slightly mindboggling. It was a mixture of old-style politics with a clever use of social media, including TikTok and Instagram, featuring characters from *The Simpsons*, *The Lion King*, and a giant green Shrek straddling Parliament House.

The planning had started well before. When the Queensland state election ended on 31 October 2020 with the Greens picking up South Brisbane to give them two seats in the middle of a Labor landslide win, they did not pack up, feel satisfied, and go home to rest. They kept going, working on the federal seats they had targeted.

Take what happened in the seat of Griffith, which the Greens snatched from Labor in 2022. Bandt reckons they doorknocked every single house in the electorate. Greens supporters delivered care packages to houses where families were struggling during Covid lockdowns. Not only that, but some of the food in the packages they provided was grown in a community garden they had established in a park that they had saved from destruction by blocking a road that would have destroyed it.

After the floods in greater Brisbane, Greens volunteers turned up at houses to help people move their furniture or rip up their carpets, often days before council workers arrived.

'They took politics from monologue to dialogue,' Bandt says of his supporters. 'They had thousands of meaningful conversations with people.'

The Greens had targeted nine seats: Richmond, Griffith, Ryan, Brisbane, Higgins, Kooyong, Macnamara, Wills, and Canberra (five held by Labor, and four held by the Liberals). They picked up three—Ryan and Brisbane from the Liberals (which Labor had been hoping it might snatch), and Griffiths from Labor—almost got Macnamara, and put up a strong showing in Higgins.

As the emergency services shadow minister, a portfolio he carried into government, Queensland Senator Murray Watt had run hard against Morrison during the March 2022 floods in New South Wales and Queensland, with accusations he was late declaring an emergency for Queensland and that he provided more money for the Coalition-held seat of Page in New South Wales than for the Labor-held one of Richmond.

Watt believed that if Teals candidates had run in Ryan and Brisbane, they, and not the Greens, would have picked them up. But there was no distinctive Queensland campaign by Labor to match the one that paid such huge dividends in Western Australia. At the next election, Watt would like to see a tailor-made Queensland-centric campaign, as there was in the west. He believes that, given the number of seats now made marginal there, Labor will have a better chance of picking them up.

That will depend on the level of resources amassed by Labor to defend what it has, whether its performance stays centrist enough on the economy to appeal to conservative voters, and whether it can craft a campaign for Queensland that won't conflict with the campaign elsewhere.

Bandt says it's a myth that Queenslanders are inherently conservative. He reckons that they understand politics is broken, and that they responded to the Greens' progressive economic alternative, combined with more ambitious action to address climate change. Plus an effective ground campaign.

Greens volunteers knocked on 260,000 doors across the country, and made 6,000 phone calls. They had an estimated 78,000 'meaningful interactions', roughly half of them in Queensland. The party received financial contributions from 40,000 individual donors, an increase of 22 per cent on the previous election. It also benefited from 20,000 volunteers helping out, an increase of 36 per cent on 2019, and 12,000 volunteers turned out on election day.

In many ways, it is the same formula as the Voices'. Thousands of committed volunteers, deep community engagement, lots of doorknocking, lots of inventive social media, and a policy patter suited to the jaded, targeted electorates. Climate, equality, integrity. Tax the rich, and spend the money on health, or education, or the aged.

Bandt welcomes the arrival of the independents, and the building up of grassroots community movements, but says the Greens got there first. 'We have been doing it for years,' he says.

He says that in two other Labor seats — Macnamara in Victoria and Richmond in New South Wales — the Greens went very close, but didn't get over the line 'this time'. He will announce target seats ahead of the next election. He sees what happened in 2022 as just the beginning if the major parties don't take the hint.

Josh Burns concedes that the Greens ran a smart campaign in his seat of Macnamara. They did not run on an anti-Labor platform; they did not say they did not want a Labor government. Their pitch was that Labor should be pushed harder on issues that the Greens cared about, while pointing out that their preferences would go to Labor.

Burns says it was a brutal national campaign, exemplified by the cage fight that was the second debate between the two major party leaders. He said that Albanese was right not to take a backward step, but that it left people feeling bruised.

'After Covid, they wanted collaboration, not confrontation,' he said, which he claimed Albanese understood, and was behaving accordingly as prime minister. Bandt was a 'little less humble,' he thought.

'The Greens had a good election,' Burns said. 'But we won 77 seats.'

To hang on in 2025, Burns has to hope that Albanese succeeds, and that he can match the Greens and the Teals with boots on the ground and clever social media.

It was Bandt who kickstarted the campaign to try to force Labor to forgo the stage-three tax cuts, scheduled for 2024–25 at a cost to the budget of $243 billion over ten years, which he said in our interview would only help billionaires like Clive Palmer.

Bandt also wasn't impressed with the austerity message coming out of the government in the early stages. He could afford to be. He wanted the money saved spent on things like free dental care. He argued that any concerns about broken promises would—or should—be outweighed by what was better for the country.

He struck a chord with that. Others, including economic commentators and independent MPs, joined the push for Labor to abandon its promise. The package as passed creates a flat tax rate of 30 cents in the dollar for anyone earning between $40,000 and $200,000 a year. Obviously, the higher the income, the bigger the cut. For a while, it looked like an irresistible force had met a moveable object.

Initially, Albanese left himself some wriggle room when he was asked to guarantee that the tax cuts would be delivered. Alert to the risks, he waited to see if there was a groundswell and where it would lead. He soon shut down the debate, affirming that there was no change in Labor's policy.

Bandt believes that the increase in the Greens' vote was more than just a protest against Morrison, combined with a hesitation about Labor. He sees it as a much more positive reaction to what the Greens were offering. Which, of course, he would.

He was shaping up for another fight over who had the more

legitimate mandate, particularly on emissions levels and which sectors would be quarantined from having to meet targets.

The Greens argue that their vote gives them leverage, which it obviously does in the Senate. To get legislation passed, Labor needs all the Greens plus the ACT independent David Pocock. Or the Coalition.

Before Bandt managed to get his party room to agree to Labor's target of a 43 per cent reduction of greenhouse-gas emissions by 2030, Albanese was puzzled by the Greens' refusal to acknowledge that they had been wrong in 2009, but, as he pointed out before parliament resumed, 'We don't need to legislate.'

In any case, he thought they would be making a big mistake if they opposed Labor's plan. Albanese held firm in refusing to make any concessions in return for the Greens' support in the House of Representatives, while accepting minor amendments from the Teals.

He had rightly assessed that Australians were fed up with climate wars, which he described as the 'most fractious and divisive issue' over the previous decade. He thought that, by the time of the next election, most people would conclude that what Labor was proposing was a lot better than nothing, and that the Liberals and the Greens would pay electorally if they did not compromise.

'It depends whether, of course, they're about what they perceive as their political interests, or whether they're about outcomes,' he said.

'And the danger for them is if people see that they are opportunistic and not seizing the chance that is there to be constructive. I'm hopeful that they will. We'll wait and see. But my job isn't to give advice to the other political parties. My job is to lead the government in the right direction. I believe if we get the policy outcomes right, the politics will look after itself, and that people want to see governments working together constructively.'

CHAPTER SIXTEEN

Team Albanese

Almost a year before the election, Anthony Albanese decided he wanted Jason Clare to be one of the two people who would speak for Labor during the campaign. The other was Katy Gallagher. Gallagher had been chief minister in the Australian Capital Territory, she knew her finance portfolio backwards, she was a solid media performer, and she was highly regarded—indeed loved—by most of her colleagues.

Clare was surprised when Albanese called him. It was August 2021, he was at a vaccination hub, and his wife was about to give birth to their second child, Atticus. He knew it would be a tough job. But if the leader calls and asks you to do something, in Clare's opinion, you say yes.

Albanese always had a high opinion of both Gallagher and Clare. They were allies, and he trusted them. He knew that Canberra-based Gallagher would be able to handle press gallery media and that her finance portfolio enabled her to be across almost every issue. He wanted to give Clare plenty of time to think about how he would approach the task, as well as to be briefed on areas outside his own portfolio.

Clare had always been one of Labor's quiet achievers, but it wasn't until he took on the campaign-spokesman role that he turned into a rock star. His regular media conferences and his appearances on breakfast television, sometimes to mop up problems, were faultless. Before the campaign, the only time he got up at 3.00 am was to give Atticus his bottle.

He had been in parliament since 2007, elected to Paul Keating's old seat of Blaxland. He had a Keating poster from 1993, with one word, 'Leadership', signed, framed, and ready to hang in his ministerial office when we spoke. He wasn't dropping hints.

Clare's name would feature occasionally in stories about who could possibly one day become Labor leader, but he was never that way inclined. He never had a killer streak. 'No ambition,' was what one of his colleagues said with a sigh.

Thoroughly likeable, handsome, and smart, with a good sense of humour, Clare just got on with his day job in opposition before rising during the Rudd–Gillard years from parliamentary secretary to cabinet minister. Curiously, he formed a friendship with Scott Morrison, also elected to parliament at the same time. They did a regular panel together on Sky, where they got to know one another.

One day, Morrison asked him what he thought about them joining up to take teenagers from their electorates to Papua New Guinea to walk the Kokoda Track. It was a couple of years after the infamous Cronulla riots, and Morrison thought it would be helpful for kids from different environments to get to know one another in a place that held great meaning in Australia's history.

Clare thought it was a great idea.

Morrison gathered four lifesavers from his electorate of Cook, and Clare brought along four Muslim teenagers from Blaxland. It was the most gruelling experience. Two people had died on the track shortly before. Two members of their team — one of them Morrison's staffer — had to be choppered out. They did

100 kilometres in six and a half days. Their guide, Charlie Lynn, a former vet, and a Liberal member of the New South Wales Legislative Council, had set a cracking pace because he needed to get back to parliament, so the pressure took its toll.

Clare was younger and fitter than Morrison, but he couldn't get over how determined Morrison was. Relentless and driven was how Morrison was described by another person on the trek.

With his glasses fogging up from the humidity, perspiring profusely from the effort, repeatedly snapping his trekking poles from the force with which they hit the ground, Morrison would keep going regardless. He was also occasionally emotional. He wept as he recounted details of the death of one of his constituents in Afghanistan. He seemed, to others, obsessed with the Anzac mythology and all things khaki and military.

Morrison would also engage in the discussions between the teenagers. One of Clare's group became the first Muslim woman to complete the trek wearing a hijab. Morrison's group was full of questions about the difference between hijabs and burkhas, and about what happened at mosques. It soon became clear, through those conversations, how big a part religion played in his life.

From where Clare stood, however, determination was Morrison's defining characteristic. His determination to finish the trek to get to the top of the mountain. And to the top of the Liberal Party.

Clare knew that Morrison would make it as leader because of the way he went about making it through that first expedition. The only surprise to Clare was that Morrison got to the leadership sooner than he thought he would. He gives Morrison credit for winning the 2019 election with the help of his 'creation' of the daggy-dad persona.

In all their dealings over the years, with two more treks together—the second in Sandakan, and the third back in PNG on the Black Cat track—Clare never encountered the daggy dad. He marvels at how well it worked.

Their friendship did not extend to lunches or dinners, or to socialising outside of the excursions. They would meet to sort out the logistics of the treks, but not much more than that. They were both conscious of the suspicions that a wider association would arouse from their colleagues. As it was, Morrison complained that Abbott had chipped him about his dealings with Clare.

However, the close contact provided valuable insights into Morrison's character. It helped Clare step into the role of Morrison in debate preparations for Albanese. He knew, for instance, that Morrison would react instinctively to the release of Labor's housing policy at its official launch by opposing it. More importantly, Clare remembered what Morrison had said before about similar schemes.

The release of high CPI figures and the Reserve Bank's impending interest-rate increase had reinforced the inclusion in Labor's launch on 1 May of a shared-equity scheme to help low-income earners buy houses. As the relevant shadow minister, Clare had worked on the policy for a year.

Although similar schemes were operating in Western Australia and Victoria, Morrison panned it, just as Clare knew he would. As well as coming up with reams of quotes from Morrison in the past supporting just such a policy, including when he was treasurer in 2017, Clare produced a video clip of himself with Morrison on Sky in 2008 where Morrison actually proposed and endorsed shared-equity mortgages.

Clare had remembered the exchange with Morrison, and someone from campaign headquarters found the footage. It was gold dust. Nevertheless, completely unfazed, with no hint of embarrassment, Morrison redoubled his efforts to destroy it. He looked hypocritical. They had forged a friendship at Kokoda, but that didn't stop Clare from skewering Morrison. It wasn't personal, Clare would say later; it was business.

Back at the beginning of the campaign, Clare had been sent out the morning after the day before, when Albanese had mucked up, to try to smooth things over. He had been watching the press conference — it was his job to keep across everything — and, like everybody else who saw it happen, felt a bit crook about it. *We've got a bit of a problem here*, he thought to himself.

Campaign headquarters immediately put him on standby. Clare watched Albanese at his second doorstop, accepting responsibility and apologising. Clare thought he handled it brilliantly. Clare did a lot of media the next day, all with a similar message: 'Politics is not a pop quiz.'

The next big moment was when Albanese contracted Covid. Clare was at a Ramadan festival in Lakemba when Albanese's press secretary, Josh Lloyd, rang to tell him that the leader had tested positive.

Luckily, Albanese had won the debate the night before, so there was a different atmosphere in Labor ranks and in the media, too. Everyone inside the party now shudders to think what would have happened if he had lost that debate then caught Covid. He might have gone on an irreversible slide. Instead, he went into isolation with a bit of momentum behind him.

Still, the news caused consternation at campaign headquarters. They had a contingency plan, but it was a logistical nightmare sorting out who went where when.

The next day, Clare was at his office at 6.00 am. The usual conference call between the leadership group-plus and campaign headquarters was at 6.15 to go through the news of the day and to work out responses. If the government had announced a policy or briefed one to the papers, they would have sorted Labor's position by 6.30 so that he or one of the shadow ministers could announce it on breakfast TV. Usually, to close off debate, they would adopt the government's policy.

That morning, it was obvious what the story was. Clare began preparing his notes for all the expected questions about testing for Covid, who else might be infected, what protocols had been put in place to protect the travelling team, including the media, and so on.

All sorted, he pressed the button to print, and managed to delete everything. His chief of staff retrieved the document, and at 9.00 am Clare fronted the media. 'All right. Well, the boss has got the bug, so you've got me,' he said.

It all went seamlessly from there, apart from a wobble from deputy leader Richard Marles on the Saturday when he grappled with a tricky question on climate.

It became one of the most important weeks in the campaign. It went better without Albanese, and not for the obvious reason. Morrison went from having a small-target opponent to no opponent—except for a few fast-moving shadows zeroing in on him on the economy and national security. When the focus was not on Albanese's shadow ministers, it was on Morrison. He could not disappear for a whole week like Albanese had.

And he had few ministers who could step in and help. Frydenberg was bunkered down in Kooyong. And instead of sending his foreign minister, Marise Payne, to Honiara to deal with an emerging embarrassment-cum-crisis in the Solomon Islands, he despatched the junior minister, Zed Seselja.

It didn't help that Payne was participating, even if in a low-key way, in the election campaign. She had appeared with Morrison in Parramatta, and word had filtered out that she had a fundraiser scheduled precisely when Seselja was sent to the Solomons. Her office denied that, saying she had a 'business dinner'.

The Coalition's leadership also had lots of red lines it couldn't cross. Morrison could not set foot in Liberal heartland seats, and Joyce was largely restricted to the Hunter Valley region in New South Wales, the Northern Territory, and North Queensland, although he did go to Nicholls.

Joyce was to Liberal voters what Roundup was to weeds, to which many serving and former Nationals would reply: 'Not our problem. It's not our job to win Liberals' seats for them.'

In 2019, it had suited Morrison and his campaign for him to fly solo. In 2022, he was front and centre of his campaign, and front and centre of Labor's. He went from being the hunter to the hunted. There was no escape for him, or from him. That week emphasised it.

It went very badly for the government on both fronts during the week that Albanese was in isolation. The pillars began to crumble, Clare said.

News broke of the Solomon Islands' security deal with China, and the March quarter Consumer Price Index showed inflation had shot up by 2.1 per cent in the first three months of the year, taking the inflation rate to 5.1 per cent. National security and the economy were suddenly front and centre. It just so happened that two of Labor's best performers, Penny Wong and Jim Chalmers were also front and centre.

Wong described the security deal as 'the worst failure of Australian foreign policy in the Pacific since the end of World War II'.

On *Insiders* on Sunday, Jim Chalmers came up with a zinger: 'Now, this is a prime minister that went to the wrong island, you know, he went to Hawaii during the bushfires when his focus should have been on the Solomon Islands. The fact that they have failed so substantially here is a direct risk to our national security. The Chinese are setting up a military base on our doorstep, and the government needs to take responsibility for that, rather than try and blame everyone else.'

Chalmers' performance during the campaign was exemplary, and despite the occasional blip he has managed to maintain top form since. He is a confident, clear communicator, one of their best. It was no accident that in the honeymoon period, Labor nudged ahead on the key economic-management measure of voters' attitudes. Chalmers' positioning of the government in the run-up to the budget, then after, was measured and candid about the even harder times he foreshadowed.

He and Albanese have grown closer, but Chalmers won't be sleeping at The Lodge any time soon.

Labor had components of its Pacific policy ready to go when news of the security deal broke. Parts of it had been done by Kristina Keneally; others, by the shadow minister for international aid and the Pacific, Pat Conroy, and the defence spokesman, Brendan O'Connor, whose debate with Dutton also dispelled doubts that Labor wasn't up to the job.

It was pulled together into one big package for release the day after Anzac Day. It involved boosting aid to the region by $525 million over four years from 2022–23 to 2025–26; stepping up Australia's support for aerial surveillance as part of the Pacific Maritime Security Program with an increase in funding of $12 million a year from 2024-25; a new Australia Pacific Defence School to provide training programs for members of Pacific Islands country defence and security forces; and expanding the program to allow Pacific nationals to work in Australia for between one and four years in rural and regional Australia.

Before the news broke about China and the Solomon Islands, Wong had contemplated dropping bits of Labor's new policy to niche markets such as the *Guardian*, figuring that the tabloids and the nightly news bulletins would not be interested in Australian aid for the Pacific. Instead, it dominated.

Labor looked like it had done the work; it was prepared. The timing was perfect, in more ways than one. Any later, and it would have been completely swamped by the CPI increase, and then by the increase in interest rates.

Preparing for the campaign, Wong says she knew the government would try to 'kill' Labor on the economy and national security. She was critical in adding heft to Labor's credentials in the foreign affairs and national security debates.

She had made important positioning speeches towards the end of 2021. She took on Peter Dutton and his departmental head, Mike Pezzullo, over the 'drums of war' controversy, which she not only believes alienated the Australian Chinese community, but also heightened tensions in the region.

Wong was also one of Albanese's closest friends and allies, going back to her Young Labor days. After the 2019 election loss, Wong had had enough. She had decided to quit politics altogether. Then Albanese decided he would run for the leadership.

She changed her mind. She came out in support of him, then she had to stay to help him win the leadership, and then win government. 'I had loyalty to him, and he had always backed me,' she said.

She always believed it was possible for him to make it, so long as he was prepared to do what he needed to do — to think about how he would engage with people, to think through problems, and to think about how to present himself.

'He has done all of that,' she said. 'People have always underestimated him.'

Another key Albanese ally is another South Australian, Mark Butler. Although they were both in the left, Butler and Albanese found they were being played off against each other by both the right and the left subgroups during the late 1990s.

Butler says it was all weird and unproductive. One day, Albanese approached him. 'This is ridiculous,' Albanese told him. 'How about working together?' So they did. Butler was elected in 2007, and the two became friends and close allies. Butler was Albanese's campaign manager when he ran for the leadership against Shorten in 2013.

The two most popular Labor figures, the two most requested for visits and party events, always, were Penny Wong and Tanya Plibersek.

Plibersek met Albanese when she was 14 or 15. He was running Young Labor, and Plibersek had just joined up, after she was persuaded by a local councillor, Hazel Wilson. Wilson had enjoyed Plibersek's speech at a school event to mark International Youth Year in 1985, where she said that policing was not the answer to tackling the problem of young people taking drugs; the focus should be on the social reasons behind the drug-taking.

Wilson told the young Tanya that her values aligned with Labor, so she should join up. Plibersek did, and she loved it. Her parents were not political, although they were community-minded. They would cook for neighbours if they were sick, or her father would carry water to the trees on the oval to make sure they didn't die in the dry weather.

Unlike some of his other acquaintances, Plibersek knew way back then that Albanese would make it. She thought that, even though he lacked polish, he had outstanding natural leadership abilities. He was a firebrand. He was confident. He could make decisions quickly, he would stand his ground, and he would stare down his opponents. He was the kind of person who would pull the pin on a grenade and hold it till his opponents surrendered, or keep holding it until it exploded. He would take everyone down with him if necessary to convince them of the rightness of his actions.

They became allies rather than best friends, not like he was with Wong and Butler. Or as close as he was with Tony Burke from the right, who also had leadership aspirations, but they never seemed to rub each other the wrong way.

There was always a bit of competitive tension between Albanese and Plibersek. That worsened in 2013, when he ran for the leadership against Bill Shorten. Although she supported Albanese, Shorten used her popularity to bolster his by saying publicly that she would make a great deputy. Albanese believed that this, as well as the fact that the party could not have two leaders from the left from New South Wales, cost him votes. She remained Shorten's deputy for six years, which helped keep Albanese at bay.

In retrospect, Shorten winning the 2013 leadership ballot was the best thing that could have happened to Albanese. If Albanese had won then, he would not have won the 2016 election against the Malcolm Turnbull–led Coalition, and he would not be prime minister now. He should have been grateful to Plibersek.

Plibersek decided after the 2019 election not to run for any leadership position. She does not regret that. She has three kids, the youngest 11, and they need her.

There was a flurry of publicity during the campaign that she had been sidelined, even though she visited 31 seats and conducted 61 media appearances. It was true that, unlike in the past, she did not appear with the leader, except on one occasion. But she was not deputy, she was not the campaign spokeswoman, and her portfolio was not a front-and-centre issue. She was also not the most popular person in the Albanese camp.

A few people around the traps thought that before the election, when Albanese appeared to be in trouble, she had been making it known she was 'there', ready, willing, and able. Just in case something happened to the leader. Whether that was fair or not, it was exactly what people were saying about Albanese when Shorten was leader. Ready, willing, and able. Just in case.

After the election, when Albanese was emphasising the need for greater civility in political discourse, Plibersek slipped up on radio by calling Peter Dutton 'Voldemort'. She did not need to be told she had mucked up. She got hold of Dutton's mobile phone number, and contacted him to apologise.

When he constructed his ministry, Albanese shuffled her out of Education. He gave it to Clare, and placed her in Environment. She was still in cabinet, it was still an important portfolio, but, as slight as it was, it was still a slight. There was no doubt he was putting her in her place.

And Environment could be difficult for her, given her battles with the Greens in her electorate — which Albanese also experiences — and what they might do if or when it falls to her to decide on any new coal or gas projects.

Albanese is much closer to his other electoral neighbour, Linda Burney. Albanese helped her get into state parliament in 2003, then backed her into federal parliament in the seat of Barton, which people thought he might run for after a redistribution made it an easier prospect than Grayndler. Burney lived 'around the corner' from Albanese, and whenever he was away, she was the one he trusted to move into his house to look after his dog, Toto. That tells you a lot about how tight they are. Toto is indisputably one of Albanese's most precious friends.

Tony Burke, seven years younger than Albanese, joined Young Labor just as Albanese was leaving it. Burke recalls that Albanese was always friendly and supportive, and always helped him at critical points in his career. It was Albanese who suggested to the leader, Kim Beazley, that the young Burke be given the immigration portfolio, which put him straight into shadow cabinet after barely a year in parliament.

In those years, there were regular cross-factional Sunday-night dinners at La Rustica in Kingston with Albanese, Burke, Jenny Macklin, Stephen Smith, Wayne Swan, and Stephen Conroy. Like Gallagher said, Albanese was good at building relationships.

Burke always wanted to be leader of the House, and pleaded to be Albanese's deputy in the job. For whatever reason, after Kevin Rudd won in 2007, he wouldn't give it to him.

In 2013, Albanese asked him for his vote for the leadership, but Burke had already pledged to back Bill Shorten. No hard feelings. After Albanese lost the ballot, he stood up and declared that he and Shorten had a deal that Chris Bowen would be shadow treasurer and that Burke would become manager of opposition business in the House. Caucus applauded.

There actually was no deal, Burke says, but Albanese locked it in for Burke. Shorten had no choice but to go along with it. Burke was mightily impressed that Albanese had looked after him, even though he hadn't voted for him.

'You don't forget that,' he says. On the night of the 2016 election, Burke rang Albanese and told him to put his hand up for the leadership. Burke hit the phones to suss out support for a bid. But by the next morning, when the count showed that Shorten had come so close to winning, Burke was the only one spruiking a challenge.

As the results were coming in on election night in 2019, Burke rang Albanese from his election-night party, the most miserable he had ever held, and told him: 'If you are not running, I am. If you are running, I am an immoveable supporter for you.'

Burke says that Albanese made two important strategic decisions from the very beginning, and then kept to them. He said that Labor had made itself the story for almost six years, winning every poll except the two that mattered. When Albanese became leader, Burke says the first thing he did was to switch the focus onto the government. If members of the media wanted to know what Labor would do, he would say: 'We are not the government.'

The second strategy was to approach the government's handling of Covid as constructively as possible. To be as bipartisan as possible in the early stages was also the right way to go.

Burke points out that the only two opposition leaders who survived the pandemic were those who showed bipartisanship and supported measures imposed by state and federal governments — Albanese, and Peter Malinauskas in South Australia. Until, of course, the mistakes were so obvious that they had to be criticised.

Then Albanese had the confidence to know when to switch course to release policies.

Now the fully fledged leader of the House, with his guitars stashed in the corner of the office reserved especially for the minister charged with the running of the chamber, Burke says he 'never doubted' that Albanese would make it.

'I thought that the Australian people would respond to someone who was real,' he said. 'His level of decency had to count for something. There was never a moment in the three years where I would have had a concern.'

At the time of my interview with Burke in July 2022, Albanese had been in Madrid for NATO, visited Paris to repair relations with President Macron, and then travelled to Ukraine to meet President Zelenskiy, where he offered solidarity and more military aid. He was heading home, where floods had yet again swamped large parts of New South Wales.

Ethnicity is important, diversity is important, but quality and experience should also be taken into account. Keneally had both in spades, as well as guts and sparkle. She worked hard to bring the Biloela family to national attention. Unlike some of her colleagues, she was never squeamish when it came to talking about asylum-seeker boats. She was not frightened to ruffle feathers.

She brought some old-fashioned razzle-dazzle to politics, one of her admirers said. She was a loyal, honest ally, who also would have been very useful to Albanese in taking the fight up to the Coalition.

Immediately behind the front lines, Tim Gartrell and Paul Erickson formed a formidable partnership. Two of Labor's best political brains, they were central to Albanese's success.

Gartrell had lived through the horrors of Latham, then basked in the success of the 2007 campaign. He knew the demands that would be placed on the national secretary as the campaign director, and he knew how important it was for whoever held that job to have a close relationship with the leader's office. When Albanese asked him to become his chief of staff, he rang Erickson and said he wouldn't take the job unless Erickson was comfortable with it. Erickson was touched by his decency.

Gartrell, six years younger than Albanese, was in Young Labor when they met. They have been close all of Gartrell's adult life. They continued their comradeship through Gartrell's university years and countless factional wars, including the drive to get left-wing candidates preselected in inner-city seats.

Gartrell was one of Albanese's branch secretaries. He says that he saw Albanese's leadership on display back then when he became his campaign manager for Grayndler and they fought off a fierce campaign from the No Aircraft Noise Party. There were a lot of angry people that Albanese insisted on fronting. He did town hall meetings and candidate forums. When protestors turned up outside Albanese's office, he would go out and talk to them. He coined the phrase 'the convoy of no consequence' to describe the mob heading for Canberra.

'He was really strong, and I thought he had a lot of political courage,' Gartrell said.

Albanese, along with John Faulkner, supported Gartrell to get a job at the national secretariat as an organiser. He worked his way up to become national secretary for Mark Latham's 2004 election campaign, and remembers watching the infamous handshake on the news, thinking it was bad, but knowing that the election had already been lost by then.

Gartrell — smart, funny, politically acute, and personable — is determined to run a collegiate office and to build deep wells of trust between the prime minister's office and MPs. He has witnessed firsthand how easily misunderstandings and rifts can derail relationships. He has played a vital behind-the-scenes role in formulating and implementing Labor's policy on the Indigenous voice to parliament. His closeness to Albanese means he can be both supportive and critical as required.

Gartrell also went back a fair way with Erickson. They first met in 2009 after Gartrell had resigned as national secretary and went to work as CEO of the polling firm Auspol. It was at a dinner with Erickson's boss, Richard Wynn, and Adam Kilgour, also involved with Auspol. The main topic of conversation was how to handle the rising challenge from the Greens. And still is.

Gartrell and Erickson worked together on the marriage-equality postal ballot in 2017, and then on the 2019 federal election. Erickson describes Gartrell as a disciplined and creative campaigner, and as a 'really decent person'.

2222222222222222

'He was always very conscious not to overstep the mark by trying to do my job for me, which would have taken a lot of discipline, especially in the early days when I wasn't really established,' Erickson says.

Gartrell paid high tribute to Erickson after the Eden-Monaro by-election in 2020, telling stakeholders that the campaign and the result showed that Erickson was capable of leading a winning federal election campaign.

Erickson's friend Ryan Batchelor, who worked for Jenny Macklin from 2005 to 2011, and then became Julia Gillard's director of policy in the prime minister's office, helped out at campaign headquarters for almost six weeks. Batchelor had been at campaign headquarters in the 2007, 2010, and 2013 elections. He told Erickson that the working relationship between Gartrell, who travelled with Albanese, and Erickson as campaign director, was 'the strongest and most professional' he had seen in any Labor campaign.

After the campaign, senior staff at headquarters clubbed together to buy Erickson a first-edition copy of the Hunter S. Thompson classic *Fear and Loathing on the Campaign Trail*, signed by the author, which they had ordered at great expense — $800 — from the US. It was a mark of their high regard for him.

He had built a close-knit team in a relatively open environment. He trusted them, and they repaid him by keeping secret all the information he shared with them. It had been a dry office — no grog allowed on the premises — with strict rules on food sharing and hygiene to try to avoid Covid.

When they presented the book to him, the chief of staff at campaign headquarters, Lidija Ivanovski, said that two generations before, campaigns were often led by people who tried to prove themselves by shouting louder, swearing more, and drinking harder than everyone else. Ivanovski said Erickson had shown that campaigns could succeed without any of that, and he had done it by building a 'positive and respectful culture'.

Fear and Loathing focussed on the 1972 US presidential campaign, mainly from the camp of the Democrat challenger, George McGovern, who lost to Richard Nixon, but was as much about pack journalism and the incestuous relationship between politicians and those who cover them. Erickson has it on his desk, and regards it as a touching if somewhat ironic gesture.

It wasn't meant to be that; it was simply meant as a thank-you, because his staff knew how much he loved campaigns. It was also recognition of and respect for his hard work, his meticulous preparations, and his talent. They described him as super-smart and super-pragmatic. And calm. And one of the few who could either persuade Albanese to do something or not do something. Having research to back his arguments helped, but he also had a very good manner.

Staff who had been there in 2016, as well as 2019, drew the comparisons. George Wright was seen as a charismatic character, while Noah Carroll was seen as remote. In 2019, in the last week of the campaign, staff were busily booking hair appointments and sorting their wardrobes for Saturday night, so certain were they that they would win.

It became a running joke in 2022, particularly when things had not gone so well, for them to ask one another what they were going to wear on election night.

'It was a white-knuckle ride,' one of them said later. There was no moment, until late on the night, when they were certain they had won.

CHAPTER SEVENTEEN

Rocking Boats

The last message that Australians heard from Scott Morrison on election day was that a boatload of refugees from Sri Lanka had been intercepted on their way to Australia, so if they wanted to keep the borders secure, they should vote Liberal.

His remarks, at a press conference that began at 1.03 pm, pre-empted an official announcement that his office was desperate to get released before his planned doorstop after he voted in his electorate of Cook.

A suitably briefed journalist asked him at 1.06 pm about 'reports' that there was a vessel on its way. In fact, there were no such reports, because the official statement had not yet been released, and nobody outside the government was supposed to know about it. But Morrison couldn't wait.

Morrison's revelation, technically an 'unauthorised disclosure', came while the operation to turn back the boat was still in progress. It also breached, in spirit at least, well-established caretaker conventions. It contradicted everything he had said as the immigration minister who boasted he had stopped the boats, when he had repeatedly refused to discuss 'on-water matters'. There were a number of reasons for that approach. Releasing information prematurely could tip off people smugglers and could endanger an operation, including risking the lives of refugees and defence personnel.

All that went overboard on polling day. With his own vessel sinking, Morrison sought to exploit fears that Labor would not be as tough on borders as he was.

Again, someone else was left to carry the can for the breaches of established procedures that day, after the head of the home affairs department, Mike Pezzullo, delivered a damning report to the new government.

Karen Andrews, who had been home affairs minister at the time, fronted to answer for it, even though, as she later discovered, Morrison could have done it all himself and accepted responsibility later for what transpired, because he had also been simultaneously the other home affairs minister.

Pezzullo's minute-by-minute account of what happened that day, showing that the prime minister's office was involved up to its eyeballs, was released by the new home affairs minister, Clare O'Neil, as the parliament was preparing to sit for the first time after the election. According to O'Neil:

> The former government had a duty to protect Australia. Instead, they sabotaged the protocols that protect Operation Sovereign Borders for political gain. Their actions undermined the integrity of this complex operation, making it more difficult and dangerous.
>
> The report found uniformed Border Force and Defence Force members, and public servants, acted with integrity and at the highest standards at all times. They should be commended for doing so.
>
> The profound compromise of a military-led operation is without precedent in Australia's history. It was disgraceful,

shameful, and characteristic of a national government which frequently pursued political interests above the national interest.

Andrews did not act illegally—something that Pezzullo readily acknowledges—however, there are those who believe that she should have refused Morrison's request for a statement to be rushed out by the department.

In her defence, Andrews says that two issues were conflated. The first was what happened with the vessel. The second was what the Liberal Party did with the information.

Andrews believes that what really tipped this story into dark places, with accusations of breaches of conventions, was the text sent later on election day by the Liberal Party's campaign headquarters—to millions of voters, Labor believes—saying:

> BREAKING: Australian Border Force has intercepted an illegal boat trying to reach Australia. Keep our borders secure by voting Liberal today. https://vote.liberal.org.au.

Andrews did not know it was being sent. No one had told her, and no one had asked her. She only found out about it when her staff showed her it was running on Twitter.

If she had been asked in advance or if her advice had been sought, she says she would have counselled against sending out the text.

'I am very conservative with these sorts of things,' she told me later, and well before she knew of Morrison's secret ministries. I am very process driven, and I probably would have said the press conference is enough.'

The boat had been detected in the early hours of that morning, between 2.00 and 3.00, as it was approaching Christmas Island. The interception occurred a few hours later.

Those overseeing the operation were fully aware of the political sensitivities on such a day, so they made a conscious decision that everything had to be played absolutely 'by the book'. As the responsible minister — the only one they knew of, at least — Andrews had to be informed.

Andrews was at a polling booth in her electorate when she received a phone call, she thinks around 9.00 am, from Justin Jones, commander of the Joint Agency Task Force Operation Sovereign Borders. They could not get a connection on a secure line, so they spoke on an open line.

She allowed Rear Admiral Jones to do most of the talking. He filled her in on the interception, and they agreed that there would be a more detailed briefing later in the day when she was back in her electorate office and could speak on a secure line. She says she went back onto the polling booth 'and left him to do what he needed to do'. Her office then alerted the prime minister's office.

Pezzullo's subsequent minute-by-minute timeline begins at 11.09 am, with: 'The Secretary directed the Department to keep an eye out for any chatter on social media or worse any leaks to the media. It could become a very late election issue.'

Andrews says she does not know why the timeline began at that exact moment, or if it had been prompted by something or someone.

However, it appears that because the details of the operation were becoming more widely known within the department and elsewhere, Pezzullo decided to act pre-emptively to caution people.

Andrews says that Morrison called her just before midday to ask that a statement be issued by Operation Sovereign Borders, stating that a vessel had been intercepted.

She says he wanted it to be factual, and argued that it was for reasons of transparency. She did not have a problem with that. She argued that it would have deterrence value. Labor had been accusing the government of scaremongering on boats, so she believed that Australians had a right to know what was happening.

'Labor was obviously a risk to borders; there was evidence the boats were potentially starting again. It was the right thing to do,' she said.

Morrison also told her that the opposition would have to be told, which she says she would have arranged anyway. But she was beaten to it.

Shortly after midday, Morrison's chief of staff, John Kunkel, who had spent the election at campaign headquarters in Brisbane, rang Albanese's chief of staff, Tim Gartrell. Kunkel told Gartrell that an asylum-seeker boat had been intercepted, and alerted him to the fact that there would be an announcement about it.

Gartrell said if it was fair dinkum, Labor would have to be briefed in advance. He expressed concern to Kunkel about a breach of caretaker conventions. Gartrell said Kunkel was reasonable, but he sounded uncomfortable.

It wasn't a long conversation. Gartrell was keen to brief Albanese and the campaign team, because he was certain that Morrison would use it to partisan advantage. He also told the shadow home affairs minister, Kristina Keneally.

Labor was suspicious that Morrison had known long before about the impending arrival of the boat. The previous day, in response to questions about the Murugappan family waiting to hear if they would be deported or allowed to go back to Biloela, Morrison talked tough about stopping boats. He said that the Murugappans, who had been in detention for four years, had not been found to be refugees, and were therefore not owed protection in Australia.

'If you grant visas to people who have illegally entered Australia, you may as well start writing the prospectus for people smugglers,' he said.

At 12.17, Kunkel rang Pezzullo and asked for a briefing to be arranged for the opposition in accordance with caretaker provisions. Pezzullo told Kunkel that, as the briefing would involve an 'operational matter'—meaning it was still underway—the home affairs minister would have to approve it.

Kunkel said he would ensure that happened. Pezzullo thought it was odd that Kunkel had rung him about such a matter. He regarded it as something well below both their pay grades. Normally, the minister's chief of staff would deal with his office and the shadow minister's office.

What Pezzullo did not know was that he had two ministers at that time. That day was difficult enough, but it would have been a lot more difficult if there had been conflicting instructions.

Andrews' office asked the department to email its press release to journalists. Pezzullo refused. He also refused a request to tweet it. He insisted that once cleared, the press release would be posted on the department's website, 'no more and no less'.

Once those requests were denied, her office did not pursue them. If they had, that would have escalated the matter.

'The most apolitical way to do it was with a factual statement. They were never asked to do anything political. Never,' Andrews told me.

'If you look at the covering letter—asking that it be sent out to journos—it was [to] the entire press gallery, not selected journalists. I don't think that's unreasonable. When they said no, that was it. The requests to amplify were not pressed. We said, *Fine, no worries.* It was not unreasonable to ask them to put it out.'

'There are a lot of interesting things in the Pezzullo report,' Andrews said.

'He makes it clear the PMO was calling the shots.'

Once again, the prime minister's office had taken control.

It was Morrison's press secretary, Andrew Carswell, who was with him at the polling booth, who was pressuring one of Andrews' media advisers to hurry up and get the release out, questioning why it was taking so long. Andrews' media adviser, according to Pezzullo's later timeline, relayed news of the prime minister's office's impatience to the department.

'A lot of people are furious,' Andrews' media adviser told the department.

Morrison couldn't wait, so sailed into his press conference. 'I can confirm that there's been an interception of a vessel en route to Australia,' he said. 'That vessel has been intercepted in accordance with the policies of government, and they're following those normal protocols …

'In the interests of full transparency in the middle of an election campaign, the Labor Party was advised of this, and a statement has been issued by the border protection authorities.' Not quite.

Morrison finished speaking at 1.07 pm, the statement appeared on the department's website at 1.09 pm, the briefing for the opposition did not take place until 2.26 pm, and the Liberal Party text was spammed around 3.00 pm.

A senior staffer who was with Morrison that day did not dispute later that the prime minister had liaised with campaign headquarters for the text message to be dispatched.

He described it as a 'quite normal and reasonable' thing to do in a campaign, especially as the matter was already public. He described Labor's response later as hypocritical, betting that they would have done exactly the same thing.

Andrews had no contact or conversation with Pezzullo until that night, when it was clear that Morrison had lost the election.

He texted her to say that the department would continue to work with her until a new minister was sworn in. He sent her another text on the Monday with a photograph of his new grandchild.

A tough operator, Pezzullo had been around long enough to know that what happened that day could have serious consequences post-election, so he made sure that everything was done in accordance with the rules.

When Dutton was home affairs minister, he and Pezzullo got along extremely well, despite the fact that Pezzullo had worked as an adviser to former opposition leader Kim Beazley.

Dutton had wanted Pezzullo to be transferred across to head up the defence department after he took up the portfolio, but there was no way that was going to happen. Even before that, when Malcolm Turnbull was considering appointing Pezzullo to run Defence, the top brass warned Turnbull that if he did that, there would be a mutiny.

At time of writing, Pezullo, who can be as abrasive as he is effective, remains head of Home Affairs. Since the election, a number of asylum-seeker boats have tried to make it to Australia. All of them have been turned back.

CHAPTER EIGHTEEN

Over and Out

It was an intimate gathering at Anthony Albanese's home in Marrickville on election night: his partner, Jodie Haydon; his son, Nathan; his chief of staff, Tim Gartrell; his press secretary, Liz Fitch; his strategic communications adviser, Katie Connolly; and Penny Wong.

Albanese wanted it 'uncluttered' and as relaxed as it was possible to be. He spent most of the night in a blue Newtown Jets footy jumper, grey skinny jeans, and calf-length, sandy-coloured ugg boots.

After months of dieting, Albanese decided to indulge himself with some comfort food. He rustled up a sauce of tomatoes, basil, and chilli, made from scratch, with spaghetti for anyone who wanted. Wong had a bowl, and even before she knew her friend had made it, thought it tasted pretty good. Others grazed on cheese platters that Jodie had put out.

The mood was subdued. There was not a lot of drinking done.

Like the rest of Australia, they settled in to watch the count on television, switching from channel to channel. Not long after the coverage began, Albanese called Paul Erickson. Online betting agencies were reporting that punters were placing bets on what tie Albanese would be wearing that night. He told Erickson to put all of Labor's money on a Rabbitohs tie. Erickson wasn't really up for jokes. 'Mate, I am trying to focus on the count,' he told Albanese.

Erickson had set up in campaign headquarters with his deputy, Jen Light; the national president, Wayne Swan; the head of the media unit, John Olenich, who was also Wong's deputy chief of staff; and media advisers Matthew Franklin, Joanna Heath, and Josh Lloyd. The mood there was more tense, and there was no drinking at all. Erickson kept his strict no-grog rule on the premises till the very end.

One wall was covered with five television sets, each one tuned to a different station. On another wall was a huge screen with a grid of all 151 House of Representatives seats, divided into Labor/Coalition wins, Labor/Coalition seats that were too close to call, and Labor/Coalition-leaning seats.

The first votes came in from Norfolk Island, where an independent had secured most of the votes. A portent perhaps. Then, at 6.35 pm, figures came in from the Thredbo booth in Eden-Monaro. In 2019, that booth had recorded a 3 per cent swing against Labor. On 21 May 2022, Labor's vote was up by 5 per cent, and the Coalition's was down by 23 per cent.

It was only a small booth, and there was a long way to go, so it was way too early to breathe out. A Parramatta booth followed soon after, showing Labor down slightly, the Liberals down by more, and the Greens up by 5 per cent. That seemed to set the pattern for the night in many seats, with the vote of the major parties down and the Greens, minors, or independents up.

The early encouraging news, the first real bit of good news, was that the Liberals had failed, despite their earlier optimistic predictions, to breach Labor's red wall. By 7.00 pm, it appeared that Labor would hold Eden-Monaro, Macquarie, and seats in the Hunter where the Coalition, using Barnaby Joyce in one of the few areas it was considered safe for him to go, had put in a big effort.

Even in seats where Labor's primary vote was looking dodgy, the campaign strategists were hopeful. Unlike in the past, they were confident that the rusted-ons were highly motivated and had voted early in pre-polls, so if it looked bad in the early count, that didn't mean it was going to stay bad.

Victoria was looking good, with strong votes for Labor in Chisholm and Deakin. Despite Liberal hopes of picking up Blair and Lilley in Queensland, there were swings to Labor in both seats. Bennelong was also looking like a gain for Labor.

The bad news was that Kristina Keneally was in trouble in Fowler, Terri Butler was heading south in Griffith, and so was Josh Burns in Macnamara. There had been a surge in the Greens' vote in both Griffith and Macnamara.

Erickson spoke with the Victorian secretary, Chris Ford. Ford said there were still 20,000 postal votes to count in Macnamara—more than 20 per cent of the total. It was clear that the Liberal vote had collapsed; some of it had gone to Burns, but a lot of it had gone to the Greens. With a large Jewish population voting early, they hoped it would come back. They deemed it too close to call.

Around 8.00 pm at Labor's campaign headquarters, they thought they had reached a stalemate, and that they would not see much movement for an hour, so they stopped to take stock. Albanese and Erickson spoke again. Erickson told him it was too early to call; they were in with a shot to gain a majority, but it was still uncertain.

Labor was ahead in Reid, Bennelong, Robertson, Higgins, and Brisbane, while Deakin, Dickson, and Boothby were close. Labor was also ahead in Chisholm, Lyons was close, and they were running a little behind in Gilmore.

They could see that Tim Wilson was behind in Goldstein, Trent Zimmerman was behind in North Sydney, and Jason Falinksi was behind in Mackellar. Erickson wasn't prepared to call it, but thought, *At this stage I would much rather be us than them.*

At 9.00 pm, the count began coming in from Western Australia. All their efforts there were paying off. Swings of between 7 and 10 per cent were showing up in their target seats. Things started to pick up. Reid was called as a gain for Labor at 9.20, Swan at 9.30, and Pearce at 9.40. Parramatta was locked in at the same time. They had their seat count at 72, with a bunch of seats too close to call, including Fowler, Lyons, Gilmore, and Brisbane.

Albanese spoke to Erickson again around 9.35 pm. It was looking very positive. They agreed that Labor would be in a position to form government; they hoped it would be a majority government, but they weren't there yet.

The most outwardly nervous person in the Marrickville household was Nathan. Albanese was described as calm, straightforward, and business-like. Zen. He and Wong, she in her black casual gear, sat together on the couch watching TV, constantly switching channels.

At 10.00 pm, Labor picked up Hasluck and Tangney in the west. It was over. Within half an hour, Erickson and his team were packed up and headed for the Canterbury-Hurlstone Park RSL club to wait for the prime minister-elect.

Labor's military-style operations, its meticulous planning — whether it was to do with which seats to target, or debate preparations, or launching in the west, or using frontbenchers to fill the void during Albanese's Covid isolation — much of it orchestrated by Albanese, Gartrell, and Erickson, had paid off.

People had been texting or calling Albanese all night, but shortly after 10.30 pm his phone lit up with Morrison's number. Everyone in the room went quiet, knowing he was ringing to concede. They strained to hear. 'Hi, Scott,' Albanese said, then walked up three steps to a small landing away from the gathering so they could speak privately.

It was a short conversation. Understandably, Morrison sounded flat. He congratulated Albanese, wished him well, and told him it was a big job. Albanese thanked him for his service to the country, and asked him to convey his thanks to Jenny and his family—sentiments he also expressed in his speech. He told him he could take his time moving out of Kirribilli and The Lodge.

They spoke briefly about the planned swearing-in on Monday, to enable Albanese to attend the Quad meeting in Japan. Regardless of who won, most of the arrangements had been made. The VIP aircraft used by the prime minister, which Morrison had nicknamed Shark One and which Albanese renamed Toto One, after his dog, was on standby.

Albanese walked back down the steps. 'That's it,' he told them.

It was an emotional moment for Albanese, a big moment, yet he didn't cry—which he reckons is unusual for him. There was no wild cheering. They hugged and kissed. Liz Fitch cracked open a bottle of champagne. She cried, and then couldn't help thinking he needed to go and get dressed.

It hit Albanese that he had won. 'Wow. We have done it,' he said. The excitement was quickly replaced by a sense of relief, which also gave way to a sense of vindication. 'We had so many people critical of the strategy I had laid out in 2019,' he said later in an interview for this book.

The dominant feeling, though, was relief. 'I felt a great weight on me because of the expectations,' he said.

Still in his footy jumper, jeans, and ugg boots, Albanese sat on his couch and decided to rewrite his speech. There were already two versions in Connolly's laptop—as he says, a good one and a bad one.

'I just decided in that moment, in a moment of complete madness, as you do, to write the speech again,' he told me.

Connolly sat on the floor with her computer, typing while he dictated.

He asked Wong to introduce him at his victory party. He was surprised that she was surprised he had asked her. Then he went to shower and dress. He reread the printed version of his speech when he came back. Morrison was making his concession speech. Albanese watched some of it.

Morrison's speech was stoic, appropriate, unembellished. On the stage, again, with his wife, Jenny, and their two daughters, there was no talk of miracles or of divine intervention—that would follow—only acceptance that it was over.

'On a night like tonight, it is proper to acknowledge the functioning of our democracy. I have always believed in Australians and their judgement, and I've always been prepared to accept their verdicts, and tonight they have delivered their verdict, and I congratulate Anthony Albanese and the Labor Party, and I wish him and his government all the very best,' Morrison said.

'Now there are many votes still to count, that is true. There are many pre-polls and postals that will still come in. But I believe it's very important that this country has certainty. I think it's very important this country can move forward.'

He confirmed he would be resigning as the leader of the Liberal Party.

'To my colleagues tonight, who have had to deal with very difficult news, and have lost their seats tonight, I as leader take responsibility for the wins and the losses. That is the burden and that is the responsibility of leadership,' he said.

Over and out.

Dressed in a dark suit with a grey tie, Albanese stepped out of his house to find more than 100 of his neighbours had gathered outside, waiting for him to emerge. As soon as they saw him, they roared. He choked up remembering that moment. He had lived on that same street for more than 30 years, and in that house from the time Nathan was six.

Albanese arrived at the club around 11.45 pm. Some staff were outside, smoking. When police took him in through the back door, and walked him through the kitchens, the remaining staff called out: 'On yer, Albo.'

There were thousands already gathered there, inside and out. They were spilling out onto the street in front. The club had already run out of the Albo ale.

Everyone who had been important in Albanese's life was there: Lindsay Keevers, his best friend from primary school; old friends Sherie and Scott Dewstow; people who had been in Young Labor with him; those who had fought alongside him in the factional wars; and his former wife, Carmel Tebbutt.

Albanese went up to the board room, where Paul Erickson, Wayne Swan, and Dee Madigan were waiting. They thought they had 73 seats by then, with hopes of holding on to other key marginals such as Gilmore and Macquarie. Erickson thought they could get to 77 seats.

Albanese was anxious to make his speech. He knew they had won the election, that they would form government with between 75 and 78 seats, and that 77 was the most likely number.

Swan was worried that the crowd was a bit too excited. He told Albanese that people had been there a few hours and were very worked up. 'They are my people,' Albanese said. 'They will be fine.'

He was nervous, only because he was worried he would get

emotional when he spoke about his mother, Maryanne, who had died almost exactly 20 years before. He deliberately kept his tributes to her as concise as possible so he could get through without breaking down.

To cries of 'Albo, Albo,' he walked briskly on stage after Wong introduced him, gave her a big hug, and then, flanked by Jodie and Nathan, began his speech. His first words were to commit to enacting the Uluru statement from the heart 'in full'.

As it turned out, Albanese had to shush a few of his people. They were yelling, or trying to show him what was on their phones.

'Can we have order, please,' he said. 'I intend to run an orderly government, and it starts here, so behave.'

Although he choked up, and at several points looked on the verge of tears, he managed to get through without crying. His speech was full of hope and inspiration.

'My fellow Australians, it says a lot about our great country that a son of a single mum who was a disability pensioner, who grew up in public housing down the road in Camperdown, can stand before you tonight as Australia's prime minister,' he said.

'Every parent wants more for the next generation than they had. My mother dreamt of a better life for me. And I hope that my journey in life inspires Australians to reach for the stars.

'I want Australia to continue to be a country that no matter where you live, who you worship, who you love, or what your last name is, that places no restrictions on your journey in life.

'My fellow Australians — I think they've got the name by now, I think they've got that,' he said, responding to the frequent punctuation of high-volume chants of 'Albo, Albo'. 'I know at the beginning of the campaign they said people didn't know me, but I reckon they've got it.'

His speech over, he went back to the board room for a few

drinks with his staff and close friends. They finished around 2.00 am. He went home, had a quiet whisky, and then went to bed

Everybody celebrated in their own way. Katy Gallagher was on the Seven Network panel. She got to her hotel room close to 1.00 am. She sat on the edge of her bed eating a $10 packet of chips from her minibar. She had had no dinner, and just managed to snaffle a glass of wine from the Seven Network staff after she saw that Chris Bowen had a whisky hidden under his desktop.

Morrison spent the night at Kirribilli with a few close staff and family. That was a hard night, filled with tears and a few regrets.

Afterwards, Carswell was full of praise for his old boss. He said the Coalition had faced a difficult pathway to victory, and that they had gained a little momentum in the final week.

'I think there was an inbuilt realism among soft voters—they wanted to draw the curtain down on Covid,' Carswell said.

'I am proud of what he has accomplished. He won't be one of those types like Malcolm or Tony. He will serve his constituents, then, once he leaves, that will be it. Scott Morrison doesn't need to have his say. A lot of what he was hit with was not politics. It's not like he has to get things off his chest. His legacy will grow and grow.

'Scott had to deal with some of the most extraordinary circumstances, in unprecedented times. His accomplishments during Covid, in particular, were profound, and will only grow in stature in the coming years. Saving lives and saving livelihoods.'

The next morning, Morrison went to the Pentecostal Horizon Church in Sutherland Shire, the same one where he had allowed the cameras to film him and Jenny praying during the 2019 campaign. He told the congregation that he was glad his last words as prime minister would be to 'our church family here'.

He choked up as he recited Habakkuk 3:17 from the Bible:

Even if the fig tree does not blossom, and there is no fruit on the vines, if the yield of the olive fails and if the fields produce no food, even if the flock is cut off from the fold and there are no cattle in the stalls, yet I will triumph in the Lord. I will rejoice in the God of my salvation.

Wiping away tears, he then recited a passage from Micah:

As for me, I will be on the watch for the Lord. I will wait for the God of my salvation. My God will hear me. Do not rejoice over me, enemy of mine. Though I fall, I will rise. Though I live in darkness, the Lord is a light for me.

'May God bless Australia. May God bless our community. And may God continue to show his favour on this wonderful church family.'

The congregation clapped him as he left the stage, but not everyone was impressed. One of his most senior colleagues had no sympathy for him.

He had led the Liberals into the wilderness. The dark passages he had quoted sounded all about him, and the tears seemed to be for himself. His colleague, never a fan, believed that in those moments people got to see Morrison for who he really was.

Albanese spent part of the next day watching a replay of his acceptance speech, marvelling at his own prose, thinking, *Fuck, how did I do that?* Normally, he reckons he is his own harshest critic, but he was rightly pleased with that one.

Albanese's victory had not come easily, it was narrow, and the pattern of voting left a lot of questions about what happened and why.

In his post-election speech to the National Press Club, Labor's national secretary, Paul Erickson, said that while Morrison came to symbolise the failures of the Coalition on climate change, on the handling of the pandemic, and on relations with near neighbours, they were institutional failures, not just individual ones.

He also pointed out that with the high level of pre-polling, it was pretty pointless to try to undertake booth analysis to determine factors such as wealth on voting behaviour.

His early analysis showed that Labor won among voters who worked full-time, among voters trained at TAFE, among renters and mortgage holders, among voters earning less than $50,000 a year, and among voters with medium-household annual incomes of between $50,000 and $150,000. Some of the biggest swings to Labor were recorded in outer-suburban and regional electorates it held, such as Greenway, Macquarie, Eden-Monaro, Dobell, Dunkley, and Corangamite, and in seats it won, such as Robertson, Hasluck, and Pearce.

'Labor gained 10 seats from the Coalition, and every Labor incumbent who was under threat from the Coalition retained their seat, enabling the ALP to form majority government,' he said.

'That said, there is clearly a message in the result for both major parties: we still have a major challenge in front of us to rebuild trust in our political institutions and restore confidence in the parliament.

'I would always like to see more voters record a primary vote for Labor, and Labor to win more seats. Our primary vote remains in the low 30s—and needs to grow.

'Queensland was one of only two states where the Labor

primary [vote] increased — but we didn't gain any seats, and we lost Griffith to the Greens. And there are challenges in Tasmania, which the party needs to thoroughly examine.'

He estimates that Labor lost around 2 per cent nationally to the Greens, not just in inner-city seats, in a campaign he described as long, brutal, and negative.

Erickson says that while the Liberals' effective advertising drove down Labor's primary vote, it did not persuade anyone to vote for Morrison. Instead, the vote for independents and minor parties went up. He believes that Labor's high-quality candidates played a part in its victory, and rejects suggestions that the small-target strategy or an agenda criticised as too timid ultimately cost the party votes.

Both major parties announced reviews of their campaigns after the election. There was a lot to consider: the roles of their leaders, their advertising, their ground campaigns, their low primary votes, the rise of the independents, and the shift to the Greens and minor parties.

Although Labor's primary vote overall ended up below 33 per cent, the party's primary vote was registering at 38 per cent on the Thursday night before election day in the 16 seats it was tracking. The actual result in those 16 seats, from across the mainland states — four of them in New South Wales, four in Victoria, four in Queensland, three in Western Australia, and one in South Australia — came in at 37 per cent.

The final track put the Liberal National Party on 36 per cent, which was exactly where the Coalition ended up. Labor's tracking had the Greens on 11 per cent; they got 12 per cent.

So its tracking was right in 16 target seats, which was comforting, up to a point. In untracked seats, its actual vote dropped a little or a lot.

In safe Labor seats that were not tracked or targeted, Labor's vote went down significantly. In working-class seats, it went to One Nation and Palmer's UAP. Labor lost Griffith to the Greens, but also lost out to the Greens in the two Brisbane seats it was hoping to pick up—Ryan and Brisbane.

In the Victorian seats of Holt and Bruce, Labor's vote dropped substantially. In Bruce, where it fell 6.6 per cent on primaries, the UAP vote went up by 4.6 per cent to 8.7 per cent, and One Nation went up by 3.8 per cent to 4.8 per cent.

In Holt, Labor's vote went down almost 10 per cent, partly explained by the departure of sitting member Anthony 'Smiley' Byrne, while the UAP went up 3.5 per cent to 9.7 per cent, and One Nation went up by 4.7 per cent to 4.8 per cent.

'A lot of working-class and ethnic voters, traditionally staunch Labor voters, were angry with us over lockdowns and vaccination mandates,' according to one Labor campaigner. Or there could be something more permanent happening to Labor's working-class vote.

One thing that everyone could agree on was that there was no longer any such thing as a safe seat.

Erickson is open to the argument that Labor could have made a better case for itself and for Albanese, but performance in government could correct some of that, and he was more than happy with the way Albanese had begun his rule.

Labor's campaign made the case against Morrison and for change, but the tactical voting that was part of the zeitgeist showed that people had worked out they didn't have to vote Labor to achieve change.

By the end, Albanese and his campaign team had succeeded brilliantly in making the case against Morrison. Scott Morrison and his team had also succeeded brilliantly in making the case against

Anthony Albanese. Where each fell down was in making the case for himself. It was, however, more important for Morrison than for Albanese to make the case for, because the election became the referendum on his character that the Liberals so feared.

The Liberals now have to work out whether, with Morrison gone, its heartland voters will become more receptive to the party, and Labor has to work out if its lower primary vote in its safest seats is a sign of things to come. Both major parties copped a battering from left- and right-wing minor parties or independents.

The good and bad news was presented to the remaining Liberal MPs on the day before the new parliament met by the party's federal director, Andrew Hirst, and the former deputy director of the Victorian branch, Tony Barry, who works for the Redbridge polling group.

The nub of it was that although Morrison was a major factor in the loss, the party had suffered significant brand damage. Barry said that the party's reputation as the better economic managers had been trashed.

Barry told MPs that the party had lost its traditional base. 'A perceived lack of leadership during Covid was at the heart of it,' he said. He said middle Australia was increasingly socially progressive, while remaining anxious about the economy, yet the Liberals were not seen to empathise with them.

The encouraging news he provided was that Labor's win, with a record low primary vote, came with no guarantee of a second term. He picked up on Labor's own concerns about the softening of its primary vote in its heartland seats, which translated into an increased vote for the Greens in inner and middle suburbs, while in outer suburbs it went to minor right-wing parties.

Barry said that after 26 years in public life, Albanese remained undefined.

'He has no political centre of gravity and no policy definition like JWH [John Winston Howard] on tax reform, support for families, and IR [industrial relations] reform.'

He warned Liberals that they needed to pick their fights carefully. He urged the Coalition to fight the next election, not the last, and warned that there was the potential for the Liberal Party to lose a generation of voters in the 18–34 age bracket.

He told them that while climate change was critical to the success of the Teals, it was also symbolic of a 'deeper values disconnect with the Liberal Party'.

Barry says that Liberal voters drifted away from the party after the same-sex marriage bill, when MPs in electorates that voted yes either abstained or voted against it.

'The climate culture wars may be ending, but the climate policy war is just beginning,' he warned.

Much the same depressing message was delivered by Hirst, who told the MPs that two big factors in the loss were the party's treatment of women and climate change.

Barry painted a sobering picture of a continuing narrow pathway because of the continuing threat from the Teals and the Greens, with the desertion of educated people, including 'professional women, doctors, not doctors' wives'.

There was a nationwide two-party-preferred swing to Labor of 3.7 per cent, taking its vote to 52.1 per cent and leaving the Coalition at 47.9 per cent. Labor won 77 seats, and the Coalition 58, with the balance made up of 16 seats held by a crossbenchers.

There were nine Liberal women left in the House. It was miserable.

In her subsequent review of the vote, Liberal senator Linda Reynolds found that:

In the previous 46th Parliament, in the House of Representatives, 13 of the Liberal Party's 61 seats (21.3pc) were held by women. With the loss of six of these 13 incumbents, seven (54pc) of these women retained their seats. In contrast, 31 (65pc) of Liberal male incumbents retained their seats. With two new Liberal women elected, in the new Parliament there are nine (21pc) Liberal women in the House of Representatives, the lowest number since 1993.

In the 46th Parliament, in the Senate, 10 (33%) of the Liberal Party's 30 seats were held by women. Of the five Senate seats lost, four were held by men and one by a woman. The loss of one woman was offset by the gain of one woman from South Australia. Therefore, in the Senate, the Liberal Party retained 10 women while having a net loss of four Senators. In the 47th Parliament, the Liberal Party has 19 (28%) female Members and Senators. Notionally a small increase from 25% in the 46th Parliament, however the absolute number of women has reduced to the lowest number since 1993.

Reynolds makes the obvious point that unless the Liberal Party regains some of its lost support from women voters, it is mathematically impossible for them to win office. One way to do that, obviously, is by increasing the number of women in the parliament, although there remained resistance, including from serving women MPs, to the imposition of quotas.

Seeing that existing targets got them to where they are now, they are in diabolical trouble.

In his summation of where it all went wrong, the Nationals' Darren Chester says that Australians were fatigued by Covid, drought, bushfires, and floods. They wanted a grand consensus, not a great divider.

He said that Labor's primary vote had collapsed, yet they still managed to win government. There was a message in that for them, just as there was a message for the Liberals from the Teals. Some of the most successful and privileged Australians voted for change.

He saw the Greens' result in previously Labor-held seats as an ominous sign.

'The further you are away from the natural environment, the more likely you are to vote Green,' he mused.

Chester managed to get a small swing to him on primaries, and more than 3 per cent on a two-party-preferred basis. 'All politics is local,' he quoted.

Next time, he thinks the federal election will comprise 151 different elections. 'Money still matters, your ground game matters,' he said. Like others, he referred to the ageing membership of the Nationals and the Liberals. One of his regular volunteers told him it would be his last time handing out how-to-vote cards. Chester was flabbergasted, thinking he had somehow offended his friend. It turned out that the volunteer was stopping because he was 90 years old.

'I don't need more party members. I need more supporters,' he said, looking with envy at the Teals.

His supporters were all exhausted after having stood at booths that needed to be manned for 1,000 hours over the voting period.

His bigger problem was that he had to find ways of winning back heartland voters and women without alienating the Coalition's conservative base.

By mid-June, three weeks after the election, Albanese still had not fully moved into The Lodge, the prime minister's official residence in Canberra.

It had been mind-spinning. He had to look prime ministerial from the moment he was sworn in, and there was even drama with that. Morrison delayed submitting his resignation to the governor-general, and there was concern that the swearing-in would have to be delayed. Fearing that Albanese's departure for Tokyo would be delayed, Government House had to give Morrison a hurry-up.

Albanese had no time to sit and savour his elevation. He had to fly to Japan three hours after he was sworn in to attend the pre-arranged Quad meeting with President Biden and Prime Ministers Modi and Kishida.

Less than two weeks later, he took a group of ministers and business leaders to Indonesia. Reports from conservative businesspeople on the trip were glowing. Albanese had performed well, as had the foreign minister, Penny Wong, the trade minister, Don Farrell, and the industry and trade minister, Ed Husic. Business leaders described Husic, who was sworn in holding the Koran, as 'very impressive'.

My first post-election interview with Albanese took place at the end of another big day. Cabinet had met in Gladstone, and the energy regulator had imposed complete control of the electricity grid for the first time in its history in an effort to prevent power shortages and outages during a particularly cold snap.

Albanese's overwhelming emotion remained one of relief.

'I'd felt a great weight on me because of the expectation that we were going to win, and because for so many people, as you'd understand, it was for them an issue about what they thought about Australia,' he said.

'This campaign, how they thought about themselves and their relationship to politics and the community. It was ... I've only run as leader once ... People were desperate for us to win — really desperate. So many ... not just party members, but people, would stop me in the street, during the campaign. I just felt it.

'I did feel positive throughout the campaign, but it was that sense of *We've done it*. We had, as well, so many people [who] had been critical of the strategy that I laid out in 2019 and that, by and large, we stuck to and were disciplined about.'

Obviously, it was much easier later for him to talk about that last night, and what followed, than the awful first day of the campaign.

'I felt terrible about it,' he said. 'I felt completely terrible because, in part, I am bloody good at ... I can tell you ... name a year, I'll tell you what the score was in the grand final. I'll tell you how much the Majura Parkway here cost—$288 million, $144 million from each level of the government.

'Any project, I'll tell you. Regional rail, it was $3.225 billion.

'I can tell you. Maths is what I do. And I felt bad about it because I should have ... it shouldn't have happened. So I just owned it, didn't make any excuses. I just owned it, which was all you can do.'

Surrounded by the benefits of incumbency, it was timely to recall Bob Hawke's words from years ago, which Albanese has taken to heart, promising not to waste a single day, given that one of the best things about being in power is the ability to do good every single day—sometimes for just one person, sometimes for millions of people.

Six days after the election, as acting immigration minister, with the full blessing and authority of Albanese, Jim Chalmers announced that the Murugappan family—Nades, his wife, Priya, and their daughters, Kopika and Tharnicaa—would be provided with bridging visas to remove them from detention and enable them to return to Biloela.

They were able to celebrate the fifth birthday of their youngest daughter as a free family. They attended a community event for Albanese that day, presenting him with a bunch of flowers and a stubby holder decorated with native flora and fauna, including a cockatoo, which he had on the coffee table at The Lodge.

Attorney-general Mark Dreyfus announced an end to proceedings against Canberra solicitor Bernard Collaery that had dragged on for four years. Collaery was facing five charges, including that he had conspired with an ex-spy and his former client, known as Witness K, to reveal details of an alleged spying operation on Timor-Leste during sensitive oil- and gas-treaty negotiations.

The same day as the Gladstone cabinet meeting, the Fair Work Commission agreed to give lowest-paid workers a 5.2 per cent pay increase, slightly above the 5.1 per cent that Albanese had said during the campaign that they should 'absolutely' receive, taking their pay to $1.05 an hour more. At his press conference that day, Albanese had to borrow a coin to hold up, as he had during the campaign.

'It was awesome,' Albanese said, and did a gentle, double fist-pump while sitting down on a sofa in a small sitting room at The Lodge. It had been his spectacular cut-through moment. He was grateful that Morrison and some journalists had ridiculed him for it.

'We could not believe our luck,' he said.

'I doubled down, tripled down … that's why I brought out the dollar coin. To double down on it. Just to be very clear — this is what it means.'

During this first interview, he was still getting used to his title.

On one of his first nights at The Lodge, he was sitting by the fire in the small lounge watching Laura Tingle on *7.30* going through 'the government's' early progress, and talking about the prime minister.

For an instant, he thought: *They are doing okay*. Then he realised she had been talking about him and his government.

When the package ended, he rang her to say he had just had an out-of-body experience.

CHAPTER NINETEEN

The Best of Friends

If any further proof was needed that Scott Morrison had lost touch with reality, not only while he was prime minister, but that his malady had lingered for months after, it came during his first conversation with Josh Frydenberg after Anthony Albanese revealed that Treasury was one of the former prime minister's secret ministries.

Almost immediately after Albanese's stunning announcement, Morrison tried to contact Frydenberg, ostensibly to apologise to his former deputy. Frydenberg ignored Morrison's first few attempts, not trusting himself to speak to him, then finally answered. Frydenberg can't actually remember Morrison using the s-word. Sorry.

What really stuck in Frydenberg's mind, and his craw, was Morrison's response in that initial conversation, when a profoundly disappointed Frydenberg put to him: 'You wouldn't do it again if you had your time over!'

Morrison replied: 'Yes, I would.'

Frydenberg was staggered. When he asked him why he had done it, Morrison had no coherent explanation, except to say that 'No one understands what it was like' — a theme he would reprise at his press conference afterwards, the one where he also insisted that he and Frydenberg remained 'the best of friends'.

Frydenberg was incredulous.

After a few days, Morrison rang Frydenberg again. He told him he had been thinking about their conversation. On reflection, he said, no, he would probably not take Treasury if he had his time over. Note, he only referred to Treasury. And there was still no apology.

When I asked Frydenberg if he still regarded Morrison as a friend, he replied instinctively: 'Yes.' When I asked him if the friendship had been damaged, the answer was the same: 'Yes.'

Despite Frydenberg's positive reflex response, that is one relationship that will never be the same again.

Morrison began in politics with few friends, and ended with even fewer. People who had stuck by him for decades, fought all his battles, gathered his numbers, prayed with him, and defended him—often at some cost to their own reputations and careers—felt used, wounded, and deceived.

When we spoke in late August 2022, after Frydenberg had spent a week in Queensland with his family, it was the first time he had agreed to speak publicly about Morrison's actions.

Frydenberg found out what Morrison had done on social media after Albanese announced it. Friends and journalists bombarded him with messages, mostly featuring the googly-eyed emoji that doubles for OMG and WTF, which is exactly what he felt. We had a brief conversation then.

He was angry, hurt, confused, dumbstruck. It was such a betrayal of trust. He debated whether or not to respond publicly. After he decided he would, and to do it first for this book, he took a few days after the family holiday to compose a response. And to compose himself.

'It's impossible properly to evaluate the decision-making during the pandemic without understanding the context in which decisions were made,' Frydenberg told me.

'We faced a once-in-a-century pandemic, an evolving crisis, laden with uncertainty as to what each day would bring. This meant we had to take and live with decisions on both the health and economic front that in normal times would never have been contemplated.

'That being said, I don't think there was any reason for Scott to take on the additional Treasury portfolio. The fact he did take it, and it was not made transparent to me and others, was wrong and profoundly disappointing.

'It was extreme overreach.'

It was a measured, carefully calibrated response from Frydenberg as he sought to convey both empathy and anger, part personal separation from Morrison — essential if he is to resume his political career — part endorsement of their decision-making during Covid, and part occupation of the high moral ground. To which he was entitled. Frydenberg, in his own words, had been 'loyal to a fault' to Morrison. And this was how he was repaid.

Although he knew that Morrison had acquired Health, he did not know he had taken on Finance, and did not know he had moved on to other portfolios, including his own.

Frydenberg was struggling to come to terms with it all. During our conversation, he was still racking his brain trying to think what, if anything, could have prompted Morrison to acquire Treasury.

The leadership chatter hadn't revved up until much later in 2021, so Frydenberg did not think it was that — although, if, as Morrison revealed, he was medicating to sleep, who knows what he was thinking.

And, as written earlier, Alex Hawke reckons Morrison was

convinced that MPs were plotting against him. Former Labor cabinet minister Gerry Hand was fond of saying that all prime ministers go mad after a while, even in supposedly normal times, and these were extraordinary times.

There were, however, two events in late April, weeks before the 2021 budget and only days before Morrison's secret takeover, which Frydenberg thinks may have contributed to Morrison's decision to acquire Treasury.

One was a news story asserting that Frydenberg was pushing back against a levy to fund aged care that Morrison was backing. Frydenberg was concerned that the story was an attempt to split them, and said so to Morrison. Morrison told him that wouldn't happen because: 'I trust you, Josh.'

The second, difficult to comprehend, given the desertion of women from the Liberal Party, was in the lead-up to that year's budget on 11 May, when Morrison was fiercely resisting a push from Frydenberg to provide extra funding for childcare. The government was already spending around $10 billion on childcare, Morrison argued, and he wasn't convinced of its 'efficacy'.

Frydenberg, working with Jane Hume, Anne Ruston, Marise Payne, and Alan Tudge, had put together a package worth $1.8 billion that would particularly help those with two or more children. Kelly O'Dwyer had used polling a few years before to convince Morrison to fund a women's package. Frydenberg twisted his arm on childcare, using implied threats.

'I am telling you as treasurer I want this, you need it, you have ministers who support it,' Frydenberg told Morrison. It was a rare win. Frydenberg was proud that he had been able to turn Morrison around on an issue where he held very strong views.

After he heard that Morrison's secret takeover had occurred on 6 May 2021, only five days out from that year's budget, a badly bruised Frydenberg, who had prided himself on his loyalty, couldn't help wondering if those two events might have triggered it.

He could not think of any other explanation, and Morrison had certainly not been able to provide one that made any sense, other than that he was getting blamed for everything anyway, and that no one knew what it was like to be him.

If Frydenberg had known about it before, he says he would have insisted that Morrison revoke his takeover. He would have told Morrison that he was the deputy leader and the treasurer—not him. Colleagues say that if Mathias Cormann had known, he 'would have gone ballistic'. As would Karen Andrews.

Stuart Robert and Alex Hawke would have also told him to back off. It would have been a brave, or foolhardy, or completely deluded prime minister to have persisted in the face of such widespread opposition. Or, depending on his state of mind, he might have raced off to the governor-general to call an election.

If Morrison had resisted, Frydenberg is convinced there would have been a challenge, because of the level of outrage in the party's moderate and conservative ranks. More likely, despite the complete absence of remorse afterwards, Frydenberg believes that Morrison would have done one of his famous 'pivots' and relinquished the additional ministries.

Once the news broke, Morrison put it out there that he had apologised to his colleagues. In a fashion. In the same way he had apologised for all his other transgressions over the years. He didn't ring Mathias Cormann—Cormann rang him; he had to be prompted to call Karen Andrews; and he never said sorry to Keith Pitt.

As late as September 2022, Pitt and Morrison had not even

spoken. There had been an exchange of text messages, initiated by Pitt, about the possibility of the Cronulla Sharks playing the North Queensland Cowboys in the National Rugby League grand final. That was it. Morrison did not take the opportunity to say sorry, and Pitt had nothing else to say to him, except for lighthearted banter about football.

Albanese's reaction was similar to most people's, and common in politics when something so extraordinary unfolds. He didn't know whether to laugh or cry when he found out the full extent of Morrison's secret acquisitions. To laugh, because the whole thing was so preposterous; or to cry, because of the affront to parliament and to conventions.

Plagued, the book by Simon Benson and Geoff Chambers, two senior journalists at *The Australian* who were given extraordinary access by Morrison to chronicle his handling of the pandemic, revealed that he had been sworn in to Health, with the knowledge and consent of Greg Hunt, and had then taken Finance. The book presented this plan uncritically as one hatched by Morrison, with the advice of his attorney-general, Christian Porter, as to how to go about it.

The book extract appeared on Saturday 13 August 2022. It lay dormant until Samantha Maiden wrote for news.com.au the next night that Morrison had taken over Resources to override Pitt on PEP 11, and Andrew Clennell reported on Sky on Monday that Morrison hadn't told Cormann he had sworn himself into Finance.

On his last day of a brief holiday, Albanese twigged immediately to the importance of the story. He rang his staff, after reading it in the paper on Saturday, to ask them to get to the bottom of it.

Albanese revealed the extent of Morrison's disregard for colleagues and conventions on 16 August. The search at the Department of Prime Minister and Cabinet showed Morrison had been appointed to administer Health on 14 March 2020; Finance on 30 March 2020; Industry, Science, Energy and Resources on 15 April 2021; Home Affairs on 6 May 2021; and Treasury also on 6 May 2021. Each appointment was made under Section 64 of the Constitution.

It was a gift. Albanese first obtained an opinion on the constitutionality of Morrison's actions from the solicitor-general, Stephen Donaghue, then appointed former High Court Justice Virginia Bell to inquire into who knew what and when, to determine whether changes were needed to strengthen the existing protections for parliament and cabinet government.

In other words, to safeguard the system from abuse by the prime minister. Morrison cooperated with Bell's inquiry after seeking legal representation, to be paid by taxpayers.

In an extraordinary summation, from someone viewed by all sides of politics as solidly nonpartisan, Donoghue found that while Morrison had not broken any laws, acting secretly was 'inconsistent with the conventions and practices that form an essential part of the system of responsible government prescribed by … the Constitution'.

'An unpublicised appointment to administer a department therefore fundamentally undermines not just the proper functioning of responsible government, but also the relationship between the Ministry and the public service,' Donoghue wrote.

Whatever political plays there were in Albanese's response did not detract from the fact that what Morrison had done was profoundly stupid and dangerous—the actions of an isolated, mistrustful, out-of-control leader—and that Albanese's ordering of an inquiry was not only justified but critical.

Morrison had been protected by a conspiracy of silence. No one who knew what he had done blew the whistle. According to Labor government ministers, public servants were 'afraid' of Morrison, saying that they lived in 'an atmosphere of terror'.

The governor-general, David Hurley, was a former military man, very close to Morrison, also deeply religious, who would urge — or rather oblige — guests at his official residences, and at events around the country, to sing to one another. Guests were alerted to the expectations of their hosts by his wife, Linda, who would announce: 'I believe that singing is a gift we give to one another.'

The foreign affairs department began forewarning new ambassadors of the Hurley tradition before they made the trek to Government House.

'You Are My Sunshine' was a hot favourite. Guests were told to face the person next to them to sing the final chorus. Sometimes it would be the familiar tune with new lyrics written by Mrs Hurley that would be printed on the back of menus and handed out to guests. No one had an excuse not to sing along.

Hurley was punctilious about this ritual he had initiated, even though some guests found it awkward or embarrassing. But he did not see it as his duty or responsibility to notify the public that the prime minister had secretly sworn himself in to five additional portfolios.

A former staffer, involved intimately for years with interactions between prime ministers and governors-general, said that Morrison's secret takeovers and the seeming acquiescence of the governor-general came about as a result of 'weakened institutions, weakened processes, and weak people'. He was referring to the public service, the governor-general's office, and the prime minister's office.

He said that writing a letter to place on record his disapproval was the very least that Hurley could have done. He said it was wrong for people to keep describing what happened as 'weird', because that minimised what had occurred.

'It was not kooky — it was dangerous,' he told me.

He said that governors-general had at different times questioned directives from prime ministers or governments, compelling them to slow down procedures and to think carefully before embarking on potentially dangerous paths. Often, that was enough to stop precipitous actions.

In the aftermath of the revelations, Morrison became an object of ridicule. He joined in Facebook posts that poked fun at what he had done. Except that they were not laughing with him; they were laughing at him.

Even Peter Dutton made a joke at Morrison's expense at the press gallery's midwinter ball on 7 September. Dutton recited all the ministries he had held — from assistant treasurer, to Health, to Immigration, to Home Affairs and Defence — over his 21 years in parliament.

'Imagine how angry I was when I found out I could have been minister for all those portfolios at once,' he said. 'All those wasted years.'

'How good is Scott Morrison?'

Dominic Perrottet couldn't resist a swipe during budget estimates in the New South Wales parliament. Asked about his response to various scandals and controversies that had beset his government, he joked that at least he wasn't like the former prime minister.

'I am not Scott Morrison here. I don't run every single ministry,' Perrottet said. 'I have ministers to do their jobs.'

Before they knew who had done what, or how it had happened, some of Morrison's colleagues were critical of his office and his department. It did not help Morrison that the person in his office dealing with the paperwork was not a lawyer and was described by colleagues as highly secretive. Other staff complained that this staffer, John Harris, was reluctant to share information and to seek advice.

Even those usually counted among Morrison's few friends in government, who had followed him religiously, literally, were dismayed.

Stuart Robert thought it was 'nuts'. He was mightily offended by Morrison's lack of faith in him personally to be able to step into those portfolios if anything happened to the ministers.

He says that lots of crazy things happened during Covid, and blamed the secret ministry takeovers on poor advice. He said that either Morrison's chief of staff or the head of his department should have stopped him.

'They should have hauled him back,' he said.

Robert said that one of the early concerns in managing the pandemic was to hold the government together. He knew that in the wake of the Spanish flu pandemic, the Scullin government had fallen apart.

'We were facing Armageddon,' he said. Even so, he did not think this was a good-enough reason to excuse Morrison's actions. 'If Armageddon happens, if all those five [ministers] get wiped out, then swear others in,' he said.

He pointed out that it would only have taken a few minutes, and that if Morrison himself had gone down, another prime minister would have been sworn in.

'It was still a crazy time, crazy things happening,' he said, including Morrison being 'crazy' for thinking he could carry the load of five ministries if anything happened to the ministers. Robert said that Morrison would have collapsed under the burden.

Confirming that Morrison had never mentioned it to him, even during their frequent prayer sessions, Robert said: 'I am not sure he thought about it that much. I don't think he even remembered it.' Asked about reports that the National Security Committee had been briefed on Morrison's acquisition of Health, Robert said it took all of '20 seconds'. Others had trouble recalling even that.

Ben Morton said he could not remember if he had been told about Health and Finance, but did not know about the other ministries that Morrison had taken over. He said there was 'a lot of hyperventilating' after the revelations. Morton said there was nothing 'Machiavellian' about it, and in countries that had fared so much worse than Australia, people would be scratching their heads wondering if, post-Covid, this was the issue that was preoccupying Australians.

Michael McCormack worried that the revelations would leave a stain on the government's management of Covid.

Alex Hawke, although not a Pentecostal, was also part of the prayer group, and had been extremely close to Morrison for many years. He says he never knew, and that he would have been 'very upset' if he had found out that Morrison had made a decision in his immigration portfolio, which came under the Home Affairs umbrella.

When Karen Andrews heard Morrison say on 2GB that he couldn't remember if he had signed himself in to other portfolios, her radar went up. She took that as a sign that he had. She called on Morrison to quit as soon as Albanese revealed it a few hours after Morrison's memory lapse.

Andrews, as she made clear in our earlier interview, was a stickler for process. She believed that Morrison had indulged in an abuse of process. She had decided early on what she would say about it if asked, even if it emerged that her portfolio had not been acquired.

He had to go. The party had to be able to draw a line under his tenure, and while he remained in parliament that was not possible.

Andrews had been attending an event at a women's shelter in Launceston when Albanese broke the news about Morrison's acquisition of Home Affairs. The phone of her press secretary, Valeria Cheglov, lit up. Andrews delivered her lines to waiting cameras on the way into a previously scheduled shadow cabinet meeting.

She told me that she did not take it personally or regard it as a slight when she found out that Morrison had taken on Home Affairs. Nor was she fussed about getting an apology. But she was mightily offended that he had not repaid the loyalty he had been shown.

'It diminished him, it diminished the cabinet, and diminished the government—all that work we did during Covid, industry stepped up, it was really good work. That was diminished,' she said.

She said that if ministers had known, they would have insisted that his extra commissions be revoked. If he had refused, she believes it is possible he would have been challenged.

'He had very strong support from ministers at the time. I thought cabinet worked well,' she said. 'Ministers were unswervingly loyal to him. We went into the election fighting it out for him and the Liberal Party. Josh Frydenberg pushed back on challenging him. There was so much loyalty given to Morrison, and he has, in hindsight, squandered all the goodwill that was there.'

She copped some negative feedback for telling him to go. But, overwhelmingly, the feedback was positive.

A tough operator, Andrews had considered running for the party's deputy leadership after the election. When it became clear that Dutton was the only contender for the leadership, she decided not to put her hand up. The party couldn't have both the leader and the deputy from Queensland.

Andrews subsequently had two words of advice for Dutton after he was installed: 'Be inclusive.'

When Morrison eventually called her to apologise, after being prompted by Dutton, it was a brief conversation. He told her he had only acquired portfolios where ministers had unilateral powers.

Andrews did not ask him why he had done it. Asked why she hadn't, she replied: 'Because there is no reason I would think was plausible.'

She was right to assume that. During his hour-long press conference, Morrison's explanations for his actions were both implausible and insulting. Also delusional. He had to take control because people thought he already controlled everything, and he was getting blamed anyway for everything that went wrong.

He said he had to take control in case there was 'some threat to the national interest as a result of unilateral action by an individual'. That individual would have been the elected person he had appointed to the cabinet who could not be trusted to make decisions in the national interest. Unlike him.

He sounded hollow, incoherent, full of self-pity and self-justification.

'There was a clear expectation established in the public's mind, certainly in the media's mind, and absolutely certainly in the mind of the opposition, as I would walk into Question Time every day, that I, as prime minister, was responsible pretty much for every single thing that was going on, every drop of rain, every strain of the virus, everything that occurred over that period of time,' he said.

'Now, I'm not taking issue with that,' he said, although it sounded very much like he was taking issue with it.

'But this was the expectation, and I think the Australian public had an expectation the prime minister had the authority to even overrule states. Now, that was not the case.

'But where there were authorities or powers that could be established, there was a clear expectation that I, as prime minister, would have sought to put those in place to protect the country and lead us through what was a very difficult period. People held me, rightly, to account for that.'

As they do all prime ministers, always, regardless of the times or circumstances.

The Nationals' Senate leader, Bridget McKenzie, was outraged when she found out, believing that Morrison had trashed important principles of accountability and transparency. The fact that it happened during a crisis was no excuse. That was a time, more than ever, when proper processes should have been observed.

McKenzie, one of the first members of the Coalition to come out publicly to criticise Morrison, who describes herself as a small-c conservative, was appalled. She described it as a 'bizarre disrespect' of the process.

McKenzie, in a relationship with Simon Benson, one of the authors of *Plagued*, says she only found out what Morrison had done when she read the extract in the newspaper.

Others responded lamely. They feared they would lose Morrison's seat of Cook if he walked, or that it would harm the New South Wales Liberal government's chances of re-election.

They skated over important principles, long-established conventions, and the public interest for what they perceived would be to their political advantage. It was shameful.

In a deliberate tactic — thought-through, but ill-judged — hours after Albanese revealed the extent of the deception, shadow cabinet decided to downplay it.

'The view was, we were best not to talk about it,' one frontbencher said later. The dominant view was: 'A day not spent talking about the rising cost of living is a wasted day.'

As if it was not possible to talk about the economy and to address a serious breach of conventions at the same time.

Warren Entsch, one of those who had urged Frydenberg towards the end of 2021 to move against Morrison, does not believe that Morrison's actions would have been enough to force a spill if they had been unearthed before the election. He believed it would have been too late. Even when he was pressing Frydenberg to challenge, he knew it was not without risk.

Andrew Bragg, who had also appealed to Frydenberg to challenge, was similarly not convinced that it would have led to a spill against Morrison.

'The interventions in the New South Wales Liberal Party and the handling of the religious discrimination agenda demonstrated a clear management style in which the later emergence of megalomania was unsurprising,' he said.

It took Peter Dutton too long to robustly condemn what Morrison had done. As the newly anointed leader of the opposition, he was loathe from the outset to launch into a public dissection of Morrison's tenure. He didn't want to wallow in the past.

Dutton had no idea how long Morrison planned to stay in parliament. All he knew was that Morrison had told friends he would probably stay for a year.

Morrison gave an assurance to Dutton that he would be constructive, 'more Howard than Turnbull', but his mere presence was enough to distract, damage, and to remind.

Dutton was trapped here, as he was on so many things. He believed there was nothing to be gained by raking over Morrison's mistakes or his unpopularity. He would not be a factor at the next election.

That sounded a lot like wishful thinking. Without a clean break from his rule, the reputational damage to the Coalition, especially to the Liberals, threatened to continue.

Dutton took a number of bad decisions early on. He made a captain's call not to support Labor's legislation for 43 per cent emissions reductions by 2030 because he feared it would split the Coalition. But if he couldn't withstand an internal dispute early on, then he probably never would.

He rejected the government's invitation to attend the jobs-and-skills summit. The Nationals' leader, David Littleproud, accepted.

Immediately distancing himself from Morrison's madness should have been automatic. As the days passed and the outrage grew, Dutton toughened up his language, separating himself a little from Morrison.

Morrison's continued presence in parliament made it difficult for the Liberals to draw a line under his tenure, and for them to separate themselves from him. But it was not immediately obvious to anyone what Morrison would do if he was not in parliament, or who would even offer him a job, given his record and his reputation.

Some of them, sounding like the last soldiers coming out of the jungle decades after the war had ended, didn't even want to criticise him.

There were more than 600 submissions to the review of the election loss conducted by former federal director Brian Loughnane and Senator Jane Hume. Obviously, Morrison was a significant factor in the loss, as was the phenomenal campaign run by the Teals. Western Australia alone will take years to win back.

Liberals estimated that they would have to get their primary vote up to 48 per cent or 49 per cent to regain the seats won by the Teals. They hoped they could do that in three years. More realistically, they thought it might take six, and in the meantime they fully expected the Teals to expand further into the regions.

Liberals unearthed plenty of not-so-fun facts. In Victoria,

more people voted Teal than voted for the Nationals. Only one in four women aged between 18 and 34 voted Liberal. 'We have lost a generation,' one female Liberal MP said, urging changes to recruitment practices and a broadening of the membership base to ensure that more women were chosen to run for parliament.

'That won't happen with a 70 per cent male membership,' she said. 'The more we talk about our woman problem, the more of a problem we have with women.'

She said the Liberals needed policies that appealed to modern women.

'The fastest-growing cohort is single women. They marry later and live longer, they won't be disrespected and ignored, and they are the best educated in the world, 'she said.

According to a former female minister, although Morrison had appointed a record number of women to cabinet, he never sought their advice. 'It was an exercise in window dressing,' she said.

The morning after the election, a despondent Simon Birmingham had said that the party needed more women and a more ambitious target on climate change.

So Dutton's captain's call to vote against Labor's climate change bill offended the moderates, while his leaving open the option of supporting the Indigenous voice to parliament offended the right.

Such is the lot of an opposition leader presiding over a deeply divided party.

There were dismal predictions from colleagues that Dutton would struggle to make it to the next election. One frontbencher, while describing him as engaging personally, said that he had 'a head like a robber's dog'. He gave him 12 months, which sounds a bit harsh.

Another believed that Dutton made the call on climate change because he feared a repeat of the history of opposition leaders elected after losing government not making it to the next election. 'He is already looking over his shoulder at Angus Taylor,' he said.

Another, not a moderate, said that the party risked looking like 'Neanderthals' on climate change.

One conservative defended Dutton's decision, saying that the Coalition had come close to fracturing over the adoption of net-zero emissions in 2021, and that they were best to zero in on 'lawfare'.

Those opposing Dutton's call, describing it as 'completely mad', think he should have simply waved the government's legislation through and saved himself for the fight over the economic impacts of carve-outs. They believed it would have been better to wait to see which industries and which sectors would be most affected by measures to achieve the reductions.

One of the first policies that Dutton announced, barely a month after the election, was to allow pensioners to earn more without losing the pension, which Morrison had left lying in the bottom drawer. At a time of severe worker shortages, Dutton said that allowing pensioners to earn $600 a fortnight, rather than the existing $300, without losing their pension might help in places such as airports and restaurants.

Albanese and Chalmers had toyed with a similar policy before the election, but weren't convinced of its effectiveness. Instead, they adopted a version of it during the jobs-and-skills summit, announcing a one-off income credit to allow aged pensioners to earn an extra $4,000 over the financial year without losing any of their pension. Whether the idea survives beyond that depends on the take-up rate and a cost-benefit analysis of the results.

Someone forgot to give the deputy opposition leader, Sussan Ley, a brief history lesson about the policy. Ley blasted the government, saying it was too little, too late, was half what the opposition was proposing, and should have been introduced 'weeks ago'. Or maybe even months before, by Morrison.

While Dutton left it open to support the Indigenous voice to parliament, the election of dynamic Indigenous Country Liberal Senator Jacinta Nampijinpa Price from the Northern Territory complicated debate about the plan. Price gave an impassioned speech urging greater action against the drug- and alcohol-fuelled violence being endured by women and children. She flatly opposed the voice. That mobilised conservatives to flag their opposition to it.

When Price finished her speech, Birmingham leaned across the despatch box and told the government leader in the Senate, Penny Wong, that this was not just a problem for the Coalition, but for Labor as well.

In a terrific speech to the annual Garma Festival in Arnhem Land, Albanese said it was possible to do both the symbolic and the practical.

'Let us all understand this, very clearly: Australia does not have to choose between improving peoples' lives and amending the Constitution,' he said.

'We can do both—and we have to.'

The problem was not just the fault lines inside the Coalition party room. A potentially far greater problem was the dysfunction in the party's infrastructure.

One person not completely depressed about the future, while acknowledging the desperate state of the party, which would take time to fix, was Queensland Senator James McGrath—the architect of one of the Liberals' greatest victories, when Campbell Newman was elected premier of Queensland.

'The greatest challenge facing Peter Dutton isn't climate change. It is the cooked state of the Liberal Party,' McGrath said.

Robert agreed with McGrath about the party's dysfunctional structure, but also reflected on its political positioning. Although they have never been friends—and even if you are, in politics it doesn't count for much, as Robert discovered—Robert promised to help Dutton keep the party anchored to the centre.

'The problems are existential,' Robert said. 'The nation has stepped to the left. It's a step change.

'The answer is not to go further to the right. We have to step to the centre, because that is where the country is. We have to be a centre-right party.'

Despite his disappointment in Morrison, Robert said the key was not to dismiss the government's achievements in handling Covid. 'We still came through it better than any country in the world,' he said.

McGrath said that Queensland and Tasmania were the only two properly functioning state divisions in the country. 'You have basically four state divisions and two territory divisions from a federal perspective that are bankrupt,' he said.

'It is a challenge as we rebuild, but this is the inheritance left for Dutton.

'I think that there is goodwill there for a rebuild. The danger is people who want to go to the right, and people who want to go to the left. I think we have the good bones, and we can come back.

'The issue the party faces is the structure on the ground. Unless there is real change, it will get worse before it gets worse. When you have factional warfare and factional warlords, the ground campaign dies.

'We are a political party. Not a debating society, not a supper club, not a bank. We are here to fight and win elections to implement Liberal Party beliefs. When we fail, Australia falls.'

Dutton's challenges were as epic as Albanese's, but without the luxury of government to address them. The character of the Liberal Party has changed, potentially forever, with no guarantee it can survive.

That change was welcomed by some, including the party's motormouth female federal vice-president, Teena McQueen, who told a conference of conservatives in October 2022 that 'the good thing about the last federal election is a lot of those lefties are gone — we should rejoice in that. People I've been trying to get rid of for a decade have gone, we need to renew with good conservative candidates.'

Simon Birmingham rightly demanded that she resign. An equivocal Angus Taylor called on Liberals to show respect. Dutton flatly declared her remarks unacceptable, and promised she wouldn't be repeating them, but did not join the moderates in seeking her resignation.

A few disillusioned small-l Liberals believe the time has come for the party to be honest and to start calling itself the Conservative Party, with a capital C.

Morrison's solution for the once-broad church that was the Liberal Party was a schism. He told people after the election that the Liberals and Nationals should unite Australia-wide along the lines of the Liberal National Party of Queensland, to create a nationwide conservative party. Then the moderates could form a separate party to appeal to electors in all the old heartland seats. Under this Morrison scenario, they could both then come together to form a Coalition and live together happily ever after. Or not.

CHAPTER TWENTY

Future Tense

At the next election in 2025, all being well, Anthony Albanese has a clear idea of how he wants Australians to see him. It sounds simple enough.

'I want them to say about me that I'm a person of good character,' he said. 'That I put the national interest first. That I'm not someone who has seen everything through a political prism. That I've restored integrity to politics. That I'm a person of my word. That I've tried to implement what I said I would before the 2022 election.'

He also has a clear idea of what he wants to be able to say to Australians in three years about what he has achieved.

First up is: 'That we have kept our commitments.'

It is difficult to quote that answer in full, because Toto, who had only just moved into The Lodge when this interview took place, kept interrupting. Albanese's answer was punctuated by 'She's a cow', referring to Toto's fluffy toy, which she kept dropping at my feet to play with, and 'She's relentless', referring to her determination, which, in some ways, probably reflects his.

If all goes according to plan, he wants to be able to say to Australians that his government has invested in clean energy, in skills, and in infrastructure to build productivity; has addressed gender equality; that the National Anti-Corruption Commission is up and running; that cost-of-living pressures have been lessened; that childcare is cheaper; that the decline in real wages has stopped; that business and unions are cooperating; and that the government has been clear about its intentions and competent in the way it has implemented its policies.

Add to that a referendum on the Indigenous voice to parliament, which he elevated early with passion and commitment, and it is a hefty agenda, filled with symbolic and practical objectives from a prime minister determined to — dare we say it — leave a legacy.

The question is, given that he faces the grimmest economic conditions for decades, the highest inflation rate, the highest cost-of-living increases, rising interest rates, Covid still impacting on the community, as well as the most uncertain national and international security environment, how much of it will be achieved?

After waiting too long to increase rates, the Reserve Bank approached its task to subdue inflation with gusto, running the risk that it would slam the economy into reverse.

There was pressure on Albanese and his main economic team, Jim Chalmers and Katy Gallagher, to bring forward measures to ease the pressure on families, including the childcare package, to extend the fuel-excise cut, and, of course, to abandon promised tax cuts and spend the money elsewhere.

Resisting those calls and sticking to the plan as well as the promises was vital — not only for the obvious reason that higher spending would only feed higher inflation — and easier to do in the early stages, when the government was still riding high in the polls.

Even if Albanese is able to implement everything he has promised, there will be the question of what comes next. Good leaders know that voters always expect more at an election than a recitation of the government's record.

A quarter of a century after the introduction of the GST, tax is the most obvious area begging for reform. That will take courage and impeccable preparation—the kind of battle plan that won him the election, with its strategic thinking and attention to the minutest details.

Albanese might get away with reworking the stage-three tax cuts, which he promised both before and after the election to implement, if they become part of a wider reform package that he takes to the next election.

As prime minister, his overarching mission has to be to restore trust in government. The fates of Keating, Howard, and Gillard, who went back on promises, or embarked on reforms for which they had no mandate, as explained by Paul Erickson to frontbenchers in February 2020 after Morrison's crash in the wake of his flight to Hawaii during the bushfires, remain as a salutary reminder. The governments they led had been in office longer, but history shows how severely voters punish governments and leaders if they go back on their word without sound economic, moral, and political reasons.

Albanese knows that if he reneges on such a significant, unequivocal pledge, the cost to his reputation could be politically life-threatening. Breaking that promise without the consent of voters would also breathe life into an opposition struggling for relevance.

Perhaps, if he has done everything in his power to fulfil his promises—going beyond a stunt a day to satisfy his ego or the demands of the news cycle, as was the wont of his predecessor—and to protect Australians from the great recessions or depressions that threaten abroad, he might be trusted to tackle tax reform.

If he fails in his mission to restore trust, the drift away from major parties to independents and minor parties, which has been building for years, will only grow.

He will fail if he shirks other tough decisions, or if he allows the inevitable tensions that will arise between him and his ministers to consume his government. He has a strong frontbench. Chalmers and Gallagher are working extremely well together in the face of the most daunting challenges. Wong is formidable in foreign affairs, and Burke, Burney, Bowen, Plibersek, and Clare are powerful advocates. Marles is steady. Clare O'Neil is impressive. So are Madeleine King, Michelle Rowland, Ed Husic, Mark Dreyfus, and Pat Conroy.

Albanese was confident enough to give his frontbenchers the licence to do their jobs. He doesn't feel compelled to hog the limelight every day, nor to overtly or covertly take over their ministries, but he makes it obvious who is in charge, as in the pre- and post-selling of the first budget to show that the document was as much his as it was Chalmers'. He consults, allows his ministers to debate publicly as well as privately, then makes the final call, as he did when he shut down debate on abandoning the stage-three tax cuts.

Although Albanese has kept up his tradition of Sunday-night dinners, which worked so well for him in opposition — with a change of venue now to The Lodge — he needs to be mindful of the jealousies and paranoia that always beset cabinets and governments.

From the beginning, Albanese was intent on showing that there was a better way of governing, that he could deliver on his commitments in a 'competent and inclusive way'. And to show that 'politics is less angry than it was under the Morrison government'.

Albanese's first task, through happenstance, was to restore Australia's reputation internationally, and not just with the French. In this interview, he was scathing about Morrison's standing abroad. Boris Johnson had just quit, and with all the accusations about his lying, there were the inevitable comparisons with Morrison. Albanese wished Johnson well, but he did not feel in the least sorry for him.

Albanese had just returned from a NATO meeting in Madrid and a visit to Paris to meet with President Macron. He said that Morrison was seen globally 'as just not being trustworthy'. And not only by Macron.

'The US was told that Labor was consulted during the AUKUS process, when we weren't. And they were told that France was okay with all of the arrangements, and quite clearly they weren't.

'Which is why ... France withdrew its ambassadors, not just from Australia, but the United States. I've been very much welcomed internationally.'

Unlike Morrison, he implied. It is true that there was suspicion abroad about Morrison initially, particularly in the US as a result of his closeness to Trump. That lessened after he and Biden met, and then flared again after the mishandling of the nuclear submarine announcement, compounded by Morrison's leaking of personal messages from Macron to try to counter his accusation that he had lied.

'And you look at some of the pictures that were shown of Morrison when he'd attend forums, and he ... there was a sort of distance there,' Albanese said.

'And the government's position on things like climate change. The sort of nonsense that [Angus] Taylor and co. would put here were just regarded with contempt internationally. They just didn't get away with it. To go to the Glasgow summit and not really have anything to say. People internationally saw the pamphlet for what it was—a glossy pamphlet with no substance. And for Johnson as the host of the conference, for Biden, for the Europeans, the Canadians. That just didn't ... stack up. And that's across the political spectrum as well.'

Albanese knows that to have any hope of coping with the problems he confronts and the personalities he needs to persuade, honest dealings and an even temperament are indispensable.

He said there was plenty thrown at him during the campaign. He remained calm, but admitted that is not always the case.

'I try not to lose my temper, but I am not perfect,' he told me.

Those who have dealt with him, including from conservative ranks, describe him as methodical and clever, without having to always be the smartest person in the room, and probably the 'most normal' of any of his five predecessors.

Albanese reckons some people have called him a bit OC [obsessive compulsive] because he likes to be well organised. 'I never put anything off until tomorrow I can do today,' he said.

'He is doing everything right,' one senior Liberal observed after Albanese's first 100 days. After dealing with him and those close to him, he concludes: 'They are not going to make the same mistakes as Rudd.'

Albanese knew it was important to set the right tone from the beginning. He had watched enough prime ministers up close to know what worked and what didn't. He was still himself, but as different as it was possible to be from Morrison.

Although reared a Catholic, he took the oath at his swearing-in rather than holding a Bible, explaining later that he firmly believed in the separation of church and state. It was deliberately pointed. He was outraged by Morrison's post-election sermon telling people not to trust government.

'I believe that government does play a role in people's lives and our living standards,' Albanese told Virginia Trioli on ABC radio.

'I say to young people all the time, get involved, because government will impact on the quality of your life, whether you get healthcare when you need it, what sort of education opportunities you have access to, what your standard of living looks like.

'And the idea that he's out there and pressing the United Nations button again—I've spent the first two months since our election … trying to repair our international relations. And that sort of nonsense, throwaway conspiracy line about the United Nations, I think isn't worthy of someone who led Australia.'

Less than two months after the election, a few remaining senior Liberals thought it would be a good idea to criticise Albanese for being overseas so much. It was, given all the circumstances, ridiculous and unfair. It only reminded people that Morrison had done a runner to Hawaii for a holiday during the bushfires. Political genius.

The shadow treasurer and wannabe leader, Angus Taylor, sensing an opportunity, with floods again devastating New South Wales, accused Albanese of circumnavigating the globe and ignoring problems at home.

What he and the others ignored was that the floods had begun while Albanese was away; he hadn't snuck off to Hawaii on a holiday while the place was being devastated without telling anybody; he had visited Ukraine, where the war made it unsafe to travel with mobile phones, so he was incommunicado; and, by the way, part of the reason he was overseas was to clean up messes left by his predecessor, including with the president of France and with Pacific nations. Details, details.

Dominic Perrottet, who looked more comfortable being with Albanese than he ever did with Morrison, shot down the accusations. Dutton also promptly closed them down.

Coming to grips with life in opposition was as hard as coming to grips with government.

Albanese said he had a lot of time during the lockdowns to think about how he would approach the job of leading the government. He didn't go around as a kid saying he would be prime minister one day. He didn't ever think it was seriously possible until 2013, and even then, according to those urging him to run for the leadership after Labor lost to Abbott, he had to think long and hard about putting his hand up.

In 2012, during the Rudd–Gillard wars, when he said that all he ever wanted to do was fight Tories, a few people commended him. At last, they said, someone with a bit of common sense had spoken up. They didn't mean for him to beat up on conservatives, and he says now that is never what he meant. He wanted Labor to end its civil war and to turn its attention to the enemies opposite, rather than within. The thought crossed his mind then that, maybe one day, he might get there.

Albanese didn't win all of the many battles he fought, but he did have to fight for everything he got, including all the positions he held in the Labor Party.

When he was elected to parliament in 1996 after a ferocious battle with the No Aircraft Noise Party, the leader, Kim Beazley, told him to run for the frontbench. He told Beazley he didn't think he would get elected. Sure enough, he wasn't. He was blocked by the Martin Ferguson left, as he knew he would be. But he reckons that most, not all, of his internal opponents later ended up as close supporters, including the right's supremo, Graham Richardson, and his sidekick, Leo McLeay.

When Albanese was assistant secretary of the state ALP, his internal enemies took advantage of his absence overseas to move his desk and belongings out of his office. When he got home, he turned up with a few of his closest allies to put the furniture back the way it was. 'I just wouldn't cop it,' he said. Richardson said to Albanese: 'I told 'em not to do it.'

'He was a bit of a wild man in his youth,' Richardson says now. 'Politically, not personally.' Asked if he could ever have imagined back then that Albanese would one day become prime minister,

Richardson said: 'No. I can unequivocally say I did not envisage it.'

He describes Albanese as a 'really decent person' whose essential nature has not changed, but who grew steadily over a long period of time.

Like many others from the right — and the left — former senator Stephen Loosley had an unhappy relationship with Albanese. Loosley was general secretary of the New South Wales ALP when Albanese was the junior assistant secretary, the slot reserved for the left. Loosley delegated the right's assistant secretary, John Della Bosca, to deal with Albanese, whom he described as a 'firebrand radical'. He was being polite.

Loosley recalls a story about Rodney Cavalier, a former New South Wales Labor government minister, regarded as being in the moderate left and no friend of Albanese's, walking in the city one day when he turned the corner and ran into Albanese. 'I didn't expect to see you here — you are like Banquo's ghost,' Cavalier said to him.

'I don't know what you are talking about. You should not be in the left,' Albanese told Cavalier.

Like so many others, Loosley never thought for a moment that Albanese would become prime minister. He says that Albanese is 'unrecognisable' now, and thinks that he presided over the best beginning to a Labor government since the two-man combination of Gough Whitlam and Lance Barnard in 1972.

'He is very measured and very disciplined,' Loosley says. 'Let us hope it continues.'

When you ask Albanese what all those battles say about him, he wears them as a badge of honour. 'I am tough,' he said.

'No one has ever handed me anything. I have been underestimated my whole life. Everything I have in politics and in my life I have fought for. It's not like I had a hand-up at any stage.

Obviously, there were people who supported me — no one does things on their own,' he said.

'But it builds resilience.'

So when Morrison would taunt him across the despatch box, trying to psych him out, saying *You wait, we haven't started on you yet*, thinking the longer he waited to call the election, the more he would wear him down, Albanese was unfazed.

'He would be trying to intimidate me, and I would say to him: 'I have fought people a lot tougher than you, mate.'

Albanese began attending Labor Party branch meetings as soon as he could walk. He would go with his mum, Maryanne, a working-class Catholic single mum, who told her son that his father had died and had given him his surname. In the 1960s, it was easier being a widow than an unmarried mother.

'She would have been incredibly proud,' he said. 'Proud of me, but proud of herself as well. It's an extraordinary achievement for her as a single mum.'

He thought his mother had only been on a plane once in her life, maybe twice, when she flew to Canberra to see him sworn in as the MP for Grayndler in 1996, then to watch him deliver his first speech. She was sitting in the public gallery. He couldn't look at her, because she was crying all the way through it. He would have started bawling, too.

He thought about that while he was on board the VIP aircraft, now renamed Toto One, which flew him back from Tokyo, where he attended the Quad with the leaders of the US, Japan, and India only days after he was sworn in. He left Tokyo as early as he could so he could to get back in time, before the day ended, to mark the anniversary of his mother's death. As soon as he landed, he got straight into C1, the prime minister's car with the flag on the front. With a police escort, he headed straight for Rookwood Cemetery.

It was 20 years to the day since she had died, and he always made a point of visiting her on the anniversary. It was dark and a little spooky. The cops left the car lights on, and accompanied him armed with a torch. They left him alone at her gravesite under a tree in the Catholic section that she had chosen. She had bought two plots — the one next to her for him, so he could be buried beside her. Her near neighbours there are Jack Lang and Fred Daly, and, of course, her parents.

He felt her presence strongly, and then did what so many of us do when we visit the dearly departed, and began a conversation. 'Hey, mum. Here I am,' he said. 'Guess what?' Although he figured she already knew. Again, because you can't do it too often, he thanked her for everything she had done for him.

He was bowled over that she had been able to pay for her plot and his out of her pension. When she died, she was six weeks ahead on her rent. That's something else he got from her. He is no spendthrift.

'I am careful with money. I bought my first house in my 20s, and I have never paid a cent in interest on any of my credit cards,' he said. 'I am fiscally very careful. And in policy terms, too.'

That thought reminded him that he had cut staff entitlements for the independents from eight to five, which had saved $1.5 million. They had asked for an extra staffer, and were outraged by the cut. He was dismayed that they had so many already. 'I was, like, *Are you kidding me?*'

A significant life-changing event, one which almost ended his, was when a Range Rover driven by an 18-year-old ploughed into his car on 8 January 2021. He thought he was going to die. By the look of his car afterwards, it was amazing that he hadn't.

One person who can attest to that is his long-time friend and former staffer Darcy Byrne, now mayor of the Inner West

Council in Sydney. Byrne was getting ready to meet Albanese at the Marrickville Golf Club for a social catch-up when Albanese called to tell him not to bother going to the club, that he had been in a car accident, and to come straight away. It took Byrne only a couple of minutes to get there.

Albanese was still sitting in the seat of his mangled car. He had been told by an off-duty nurse not to move. He was calling people to tell them what had happened, including Jodie, who arrived soon after.

Byrne says that if the impact had been 30 or 50 centimetres the other way, it would have been 'lights out'.

Despite what had just happened, and the fact that he was in a lot of pain, Byrne says Albanese was cool, calm, and collected. Byrne saw him again a couple of weeks later. He said it was obvious that the accident had changed him, given him a different perspective on life and his political career.

He began to look after himself better. He dieted. He also seemed more resolved to be better and to do what he thought was right. He had been given another chance at life, but he wouldn't get another go at an election.

Byrne, who went to work for Albanese the week that Rudd was deposed as prime minister, and left after the 2019 election, describes Albanese as 'very, very tough'. Byrne says the fact that Albanese had never been burdened by a 'Messiah complex' would serve him well in office.

He says that Albanese has surrounded himself with good people who know him well, who do not hesitate to tell him where he has gone wrong. That can sometimes lead to what are euphemistically known as robust exchanges; however, Byrne says one of Albanese's best qualities is that he can have arguments with people without leaving their relationships permanently scarred.

Byrne reckons that Albanese's great friend and mentor Tom

Uren was probably the only person who ever truly believed that Albanese would become prime minister.

Asked when Byrne knew it would happen, he jokes: '21 May.'

In our second interview, Albanese said he knew even after the 2019 election that Morrison was beatable. That was partly because he could see clearly where Bill Shorten had gone wrong, which was in trying to 'govern from opposition'.

'I had a very clear idea of how we should position ourselves at the election in 2022,' he said. 'Just as I think I have a clear idea of how I want us to be positioned by the next election in 2025.

'Now, you can't stick rigidly to that, because the world's not like that. Events are dynamic, and you have to respond to events as they arise. And we didn't know at that point, for example, that the pandemic would come, but if you go back and look at my speech when ... on the day I became leader, I spoke about being Labor leader, not being opposition leader.

'I spoke about putting the national interest first. I spoke about some of the national policy priorities that we would have, and I think that the tone that you set as a political leader is important.'

He scoffed at attempts by Morrison and his ministers to brand him as being on the extreme left by using what he had said or written as a university student.

He quoted Uren saying to him: 'You have to learn something every day. You need to get better as a person every day. You need to grow as a person.'

'And I've taken that to heart as something that I try to do. So when some people say to me, "Have you changed from 1985 or 1995?", I say: "I hope so."'

This second interview took place the day after Japan's former prime minister Shinzo Abe had been assassinated.

At his press conference paying tribute to Abe the previous day,

Albanese made it clear that he would not change his behaviour as a result of the assassination.

'We need to in this country go about our business. I think that is a very good thing in Australia that you can go out and walk the dog, not by myself, but with some protection these days,' he said.

'That's a good thing. And we need to make sure that part of our democracy is being able to go around. We've just had an election campaign where Mr Morrison and myself, and the candidates around Australia, met Australians from all walks of life. That's a good thing. We need to make sure that in cherishing our democracy, we're not put off from engaging.'

When I arrived at The Lodge on that brutally cold Sunday morning, he was outside throwing a tennis ball for Toto, who loved her new digs.

He was wearing a short-sleeved T-shirt, and, after I left, having added a sleeveless puffer vest, he was heading off to walk Toto, accompanied by members of his personal-protection squad. Touch wood, the most fearful thing about living in Canberra is catching pneumonia.

The fault lines in the government and the opposition were obvious even then. The Liberals were struggling to cope with reality, and Labor had the harshest reality imaginable to contend with.

The goodwill and the relationships that Albanese has built inside Labor will be tested by the strain of multitudes of difficult decisions that he and his government will have to make all day, every day. There are times he will have to bend to popular opinion, and other times when he will have to ignore it, and be smart enough to know when to hold firm and when to compromise.

The death of Queen Elizabeth drew the inevitable, immediate questions about a referendum on Australia becoming a republic, which he promptly dismissed as inappropriate before pointing out that he had never promised it for this term and that his priority was the Indigenous voice to parliament. He wisely dismissed calls for the two to be dealt with simultaneously. That would only guarantee the defeat of both.

The cancellation of a parliamentary sitting week in the wake of the Queen's death temporarily threw out his schedule, and his declaration of a public holiday drew moans and groans from business about the costs.

He stuck to the absolute letter of the prescribed protocols laid down years before, determined not to show disrespect, or to inflame the monarchists or those tempted to side with them. Those battles will be fought another day, and he needs to bank as much goodwill as he can between now and then from the middle ground.

He could prove to be the reverse of Morrison — to be a much better prime minister than campaigner. It is in his hands.

Albanese will make mistakes. That is inevitable. Plenty will go wrong, and occasionally it will be his fault. The lessons of the first day of the campaign should stay with him: admit the error, fix it, and keep going. But months after his election, those early words of Tony Burke that he had grown in the job were at least holding true. Labor's and Albanese's position in the polls had improved. Voters seemed more than content with their choice.

Jay Weatherill, a former South Australian premier, co-author of the review of Labor's loss in 2019, and one of the architects of the childcare policy, says that new governments have a 'golden' period of around six months to set about implementing their policies and to define the character of their administration.

Conscious of that, Albanese moved quickly to implement his agenda on climate, integrity, and childcare.

One very big mark in Albanese's favour was that he has never looked as if he was searching for a character to play. Or tried out a different one every day for the cameras, supposedly to maintain contact with reality — which didn't work out so well for his predecessor.

'I am who I am,' he told me. The challenge, given the demands of the prime ministership, along with the luxuries that accompany it — people to shop, cook, and clean for you, and to drive and fly you wherever you go — will be to stay in touch with his old self, with everyday people and the issues that concern them. He has to keep people around him not frightened to prick his bubble when he gets too full of himself, or who know how best to get him back up when he's down.

He will try to keep playing tennis at his local club, even though there is a court at The Lodge, and he will put some effort into maintaining contact with his friends from childhood and his old neighbourhood. There is no danger he will forget where he came from.

On the first parliamentary sitting day, Albanese provided an insight into how he intends to approach his new job, which he says without hesitation or qualification that he is 'loving'.

'I say to everyone here, all of my parliamentary colleagues, don't miss the chance. Because you're not here for that long. None of us will be,' he said.

'And when you're sitting on the porch thinking about what you did, you can either have a source of pride or a source of regret.

'No middle path. No middle path. Make it a source of pride.'

He might have had trouble sometimes as opposition leader and as a campaigner to find the words to move people, but he certainly got the hang of it as prime minister.

He was talking about why an Indigenous voice to parliament mattered. He could do a lot worse than allow those sentiments to guide him throughout his tenure, and to apply them to everything he does.

Acknowledgements

There were so many conflicting emotions in the lead-up to the creation of *Bulldozed*. It was a book I was desperate to write while also dreading having to write. After making a commitment to myself, my family, my friends, and my publisher, Henry Rosenbloom, that there would only be another book if Scott Morrison lost the election, I had little choice but to start typing.

If Morrison had won, there would have been no story, and while I would have been free of the burden of having to write *Bulldozed*, it would have triggered a crisis of faith in Australian voters. I had spent more than three years writing about Morrison in my weekly newspaper columns, talking about him on TV and radio, trying to give people an insight into his character and to critique his prime ministership—which, it has to be said, was woeful.

He was the worst prime minister I have covered, and I have been writing about all of them since Gough Whitlam. He simply wasn't up to the job.

The secret ministries showed what a dangerous, deluded path he had been walking. Victory would have confirmed his sense of righteousness. There were few brakes on him before, and there would have been none after. God knows what he would have done.

If he had won, there literally would have been nothing left for me to say, nothing left for me to write. There would have been no point in continuing. The people would have spoken, and I would have accepted their verdict.

My fears were unfounded. As always, the people got it absolutely right. They had worked him out.

Then, with the encouragement and support of some people, and the considerable trepidation of others, including myself, I knuckled down to a very compressed timetable to try to tell the story of what happened and why. On both sides. Why Scott Morrison lost, and why Anthony Albanese won.

I want to express my deep thanks to the many dozens of people from all sides who spoke to me, either on the record or on background. It has been an extraordinary period in Australian political history, and trying to make sense of it all without the assistance of a few brave insiders would have been impossible. It is a shame that there were others still too frightened, too angry, or too calculating to speak out.

Most of this book had been written before Morrison's secret ministries were revealed. Most of the interviews had been conducted. In one sense, it did not reveal anything new about his character, either to me or to many of those who had spoken to me. A few people I went back to decided there was nothing more they could say about him. Others were even more dismayed.

Even after all these years, it is still surprising to me how selfish some politicians are, how cruel some of them can be to one another, and how dishonest or hypocritical they are in public. Fortunately, there are many more who are decent, honest, and motivated to do the right thing.

Morrison refused my requests for an interview. My association with him began more than a decade ago, then ended not long after he became prime minister.

I apologise for whatever part I played in his rise. All I can say is that I tried to make up for that later, after I got to know him better, but by then a lot of damage had been inflicted on the body politic.

Whatever my achievements, none would have been possible without my friends and my family. None of it would mean anything without them.

My husband, Vincent, initially wary of having to endure life with me during the agony and agony (precious little ecstasy) of writing another book, was nothing but supportive and encouraging, certain I would get there, and certain that the final product would be worth it. We shall see. My everlasting thanks to him for his support and his faith in me.

Vincent, my brother, Steve, his wife, Dana, my nephews and nieces, Andrew, Peter, Laura, Maria, Thomas, Christian, Nicki, and Steven, mean the world to me. Their encouragement and understanding have kept me going and made it all worthwhile. I am eternally grateful to my brother for helping create such a beautiful family.

My thanks also to our wonderful extended family—Marion and Kevin Forrest, Franca and Raffaele Forte, Greg, Maria, Audrey, and Catherine Oddo—for their support.

Laurie Oakes has shepherded me through four books. He has provided a quote on the cover for each one, and excelled this time by providing its title as well. Like him, it is absolute genius.

Having one of the best journalists that Australia has ever produced as both a great friend and mentor for so many years has made me one of the luckiest people alive. I cannot thank him enough.

My friendship with Elissa Fidden began around the same time. Along with Oakes, she is keeper of most of my secrets. Elissa and I have lived together, travelled together, shared great joy and immense sorrows, all of which have deepened and enriched our friendship. Long may it continue.

Thank you to Kerry-Anne Walsh, for hand-knitted beanies, fingerless gloves, and so much more. She has been a most generous and thoughtful friend. Laura Tingle had more confidence in me than I could ever have in myself. I thank her for that and other things, too. My gratitude, too, goes to Dennis Atkins for so generously sharing his peerless historical and current knowledge of political events and players.

My departure from *The Australian* sparked some commentary. A few of my 'fans' were glad I was gone. Others were kind enough to praise my work and hoped it would continue. The messages from Virginia Trioli, Sabra Lane, Michael Rowland, Leigh Sales, David Speers, Sam Clarke, Robyn Powell, and so many others were surprising, humbling, and very welcome. The wonderful Margie Easterbrook, who became my op-ed editor on *The Age* and *The Sydney Morning Herald*, was one of the first to get on to James Chessell to urge him to hire me. I thank her, and then later Patrick O'Neil, for guidance and support during my transition. Expat former colleagues and friends Trevor Hawkins and Phil Beard have provided often hilarious, always pertinent, perspectives on events here and there from Singapore and the UK.

A few friends have been lost along the way. Denis Page, a source of material and moral wellbeing, died a few months before the election. We miss him and his wise counsel. Thankfully, we still have Denise, Charles Mailler, Lajla and Beat Sidhu, Rob and Chris Hunter, Beverly Swift, Bob Nader, and Sue and Tony O'Leary.

I can never thank enough my publisher, Henry Rosenbloom, who took a punt on me for my first book, *So Greek*, published in 2010. He has stuck by me ever since, and edited all four books. Henry and his team at Scribe—Cora Roberts, Sarina Gale, and so many more — have been magnificent. I could not have asked for better. Any mistakes or shortcomings are all mine.

This is also my fourth book supported by the indispensable technical expertise and good humour of Matt Peacock. Matt reminded me recently, after I had told him that if anything happened to me, to come home and send the manuscript to Henry, that I had told him exactly the same thing on the previous three occasions. That says everything about how authors feel towards the end of the process.

Jessie Ding, Stephanie, Toby, Alberto, and the rest of the crew at Beess, a treasured community gathering place, helped us keep our sanity and our caffeine levels stable before, during, and after lockdowns. Heartfelt thanks to Antonio Di Dio and Walter Abhayaratna for the regular maintenance checks.

I have promised friends and family that this will be the last book. They will say they have heard it all before, but there is no doubt the day will come soon when I stop working and I stop writing.

That will come as a relief to some — friends and foes alike. For me, it will be a sad day. I remember clearly my first day, so many decades ago, leaving our tiny house in Doveton, clutching my portable typewriter, to begin my cadetship on the *Dandenong Journal*. My brother, Steve, and father, Andreas, had already left for work. My mother, Elpiniki, and my sister, Christina, kissed me goodbye and wished me good luck as I left to catch the bus.

I loved it right from that very first day, and I know that if/when it ends, I will miss it terribly.

⟩